Followers of the New Faith

FOLLOWERS
OF THE NEW
FAITH

✣

Culture Change and the Rise of Protestantism
in Brazil and Chile

Emilio Willems

VANDERBILT UNIVERSITY PRESS: 1967

Copyright © 1967 by
Vanderbilt University Press
Library of Congress Catalogue
Card number 67–27517

Printed in the
United States of America by
Baird-Ward Printing Company
Nashville, Tennessee

Preface

✤ This book is an attempt to understand the emergence and development of proselytic Protestantism within the context of two Latin American cultures. It claims to be no more than exploratory in its methods and tentative in its results. To place the development of Protestantism (or any other religion) in the context of a particular culture is to assume that the questions of why, where, how, and when Protestant denominationalism arose are tied in with what has been happening to institutions and customs which, at first glance, seem unrelated to religious behavior. An attempt will thus be made to see the acceptance and dissemination of Protestant creeds as something that may be conditioned or prompted by changes in the traditional ways of life of the two countries under scrutiny. On the other hand, the possibility must be admitted that, once established, the new religion may generate modes of thinking, feeling and acting that deviate significantly from traditional ways of life.

The contextual approach is implicitly "structural-functional," in the broadest possible sense. Here, emphasis is placed on what Protestantism "does" to the societies of Brazil and Chile and what specific conditions in the texture of these societies have been instrumental in generating the Protestant deviation from religious norms and folkways.

Since the cultural changes we are dealing with occur in time and space, our inquiry is bound to have historical depth and geographic range. In view of one of our leading hypotheses, both approaches seem equally important, but this book is most emphatically *not* a history of Brazilian or Chilean Protestantism, nor does our ecological inquiry claim complete coverage of such vast territories and their largely unchartered cultural variability.

Such psychological phenomena as the conversion experience or spirit possession are here considered as given rather than as objects of specific inquiry. In other words, the questions we shall attempt to answer refer to the social and psychological functions of spirit possession, for example, rather than to its psychological nature. Whatever spirit possession may be, in purely psychological terms, it cannot be denied that it somehow affects the people who experience it.

Furthermore, none of our hypotheses is in any sense concerned with theological propositions, and the outcome of our inquiry is not to be construed as an implicit endorsement of any theological doctrine. "No religions are false; all answer, though in different ways, to given conditions of human existence." These well-known words by Emile Durkheim reflect the position of the author facing a religious system as an object of research.

It would be invidious and misleading to present this study as a confrontation between Protestantism and Catholicism. That portion of the Brazilian and Chilean population reported as "Catholic" by the national censuses shows such variation in the practice of religion as prescribed by the Catholic church that, in the present context, it can only be described as non-Protestant. The Latin American habit of classifying oneself as "Catholic," whether pious or lax, agnostic or openly anticlerical, sharply contrasts to the Protestant self-classification which is based predominantly on active church membership and communicant status. Thus, to the extent that comparisons are made, they refer to Protestants and non-Protestants.

A variety of research techniques has been used. The use of secondary materials, although extensive, was preceded by a critical evaluation of the sources as well as the methodological aspects of the various publications quoted in the text. Description of such activities as street-corner proselytism, religious services, the manifestations of spirit possession, performance of healing rites, meetings of religious leaders, and the like is always based on direct observation of these events, either by the author himself or by one or several of his research assistants. Whenever feasible, attendance of or participation in those activities was repeated and observations cross-checked with previous ones to obtain a reasonably accurate picture of the occurrences. The extensive use of informants constitutes another important source of information. Since nearly fifteen months were spent in the field, it was possible, not only to interview the same informants several times, but also to add new informants and to change interviewers.

The use of informants, prime source of data in anthropological field work, raises an interesting question. Although considered sound in studies of small communities, it becomes increasingly unreliable as the aggregate under scrutiny increases in size and complexity. While resort to direct observation and informants may be considered routine procedure in the small communities on which data were either available or had to be obtained for the purpose of this study, considerable doubt may arise about the validity of such techniques when used in the metropolitan areas of Santiago or São Paulo, for example. As a rule, however, the individual Protestant congregation, even in the largest city, turned out to be rather small and tightly integrated. The church, particularly the sect, absorbs so much of the available time of its members that they get to know one another quite intimately. The typical Protestant congregation thus resembles, in some of its basic aspects, a small community rather than the typical urban parish of the Catholic church with thousands of members, most of whom are no closer to one another than the attendants of an artistic performance or a political rally. In other words, the individual Protestant congregation may be approached as if it were a small community, and in our experience the data gathered from informants seem no less reliable than those provided by members of a peasant village, particularly in so far as religion and its behavorial concomitants are concerned.

The possibilities of studying individual urban congregations, however, were obviously limited, and the question may be raised whether the data thus obtained may be considered representative of *all* congregations or churches in a given area. To answer this question, further studies will be necessary. Our generalizations and conclusions are admittedly tentative and in need of further testing. Even the use of extensive census data, though corroborative in many respects, is not of the kind to satisfy "hard-nosed" social scientists.

Since all field work was carried out in 1959 and 1960, the results presented here may not reflect some recent developments. Thus, for example, political involvement of Chilean Protestantism has almost certainly increased. In 1960, most interviews of Protestants—leaders as well as rank-and-file members—showed a cautious reserve and often undisguised suspicion regarding the program of the emergent *Partido Demócrata-Cristiano* (Christian Democratic Party). In view of the extraordinary growth of this party and its electoral victories, it seems unlikely that it should not have attracted a substantial proportion of the Protestant electorate.

There are many to whom I would like to express my indebtedness. Some of these wished to remain unnamed. In Chile, I had the assistance and the collaboration of Fernando Moraga, Elbert Reed, and the Reverend Valenzuela, among many others. In Brazil, José Fabio da Silva Barbosa, José Maria Lopes, and Koy Yuasa acted most effectively as research assistants. The Reverend Nataniel Nascimento and Professor Julio Andrade Ferreira were most helpful in organizing meetings and interviews with numerous members of the clergy and with the student bodies of two theological schools. I am particularly indebted to the Rockefeller Foundation for financial support.

Any factual errors or misinterpretations are attributable only to the author and not to those who have so generously contributed to this endeavor.

Definitions of Portuguese and Spanish terms used in this study may be found in a glossary at the end of the volume.

E.W.

Contents

PART I: INTRODUCTION

1 The Missionary as a Cultural Innovator   *3*
2 Sociocultural Characteristics of American   *5*
  Protestantism
3 Latin America as an Extension of the American   *10*
  Frontier
4 Leading Hypotheses   *12*

PART II: COMPATIBILITIES AND INCOMPATIBILITIES

5 The Sociocultural Dimensions of the Problem   *19*
6 Structural Aspects of the Recipient Societies   *21*
7 Potential Role of the Middle Class   *26*
8 Marginal Groups: Rebellion and Messianic   *30*
  Movements in Brazil
9 The Catholic Church and Social Control   *34*
10 The Viability of the Protestant Ethic   *45*

PART III: SOCIOCULTURAL CHANGE AND THE
DEVELOPMENT OF PROTESTANTISM

11 Changing Conditions of Protestant Growth   *57*
12 The Ecology of Protestantism in Brazil   *68*
13 Internal Migration and the Growth of Protestantism   *83*
  in Brazil
14 The Ecology of Protestantism in Chile   *86*
15 Excursus on Protestantism in Traditional Society   *93*

PART IV: ADAPTATIONS AND SELECTIONS: THE
NATIONAL CHURCHES AND PENTECOSTAL SECTS EMERGE

16 Schisms and Nationalism   103
17 Schisms and Nationalism: 118
     The Brazilian Pentecostal Sects
18 Protestantism and the Lower-Class Culture   122
19 The Religious Determinant   131
20 The Functions of Pentecostalism   133
21 Cohesion and Security   144
22 Protestantization as a Selective Process   153

PART V: PROTESTANTISM AS A FACTOR
OF CULTURE CHANGE

23 Inherent Changes and Contingent Changes   163
24 Changes in the Community Structure   165
25 The Protestant Family   169
26 Economic Changes   173
27 Excursus on Protestantism and Social Class   197
28 Political Behavior   220
29 Protestantism and Education   231

PART VI: CONCLUSIONS

Conclusions   247
Appendix   261
Bibliography   277
Glossary   283
Index   285

PART I

Introduction

1
The Missionary as a Cultural Innovator

✤ Protestantism was late in coming to Latin America. Whether brought by immigrants or missionaries, it arrived at a time when Latin American culture had already been molded to its unique shape. With the exception of a few abortive attempts at conquest by French and Dutch Protestants, the colonies of Spain and Portugal had been effectively isolated against heresy. The peoples of Latin America had never been given opportunity to sample religious creeds and practices different from their own. True enough, they had absorbed Indian and African influences, but this they did in their formative phase when the European settlers, the Indians, and Africans still depended upon each other for a mutually acceptable *modus vivendi*. When political emancipation came they lacked the experiences and consequently the protective devices that characterize the ideological positions of the battle-hardened churches of Europe.

The beginnings of Protestantism in Brazil and Chile were inconspicuous enough. Since the early decades of the nineteenth century there were business communities of European, mostly British, subjects in the major cities of either country. They were allowed to have their religious services and chaplains, and a few of these Protestant congregations, such as the Presbyterians of Valparaiso, eventually developed missionary activities among the local population (Vergara, 1962: 40ff.).

Protestant immigrants also trickled in during the second quarter of the nineteenth century. Although their numbers increased after 1850, it soon became obvious that they were not proselytically inclined. These largely German-speaking settlers not only confined themselves to certain areas but were also committed to a self-imposed blend of nationalistic and religious values. The Prussian Evangelical Church succeeded in transferring to Latin America the idea that *Deutschtum* and the Gospel depended on each other for survival. Attempts at depriving the people of the German language and German traditions were held to be equivalent to deliberate destruction of their religiosity, and to touch their religious creed would have meant disintegration of

3

their *Deutschtum*. Protestantism thus tended to remain strictly a German concern, preached and taught by Germans, in German, and to people of German ancestry. These self-imposed restrictions prevented these churches from developing the very kind of religious proselytism which characterizes other brands of Protestantism in Latin America. German Protestantism was obviously designed for survival rather than expansion (Willems, 1946: 476ff.).

The diffusion of Evangelical creeds received direction and impulse by missionaries who, after 1850 approximately, began to extend their endeavor to Latin America. Although some nationals from other Western countries joined their effort, the task was to be performed largely by missionaries from the United States. The North American versions of Protestantism therefore came to be prevalent in most countries south of the Rio Grande.

Although widely recognized and sometimes emphasized, the role of the missionary as an agent of cultural diffusion has never been thoroughly investigated. The missionary shares with other agents, such as merchants, administrators, doctors, nurses, teachers, and technicians of various kinds, a common characteristic: they all intend to change certain aspects of what they perceive to be the "native" way of life. Singling out the aspects with which they are prepared to deal, these innovators are more or less convinced that they have something to offer that the natives "need": tractors, a new fiscal policy, soil conservation, scientific forestry, washing machines, child care, or a different approach to the supernatural. The innovators pursue their task for different reasons and in diverse ways, whether the recipient society is aware of the imputed needs or not. They all have stories to tell about native receptivity and resistance, indifference and eagerness, misinterpretation and distortion of intentions, about co-operation and lack thereof. All innovators attempt to accomplish something in the way of changing native ideas and knowledge, habits and attitudes. They are all more or less committed to their specific task, but none is quite ready or willing to go as far as the missionary does. Self-denial is not expected of the administrator, doctor, or technician, but if he practices it in an attempt to win the natives over to his "cause," he may figuratively be called a "missionary." Within Western civilization the accepted role of the missionary is that of one normally committed to disseminate his creed at any cost. He is not supposed to be discouraged by obstacles that may deter other agents of culture change. Not even the sacrifice of his life appears to be incommensurate to the importance of his task.

In order to scrutinize the proposed task of the Protestant missionary as a cultural innovator in Latin America, it seems necessary to specify the "message" he wishes to communicate, as well as the setting or framework of ideas and attitudes in which the "message" is presented to the recipient society. Unless the missionary intends to work among unassimilated Indians, he shares common ground with Latin Americans in so far as these participate in the symbolic universe of Western Civilization, including, of course, Christianity. Such words as "redemption," "immortal soul," "grace," "sin," "Christ," "cross," "Holy Spirit," "heaven," and "hell" ring familiar to Latin Americans. Unlike his predecessors, the Jesuit fathers of the sixteenth century, the Protestant missionary does not have to grope for words to translate those concepts into native languages in which they were more often than not misinterpreted. The nomenclature is there; people know the Decalogue, erect churches, and worship collectively the Christian God.

The role of the Protestant missionary in Latin America is more that of a reformer of a creed which, it is believed, has strayed from the truth as established by the Holy Writ. A historical parallel with the European Reformation may not be inappropriate, especially in view of the fact that toward the end of the nineteenth century the Roman Catholic Church had deteriorated to such an extent that a vast reform was carried out by Rome to bring clergy and laity back to the fold.

2
Sociocultural Characteristics
of American Protestantism

♣ One starting point of this inquiry is to be seen in the fact that it was predominantly North American Protestantism, represented by American missionaries, that found its way into Latin American culture. Brought to the United States by groups of English dissenters, the prevailing forms of American Protestantism constitute the outcome of long processes of reinterpretation and adaptation to the modes of life of the American settler. These processes eventually crystalized in a set of principles, values, and attitudes which the first waves of missionaries sought to implant in the southern hemisphere. Their discrete character, compared with the brands of Protestantism predominant in continental Europe and European settlements in South America, may be seen in the way relationships with the supernatural were conceived, as well as in the social implications which were thought to derive from such relationships.

In America, Christianity was largely reinterpreted in terms of two major patterns: evangelicalism and revivalism. "Evangelicalism was a theological emphasis upon the necessity for a conversion experience as the beginning point of a Christian life, while revivalism was a technique developed to induce that experience." (Hudson, 1961: 78.) The conversion experience was thought to be pronouncedly personal as well as emotional. The basic traits of the revival pattern had of course been shapened by the "Great Awakening" of the eighteenth century. The emotional upheaval of the personality, intended to purify the individual and to establish communion with the deity, had been sanctioned as an integral part of American religious traditions.

Yet what might have been interpreted as the final objective of religious practice was regarded only as a beginning. According to Hudson (1961:81),

This emphasis upon the need to translate faith into action provided the basis for enlisting the full participation of the laity in the counteroffensive of the churches. Its practical effect was to channel the whole impulse of the religious life into active support of the highly organized system of voluntary societies. The voluntary societies, in turn, became a major instrument of the churches in their endeavor to fashion a Protestant America.

The belief in the priesthood of all faithful changed the position of the laity vis-á-vis the clergy. From a mere believer and recipient of sacramental benefits, the layman came to be a dynamic factor in the propagation of the faith. In frequent meetings he gained considerable experience in addressing and conducting assemblies. The Sunday School pattern was particularly apt to impart self-confidence to the layman. Ignorant he might be, but this really did not matter so long as God's spirit was guiding his teachings (Hall, 1930: 243).

The assumption that no mortal man and no human institution can be regarded as infallible (Hudson, 1961:14) laid the foundation to the *liberty of free disquisition*. It enabled the individual to seek the truth and to make his own choice and decisions with regard to the supernatural. This includes not only free choice among existing religious bodies and doctrines but also the right to dissent. The logical result of this principle is the acceptance of a "pluralistic" society of divergent creeds.

The assumption of institutional fallibility found its logical corollary in the demand that the power of the church be limited. Ecclesiastical absolutism was feared as much as political absolutism. Yet, on the other hand, "to strive, however imperfectly, to be Christ's church" it must be free, not only "from domination by a priestly hierarchy, but also from the control and the direction of the state." The role of the state was limited to that of a guarantor of protection and security (Hudson, 1961: 14–17).

Freedom from clerical domination involved a new role of the laity in the control of church affairs. Hudson (1961: 26–27) reports that the early ministers

were far removed from the status-giving context of an ordered church life and were largely dependent upon the support they could marshal among the laity both for the formation and maintenance of a particular church. Under these conditions, the ministerial office conferred little authority beyond that personal authority which a minister might be able to command by virtue of his own character, wisdom, ability, and example. Thus the transplanted churches, whatever their traditional policy, tended to become independent self-governing units which resisted subsequent attempts to regularize their status by subordinating them to a wider ecclesiastical jurisdiction.

Local autonomy and lay control became two major structural factors to shape the emerging forces of American Protestantism.

The consistent pursuance of the aforementioned principles eventually led to the "breakdown of the parish system" and to the recognition of "denominationalism." Since the assumption of institutional fallibility and insistence upon the liberty of free disquisition or the right to dissent originated discrete bodies of believers each following its own version of the revealed truth, the traditional parish system, "by which a whole community was embraced within the church and subjected to its discipline" (Hudson 1961: 27–28) had to give way to the principle of denominationalism which divided the individual communities into distinct ecclesiastical polities. These however were integrated by the principle of mutual toleration deriving from the assumption

that the true Church is not to be identified exclusively with any single ecclesiastical structure. No denomination claims to represent the whole Church of Christ. No denomination claims that all other churches are false churches. Each denomination is regarded as constituting a different 'mode' of expressing in the outward form of worship and organization that larger life of the church in which they all share. (Hudson, 1961: 34.)

Religious pluralism became firmly anchored in the structure of American Society.

Another aspect of American Protestantism is often seen in its relative lack of interest in "professional scientific theology." Evangelic action and religion as an emotional experience of the individual rather than "intellectualization" of man's relationship with God characterized the American churches of the nineteenth century. American Protestantism is "weak in theology, but strong in action." (Sweet, 1947: 110.)

The ethical components of American Protestantism were inherited from the "Reformed or Calvinistic tradition as it found expression in English Puritanism and the related Presbyterianism of Scotland and Northern Ireland." (Hudson, 1961: 18.) Strong emphasis was on moral discipline and righteousness. These values gained in scope and practical relevance during the evangelization of the American frontier.

Sweet (1947: 50) noted that

Frontier Baptist, Methodist, and Presbyterian churches disciplined members not only for personal lapses, such as drunkeness and immorality, but also brought them to book for fraudulent business dealings, such as selling unsound horses, removing boundary stones, or cutting down corner trees.

Insistence on moral discipline seems related to the revival pattern, and both play a conspicuous role in the struggle for the soul of the frontier settler.

Among the "historical" churches, the Baptists probably were the most radical opponents of traditions such as those of the Catholic and Anglican churches. Baptists conceive of sacraments "as signs of a covenant simply, without magic grace-imparting power." (Hall, 1930: 129.) There is a strong emphasis on lay preaching, and on complete autonomy of the local congregation.

"Methodism", we are told by Hall (1930: 197),

retained the bishop, but only as an administrative officer, it retained the
sacraments, but simply as beautiful memorials of Christian dedication and
social service, it retained a certain amount of ritual and churchly order,
but as administrative machinery rather than as remainder of historic continuity with a priestly past."

Like the Baptists and Presbyterians, the Methodists took up the revivalistic type of religiosity which "was expected, worked for, prayed
for, and its machinery and mentality carefully studied."

It has often been recognized that the prevailing forms of American
Protestantism bear the marks of English Dissent. The "Great Awakening," writes Hall (1930:159),

was an essentially dissenting movement; its message, its individualism, its
whole conception of Christianity breathed the air of English Dissent, and
thus prepared the minds of those influenced by it to resist the claims and
oppose the power of an upper-class England.

English Dissent, like its heirs, the American churches, may be considered a symbolic rebellion against the traditional social order. Its
value system stood for the rights of an oppressed class and opposed
that of the Anglican Church which was identified with the ruling class.
In America, its symbolism related to political emancipation and the
recognition of the rights and privileges of the common man (Sweet,
1947: 14). As in England, this brand of Protestantism became the religion of the poor. As Sweet (1947: 69) noted,

Some of the ethical and psychological characteristics of the religion of the
poor are emotional fervor, spontaneity of religious feelings, and the rejection of abstract creeds and formal ritual. Another is the development of
lay leadership and the stress placed upon the simple virtues, such as mutual
helpfulness, rigorous honesty, equality, and sympathy.

Revivalistic emphasis upon "the equality of all men in the sight of
God" contained a strong appeal to the American masses striving for
social recognition. And in order to achieve social recognition, the
"simple virtues" including righteousness, hard work, and temperance
were selected as means whose motivational effectiveness was reinforced by supernatural sanctions.

Without telling anything new, the foregoing remarks are merely intended to restate the frame of mind as well as the concrete beliefs

and practices which characterized the emissaries of American Protestant churches, particularly Methodism, Presbyterianism, and Baptism when, in the second half of the nineteenth century, they initiated their missionary endeavor in South America. Their objective was not so much to save the Latin Americans from eternal damnation as to preach "a gospel designed to produce an emotional experience sufficiently powerful to give the life directions toward righteousness, and what that gospel is depends much upon the level of culture of both the preacher and his audience." (Hall, 1930: 247.)

3

Latin America as an Extension of the American Frontier

✛ To understand the frame of mind in which the early missionaries sought to lay the foundations of their creeds in such countries as Chile and Brazil, one must be aware of the fact that their attempts were, to a large extent, continuous with the evangelization of the American frontier. Indeed, the early South American missions may be conceived of as an extension of the frontier.

The history of the Presbyterian, Methodist, and Baptist churches in those countries unmistakably bears witness to the same proselytic fervor which characterized the "Baptist farmer-preacher," the "Presbyterian teacher-minister," and the "Methodist circuit rider." The image of the Methodist circuit rider comes very close indeed to the role of the typical Protestant missionary who endeavored to spread the Gospel throughout the immense hinterland of Brazil where horse and mule were the sole means of transportation.

As in America, the missionary proceeded on the assumption "that man and God must work together to build a decent world; that no situation could be so bad that man with God's help could do something about it." (Sweet, 1947:48.) The message of redemption carried supernatural *and* socioeconomic implications. Education, thrift and hard work were integral parts of the attitudinal and institutional complex that the missionaries sought to implant among Latin Americans.

Along with values concerning religious doctrine, cult, and individual conduct, the early missionaries tended to introduce a series of organizational devices designed to shape the individual converts into a coherent structure. Their perception of the way in which believers and pastor ought to be integrated into a single, enduring social unit reflected not only the structural principles of their particular denominations but also those which prevail on the communal level of American society in general. In the light of contrasting Latin American structural principles, the following may be pointed out: the assumption of ethical equality of the members of a community regardless of wealth, educational background, or occupation; the assumption that the individual members of a community are morally and intellectually capable of solving their common problems in a responsible fashion; the assumption that leadership does not imply restriction of freedom of expression and judgment. A leader's initiative should be inspired by group opinion; he should help people, of course, but above all he should teach people to help themselves. And a leader should be accessible to all members of the group.

These principles are given expression in the belief that the local congregation was to have considerable if not complete autonomy and belief in a constitution that would grant fullest participation of all members in the selection of church functionaries and in the conduct of current affairs. As conceived by the missionary, the life of the congregation was implicitly dependent upon the assumption of individual responsibility of its members. The missionary's role was to be that of a *primus inter pares* whose presence should encourage rather than stifle expression of individual judgment and participation in church proceedings. The only model available to the missionary was that of American congregations, and regardless of the obstacles he might have expected to meet, eventual success would mean the formation of a congregation with an associational and institutional life similar to that of a Presbyterian, Methodist, or Baptist congregation in the United States. The existence of these models in the mind of the early missionary may be inferred from their actual projections which indeed bear a remarkable resemblance to American congregations, not as they are now, but as they were half a century ago. It would be a serious mistake to conceive of the missionary as an invariant factor in time, unaffected by the changes that transformed the historical churches in the United States.

4

Leading Hypotheses

❖ The social scientist today is expected to have a set of hypotheses neatly formulated before he becomes involved in field research. If the field is largely uncharted, however, and the researcher approaches it with an open mind, previous hypotheses often tend to fade away or change, new ones emerge and supersede one another until eventually tentative interpretations of empirical findings suggest the selection of a final set of assumptions that seem worth testing.

This is what happened in the present study, except that previous contact with proselytic Protestantism in Brazil made it possible to maintain at least one broad hypothesis: In a series of research projects carried out in rural São Paulo between 1945 and 1948, we found that small Protestant congregations representing various churches and sects deliberately abandoned or changed customary ways of behavior which had gone unquestioned for several generations. These initial observations, which actually motivated the present inquiry, pointed to cultural changes in which Protestantism appeared to be instrumental.

Critics of the Protestant movement in Latin America have often affirmed its incompatibility with the historical and cultural traditions of the Southern Hemisphere. Protestants themselves have frequently contrasted their own way of life to that of the surrounding non-Protestant world. In fact, many of our Protestant informants tried to convey the impression that theirs was a way of life that had no roots in the society of which they were a part. Unconvinced by the apparent incompatibilities between native traditions and Protestant values, and encouraged by the fact that cases of religious dissent stressing social reform had been recorded by historians, we began to probe for compatibilities, *on the assumption that Protestant dissent had its antecedents, if not its roots, in structural peculiarities of the traditional society, even in some of its customary ways of coping with the supernatural.* Attempts to verify this hypothesis will be made in the first part of this volume.

In the course of our field work it became abundantly clear that Protestantism, particularly its sectarian varieties, were thriving in those areas of either country where exposure to cultural change had been long and intensive. Statistical data on the distribution of Protestants confirmed that industrialized modern metropolitan areas and, to a lesser extent, rural frontiers had indeed the largest Protestant populations. A new hypothesis thus came to be formulated: *Heavy concentrations of Protestants* are correlated with changes strongly affecting the traditional structure of the society; conversely, Protestantism may be expected to be relatively weak in areas that have had little or no exposure to such changes.

Thus a seemingly contradictory possibility began to take shape: Protestantism "causing" cultural change and "being caused" by culture change. To solve this apparent paradox it was assumed that historically Protestantism emerged as a by-product of changes affecting the social structure and values of nineteenth century Brazil and Chile (foreign immigration and progressive secularization of the culture, for example). Once established, Protestantism began to act in a very limited way as a factor contributing to sociocultural change. Then industrialization, urbanization, internal migration, and the opening of rural frontiers not only generated conditions increasingly favorable to the growth of Protestant denominationalism but also gradually reinforced its active role in the process of sociocultural transformation, mainly because the changes intended by Protestantism proper received impulse, direction, and additional meaning from the general changes modifying the traditional social order. In other words, the value orientation described earlier as the "Protestant ethic" was assumed to be particularly rewarding under the conditions prevailing in the emerging industrial order. The verification of these hypotheses will be attempted in the second part of this volume.

While our concern has so far been with major Protestant concentrations, field experience and a careful scrutiny of census data suggested that in some regions of Brazil at least Protestantism had been moderately successful in traditional rural settings. It was hypothesized that absence of the feudal elements characterizing the traditional social order was sufficient to allow the development of Protestant dissent and that such permissive conditions prevailed in rural areas where medium-sized agricultural holdings were relatively numerous. A separate chapter deals with these hypotheses.

Upon probing the history of the Protestant movement in Brazil and Chile, one cannot help being impressed by the number of schisms and the proliferation of churches and sects. Most of them seem to push in one of two directions: away from foreign-controlled church bodies and toward "national" church organizations, or away from the historical church and toward sectarian dissent as reflected in the Pentecostal movement. It was hypothesized that the dynamics of Protestantism, particularly internal competition, conflict, secession, and sectarianism in general, were attempts, deliberate or not, to seek out those versions of Protestantism which proved to be most congenial to the particular needs, desires, or aspirations of the recipient societies. The third part of the book will concern itself with this hypothesis.

Returning to the hypothesis that Protestantism "causes" culture change, a somewhat more precise formulation seems to be in order. The basic assumption is that the acceptance and practice of a Protestant code of behavior tend to redefine the social relationship Protestants establish or maintain with one another and with non-Protestants and that, since these redefinitions are primarily concerned with reciprocal responsibilities, the changes they produce tend to affect family structure and the socialization of the child, economic behavior, political behavior, the class structure, and the structure of voluntary associations. The relevance of such newly adopted organizational patterns and modes of behavior is perceived in terms of both the decaying structure of the traditional, feudal, patriarchical society and the emerging industrial and urban order. In other words, the assumption is that Protestantism rewards ethical discipline by providing what the traditional society denies and the emerging industrial society promises.

The scope of these hypotheses seems broad enough to support the claim that our inquiry attempts to understand Protestantism within the context of Latin American culture and in terms of that culture. The decision to choose Brazil and Chile is based primarily on the fact that both countries have relatively large and old-established Protestant churches. Furthermore, if there were significant differences in the reaction to Protestantism they would probably show up in a comparison between the response of Portuguese America and that of a Spanish American country.

Most of the empirical data presented in subsequent chapters are not compelling to the point of satisfying a "hard-nosed" social scientist. Of course, Max Weber always looms in the background of studies such as ours. Far from denying his powerful influence, we wish to make it clear that the present study is not intended to test Weber's hypothesis affirming a relationship between Protestantism and the emergence of modern capitalism. In the first place, it would be difficult to determine whether the emerging industrial order in Brazil and Chile may in fact be identified with what Max Weber called the spirit of modern capitalism. Numerous and rigid government controls prevent the economies of these countries from developing the characteristics Max Weber (1924: 238–240) regarded as essential attributes of modern capitalism. Furthermore, capitalism in Weber's sense is inseparably tied in with industrial entrepreneurship, and proselytic Protestantism, regardless of its social ascent, has hardly reached a social level where it could possibly find expression in industrial entrepreneurship.

PART II

Compatibilities and Incompatibilities

5

The Sociocultural Dimensions of the Problem

✠ The scope and implications of the changes which the Protestant missionaries attempted to introduce in Latin America cannot be understood unless they are examined in the light of the social structure and basic value orientations of the recipient societies. It is not our intention to magnify the relationships between missionaries and neophytes to the proportions of an encounter between "American culture" and "Latin culture." What the missionaries stood for clearly represented a highly selective though significant sample of American culture. Their contact was limited to those sectors of Brazilian and Chilean society that were approachable and proved receptive to their preachings. Neither geographically nor socially did they completely cover these societies or their ways of life. One might say that the missionaries were restricted to such aspects of the native culture as were embodied by the lower social strata and their ways of feeling, thinking, and acting. The lower strata of Chile and Brazil were nevertheless parts of a cultural whole, and without recourse to certain basic characteristics of that whole, their way of life will remain unintelligible.

It has often been recognized that success or failure to introduce and disseminate new values and attitudes into a society depends upon the compatibility or incompatibility of such elements with values and attitudes already existing in that society. If an innovation is accepted in spite of obvious incompatibilities, it is assumed that the gains or rewards people hope to attain by giving up customary forms of behavior are felt to be worth the distressing personal and social experiences usually deriving from such changes.

The question of whether American Protestantism is compatible with "the Latin American way of life" cannot be answered in this oversimplified manner. By breaking down "American Protestantism" into a number of previously specified patterns, however, and comparing them with corresponding patterns found among the lower strata of Brazil and Chile, it may be possible to detect affinities or disparities. Considering that a century has elapsed since the implantation of proselytic Protestantism in those parts of Latin America, and

19

changes of almost revolutionary proportions have affected their traditional way of life, it would be unrealistic to assume that exposure to the patterns of American Protestantism should have produced invariant responses. In fact, it will be hypothesized that the accelerated occurrence of major changes in the native social structures and basic value orientation generated conditions that turned out to be increasingly favorable to the dissemination of Protestant creeds.

This is not to say that the message of the missionaries was not affected by changes in the historical churches of America. But until the turn of the century and shortly thereafter, the orientation of the American missionaries, regardless of denomination, might be defined broadly as fundamentalist and puritanical. By that time the Protestant churches, especially in Brazil, had attained, or were striving for, national autonomy. They were increasingly able to carry on their task with native personnel, and the native clergy attempted to maintain the same puritanism and fundamentalism that had been imparted to them. Although the American missionary did not by any means vanish from the scene, his role tended to become more and more peripheral and, to some extent at least, more specialized in such fields as agriculture, medicine, and education.

Religion as an emotional experience, mediated through the pattern of revivalism, was bound to fascinate the Latin mind. Official as well as folk Catholicism offer numerous avenues for emotional expression, from pilgrimages to miraculous shrines and the ceremonies of the Holy Week to the miraculous feats of visionaries and thaumaturges who sporadically emerge and often carry their followers to the frenzy of religious exaltation and fanaticism. In fact, as subsequent chapters will show, the desire for emotional communion with the deity, inherent in the Protestant conversion experience, eventually led to the emergence of the Pentecostal sects whose phenomenal growth both in Brazil and Chile has reached the proportions of a religious mass movement.

6

Basic Structural Aspects of the Native Societies

✠ The two other major characteristics of American Protestantism lie in the field of social organization and ethics. The organizational components concern the position of the laity within the church, especially vis-à-vis the clergy; the moral autonomy of the individual, particularly his right to dissent; local autonomy of the congregation, hence its freedom from superior ecclesiastical domination; the denominational system instead of the parish system and consequently the need to share the same community with other denominations. Most if not all of these traits imply the capacity of concerted action at a sociocultural level determined by the composition of the individual congregation. Since the lower social strata were (and in most congregations still are) strongly predominant, the question arises whether the pattern of spontaneous concerted action was in any sense compatible with the customary ways of behavior of these strata.

In view of the salient characteristics of the preindustrial social structure which Brazil and Chile shared with the rest of Latin America, the answer seems to be negative. The colonial system of granting huge portions of land to privileged individuals laid the foundations of a social structure which put small groups of owners in almost absolute control of the landless masses. Abolition of the *encomienda* (landgrant) system in Chile and of slavery in Brazil did little, if anything, to reduce the profound cleavage between the two classes that were bound together by a traditional relationship variously named "paternalism," "feudalism," "patrón system," or "hacienda system." These terms may not be exactly synonymous, but they all imply a social structure gravitating around the large agricultural estate. Within its orbit the feudal tradition of reciprocal loyalties between the owner and his family on the one hand, and the resident labor force on the other survived its colonial precedents with little change.

The tendency to see in this sort of social organization an analogy to the father-son relationship suggests not only correspondence of benevolent though stern authority with dutiful obedience and filial respect, but it is actually meant to convey the idea that paternalism closely follows the structural model of the patripotestal extended family which constitutes one of the most conspicuous aspects of the Iberian cultural heritage. The hacienda owner or patrón plays a role comparable to that of an authoritarian father, and his *inquilinos* (Chile) or *colonos* (Brazil) owe him the kind of obedience expected from subservient children. Their mutual relationship is thus more than an impersonal labor contract in the legal sense of the term. It comprises moral in addition to legal responsibilities which go far beyond the rendering of stipulated services and their remuneration in kind or money wages.

It ought to be emphasized that the reciprocal recognition of largely unspecified moral obligations did and does not by any means prevent the hacienda owner from exploiting his laborers, as it did not prevent the head of the patripotestal European peasant family from exploiting his own children. In fact, paternalism may be considered a convenient organizational device to veil economic exploitation and to make it mutually palatable. Quoting Céspedes del Castillo, José Medina Echavarría emphasizes the exercise of authority as the principal function of the hacienda. The following passage is translated from Medina Echavarría (1963: 36):

> Over each and all, from his eldest son to the least of his slaves, the chief of the *hacienda* exercises his authority, at once tyrannical and protective, in degrees varying according to complex factors and circumstances. At once tyrannical and protective signifies authoritarian and paternal. And this image of the relationships of subordination—protection and obedience, arbitrariness and graciousness, faithfulness and resentment, violence and charity—which in its origin is a replica of the characteristics of the far-off monarchical domination, was maintained intact for a long time after the King had been replaced by a President of the Republic. The model of authority created by the *hacienda* spread and penetrated through all the relationships of command, embodying in the paternalistic employer the notion of authority persisting in the popular mind.

In other words, the pattern of authoritarianism had a far-reaching influence in shaping the social structure even outside the hacienda system proper. The preindustrial Latin-American town was and still is traditionally composed of a relatively small core of absentee landlords, merchants, professional people, artisans, and bureaucrats, and a rather undifferentiated lower class composed of unskilled or semi-skilled laborers who hold only a precarious niche in the economic order. Occupational opportunities are few and of a highly unstable nature. Most lower-class families make a precarious living dependent on such odd jobs as water-carrying, street-cleaning, gardening, peddling of lottery tickets, vegetables, charcoal, or firewood, and many are merely beggars and prostitutes. In many Brazilian towns these people are called *biscateiros*, i.e., people who drift from one odd job to the next, and who depend for their livelihood upon the good will and the charitable inclinations of the occasional employers of their services.

A recent survey of Pirambú, a lower-class suburb of Fortaleza (Ceará)—still predominantly preindustrial—yielded the following occupational figures:

Heads of families gainfully employed	3,263
Washerwomen being the sole breadwinners of their families	1,337
Biscateiros	1,026
Unemployed heads of families	2,396

Source: Ribeiro, MS: 13.

With these they maintain a personal relationship not unlike the one that binds the hacienda worker to his patron. In Brazilian towns, members of this class indeed address *any* member of the middle and upper class as *patrão* or *patrôa* (feminine). There are many institutional manifestations of the reciprocal moral obligations which bind these two sectors of the preindustrial urban population together. Religious brotherhoods, such as those responsible for the maintenance of the local *Santa Casa* (hospital) where the indigent find free treatment, and religious fiestas such as the Feast of the Holy Ghost where the poor are lavishly entertained and fed by those who can afford to be generous, are but a few manifestations of a moral order that cuts across traditional class lines

The social structure of the hacienda may be regarded also as a slightly simplified miniature model of the traditional political structure, not as represented by its legal façade, but in its everyday operations and especially in the ways by which, regardless of constitutional appearances, the many are manipulated by the few. Here again, colonial precedents had decisive effects upon structural arrangements instituted by the republics. Deprived of political initiative and any semblance of self-government by extreme political centralization, the Latin American masses had grown to expect decisions both petty and important from Spain and Portugal. Political emancipation substituted Creoule oligarchies for the king, but the relative position of the subordinate classes failed to change. True enough, revolution as a political instrument was incorporated in the traditional culture, but whenever it was meant to change anything at all it merely became a means to force additional responsibilities upon the central government rather than to implant and develop responsible self-government on a local or regional level.

Like paternalistic landlords, the republican governments are expected to perform the role of universal providers; whatever institutional shortcomings there may be at the community level, they are invariably blamed upon the government, and the expediency of a local political leader is measured in terms of roads, bridges, hospitals, schools, and other public works, the financing of which he succeeded in "wrestling" from the central government. Such improvements are grudgingly conceded, and few communities, *departamentos*, or provinces receive an adequate return from the taxes contributed to the national treasury. As Spain and Portugal siphoned off the riches of their American colonies, the republican governments have shown considerable resourcefulness in channeling the flow of taxes toward the capital cities whose development seems out of proportion to that of the rest of the country.

Paternalism still persists within and outside the hacienda, even under circumstances in which it seems oddly at variance with technological and managerial innovations. To investigate the *patrón-inquilino* relationship we selected four Chilean haciendas that had undergone many changes and were up to the standards of scientific agriculture and modern management. We entertained the hypothesis that labor relations had been adapted to meet the requirements of strictly capitalistic enterprises. This hypothesis proved untenable because the labor relations on those haciendas had changed very little and were still very much of the paternalistic type. Whenever the *inquilinos* find themselves in a difficult situation they come to the *patrón*, be he owner or manager, for advice and assistance. Such personal troubles as sickness, childbirth, marital troubles, weddings, deaths, conflict with neighbors, and loss of property were thought of as problems requiring assistance of the *patrón*. In the vicinity of one of these haciendas there was a village of small landholders who were in no way dependent on the hacienda owner. But the villagers were the descendants of *inquilinos* who had once worked for the grandfather of the present owner, and they still came to him for advice and aid in their personal troubles. The economic relationship had long since been severed, but their feudal loyalties continued almost undiminished. Even if the *patrón* could do little or nothing to solve their personal problems, they obviously derived a feeling of security from the fact that somebody would lend a sympathetic ear to their difficulties.

In so far as paternalism means reliance upon superior authority for decisions on trivial as well as important matters, it seems at variance with the Protestant idea of the self-governing autonomous congregation whose individual members are expected to assume full responsibility and to concur in the process of making all those decisions which the continuity and expansion of the church may require. If the membership of early Protestant congregations was overwhelmingly composed of the same people who lived in a stable or unstable paternalistic relationship with a *patrón*, and who looked up to all representatives of superior authority as universal providers and decisionmakers, how could they be expected to have adopted a diametrically opposed way of behavior as soon as they joined a Protestant congregation?

The possibility of such a sudden and radical change seems even more remote when the structure of the Roman Catholic church is taken into account. There is no liberty of free disquisition, but a rigid doctrine binding the individual through his baptismal vow. The Catholic church is not run by the laity, but by a sacerdotal hierarchy whose authority cannot be questioned. In doctrinal matters, the Pope is infallible and the church cannot be wrong. Local parishes are not autonomous but subjected to higher ecclesiastical jurisdiction. The idea of different denominations expressing differing versions of the same general truth is unheard of, and, like the church, the parish is a monolithic structure which tolerates no deviations from the established doctrine. Furthermore, both in Brazil and Chile, the Catholic church was closely associated with the state; Catholicism was the official religion of the state and as such defined and protected by the constitution. This association brought the church into the orbit of the ruling class, and, rightly or wrongly, the lower strata of the native societies came to perceive the ecclesiastical hierarchy as a factor that reinforced rather than challenged the power position of the landholding aristocracy.

7

Potential Role of the Middle Class

✤ Two qualifications seem in order at this point. One refers to the assumption, implied in the preceding pages, that the paternalistic system of the traditional agrarian society encompassed the *total* population of preindustrial Brazil and Chile. The other bears on the actual position of the Catholic church, particularly its effectiveness as a controlling power within the structure of the two societies.

As a matter of fact, there always was a population sector the components of which were marginal to or relatively independent of the landholding upper class. The term "two-class society" in the rigid economic and occupational sense does not apply to either country. The middle strata may have been numerically weak and politically impotent, but they existed, even in colonial times. Nor was their existence restricted to the urban centers. The statement that there was or is no "rural middle class" anywhere in Latin America does not gain in veracity merely because the people who belong to it fail to conform to what Americans and Europeans consider "middle class." The tables I to IV in the Appendix clearly show that the structure of Brazilian and Chilean rural society cannot adequately be defined in terms of the now popular dichotomy *minifundio-latifundio*.

There clearly is an intermediate stratum of small and medium-sized landholders. In the case of Brazil, all those holdings of ten hectares or less may be excluded as too small to warrant the classification of their owners or operators as members of the rural middle class, although there are of course many holdings within this category that afford a level of living considerably above that of the landless rural masses. The next larger category, however, (10 to fewer than 100 hectares) lies so far above the *minifundio* and so considerably below the *latifundio* that their owners or operators may safely be included among the rural middle class. In 1960 there were 1,494, 548 such holdings in Brazil. Even if allowance is made for the fact that a certain (unfortunately unknown) proportion of landholders own more than one farm, there still remains a sizable number of people who definitely belong to the middle stratum of Brazilian rural society. This statement is not meant to imply that these farmers are particularly progressive or prosperous, that their level of living is comparable to that of American or European middle-class farmers, or that they are capable of organizing themselves into co-operatives and unions, political parties, or the like. Our contention merely is that, subjectively, they perceive themselves as superior to the *agregados* and inferior to the *fazendeiros*, and, objectively, by their level of living, they cannot be identified with either stratum. Furthermore, the assumption that this rural middle class is restricted to areas of recent European colonization in the three southernmost states of Brazil is obviously erroneous. The agricultural census of 1960 shows that there were 161,673 medium-sized farms in Bahia, 199,405 in Minas Gerais, 139,620 in São Paulo and 50,850 in Pernambuco, to name only a few major states listed among the "traditional areas."

Comparison between the census figures of 1920 and 1960 shows that the number of medium-sized farms not only increased from 157,959 to 1,494,548, but also that their portion of the total area utilized for agricultural purposes increased from 8.9 percent in 1920 to 17 percent in 1960 (See also Milliet, 1939:73–117).

So far as Chile is concerned, the holdings of fewer than five hectares probably fall in the category of *minifundia*. Of the following three categories, only farms measuring from 21 to 50 hectares may safely be considered medium-sized. There were 12,495 of those in 1916. Actually, a considerable proportion of farms in the 5 to 20 hectares category ought to be included among the medium-sized holdings, and probably most farms ranking in the 51 to 200 hectares class may be included in that category. If we add these two categories to the first one, the total amounts to 46,718 or 51 per cent of a total of 91,309 holdings.

The Chilean agricultural census of 1955 reported 82,800 holdings measuring from 5 to 199.9 hectares, or 66.6 percent out of a total of 124,400. The arable area represented by these holdings totaled 1,615,-602 hectares, or 29.3 percent of all arable land covered by the census.

It would seem that, even allowing for a wide margin of error, the existence of a rural middle class in either country cannot be denied. Unfortunately, the values and attitudes of the people included in that class are almost totally unknown, except for the state of São Paulo. According to Antonio Candido, the agrarian structure of this area began to take shape with the stabilization of land tenure during the eighteenth century. It marked the beginning of a stratification process into *fazendeiros* e *sitiantes*. Although generally derived from the same family lines, the *fazendeiros* developed a large-scale commercial agriculture based on slavery, while the *sitiantes* operated their holdings primarily on the basis of a subsistence agriculture without slaves. The *fazendeiros* legalized their holdings, the *sitiantes* were often unable to secure legal titles to their land and frequently became victims of trickery and despoliation. The growth of the plantation economy and its association with political power tended to marginalize and isolate the *sitiantes* without extinguishing them as a separate rural class which obviously preceded the modern version of the *sitiante* (Muller, 1951) by almost two centuries. Independence and refusal to accept the values of a changing economy are two of the basic characteristics of the traditional *sitiante* (Candido, 1964:58 ff.).

Whatever the origin and historical precedents of the contemporary rural middle class, it is our contention that the way of life of its members enables them to choose the alternatives presented by the organizational patterns and ethical precepts of the emerging Protestant congregations. This statement does not imply unwarrantable claims. Put in terms of whether Protestantism held a particularly strong appeal for the rural middle class, the answer can only be negative because the vast majority of its members did not adhere to any Protestant creed. In another part of this study, however, we shall present data suggesting that it played a strategic role in the adoption and dissemination of Protestantism in so far as locally influential individuals not only accepted the new faith but were instrumental in establishing "preaching points" or in supplying land, building materials, and money for the erection of the first churches. Where medium-sized holdings prevailed, one of our hypotheses states Protestant nuclei would sometimes develop and eventually grow into larger centers from which migration would spread the new faith to other areas.

In connection with peasant landholders, two native institutions ought to be mentioned which may be considered as structural precedents for the type of the spontaneously co-operative and egalitarian organization found in Protestant congregations. These two institutions, the religious brotherhoods and the exchange of labor, constitute multifunctional links among scattered and loosely integrated peasant farmers. The *mutirão*, or festive working party among neighbors, is quite common all over Brazil. It alleviates the shortage of labor existing in many regions or simply takes the place of wage labor in areas where subsistence farming is of vital importance. In Chile, the festive labor party is called *mingaco*, and both countries also know its nonfestive counterpart, the *troca-dias* in Brazil, and the *vuelta de mano* in Chile (Erasmus, 1956).

The religious content of the brotherhoods, centered around the cult of a saint (typically Saint Benedict among Brazilian peasants), appears irreconcilable with Protestant teachings which label such manifestations of religiosity as "idolatry." But the brotherhoods, such as the one described by Wagley (1964:199) are also effective fund-raising organizations, and provide means for the maintenance of church buildings. In fact, many rural (and urban) churches in Brazil were erected and are still owned by religious brotherhoods, often to the chagrin of the parish priests who try in vain to gain control over these sanctuaries. The astonishing capacity of many Protestant congregations to raise funds for the construction and conservation of churches would be hard to explain without reference to the precedent established by the religious brotherhoods.

The structure of the festive labor party in both countries is equally incompatible with Protestant precepts, at least to the extent that it involves heavy drinking and dancing. But again, as a form of spontaneous and reciprocal co-operation among neighbors it seems to be a close lineal ascendant of the manifestations of solidarity found in rural Protestant congregations. In fact, where there are enough Protestants in rural neighborhoods some form of nonfestive labor exchange is usually practiced.

So far as Chile is concerned, Vergara traces the rapid acceptance and dissemination of Protestantism back to the organizational capacity of the lower classes which, in contrast to Brazil, have generated not only a greater variety of voluntary associations but particularly those that are equipped to cope with social problems arising from changes of the social structure. Vergara (1962:234–235) notes that

The Chilcans often appear to be a conglomerate of indolent people, resigned to their fate, sometimes miserable and without responsibility or initiative. Nevertheless, this same people has demonstrated more than once in its history not only its valor and endurance . . . but also its ability to organize, to direct, to excel in all fields of human endeavor whenever it awakens to the task.

To confirm this I could cite countless examples such as co-operatives of all kinds, of consumption, construction and savings, totally integrated by humble people with little education, workers or peasants who received no more than a technical orientation of auxiliary personnel. One could mention, too, all those small neighborhood and town organizations, without legal authority, but which often are effective means of progress. They call themselves *juntas de vecinos, comites de luz o de agua, centros de madres, clubes deportivos.* Furthermore, how many attempts [are made] by workers to find a solution of the tragic housing problem! I know a very poor locality which was totally organized by its founders, all laborers who had but very limited funds. The parceling of the land and the layout of the streets needed very little correction when technicians took over the matter. In another locality, an autonomous organization resulting from the private initiative of its inhabitants led to the creation of a school, a polyclinic, and an internal police for the security of its people at night.

Vergara's impressions suggest scarcely more than the ability of the Chilean lower classes to generate voluntary associations when needs arise. Even if their capacity for self-organization is superior to that of Brazil's lower classes, there is no evidence that such a difference has impaired or delayed, to any noticeable extent, the development of Protestantism in Brazil.

8

Marginal Groups: Rebellion and Religious Movements in Brazil

✤ While the rural middle class has occupied a definite though modest niche in the established social order, another sector of the population of both countries was clearly marginal and, to some extent, manifestly hostile to the established society. It was composed of people without property, employment, or occupation; of vagrants, beggars, bandits, and in Brazil, fugitive slaves who made the countryside unsafe for travelers and constituted, in colonial times and throughout the nineteenth century, a social problem of tremendous proportions. The "rural plebe," as Oliveira Vianna called these marginal masses of Brazil, supplied the human elements for the kind of private warfare in which the powerful landowners of the Brazilian hinterland so frequently engaged. Census data referring to the population of the provinces of Rio de Janeiro, Minas Gerais, São Paulo, Pernambuco, Bahia, and Ceará, in 1882, reported a total of 4,907,293 males between 13 and 45 years of age. Of these, 2,822,583 or 57 percent had no occupation of any description (Oliveira Vianna, 1, 1952:251–252). Political strife, banditry and social unrest held these masses in a perpetual state of lawlessness and rebellion.

Similar conditions seem to have prevailed in Chile. The struggle for independence, especially the period named the Anarchy (1823–1830) exacerbated internal strife and increased the general insecurity in the cities and the countryside (Encina, X, 1951: 43, 217). In the frontier areas of southern Chile, banditry remained a major problem until the last quarter of the nineteenth century (Encina, XVIII, 1951: 270ff). In addition to widespread delinquency, there was and still is the problem of a large *lumpenproletariat* composed of migrant workers and those who were expelled from haciendas and became drifters and vagrants. Thousands of these have invaded the fringe areas of the Chilean cities where they live, like many of their Brazilian counterparts, in the indescribable squalor of the *callampas*, or mushrooming shantytowns. Their rebellious state of mind occasionally explodes into action in times of political crisis, such as the resignation of President Ibañez in 1931, when the mob for a few days dominated Santiago, and "bandits and robbers" massacred the police in the streets (Olavarria Bravo, 1962: 297).

In view of these facts, the image of a paternalistic but sternly authoritarian elite controlling the submissive and apathetic masses appears to be a gross oversimplification of a far more complex reality. The traditional agrarian society of Brazil and Chile simply failed to mold the whole population to the image of a rigid social order.

So far as Brazil is concerned, the existence of a population sector marginal and fundamentally hostile to the established order has considerable bearing on the sporadic emergence of religious movements. Characteristically, at least two of these movements, the rebellion of Canudos (1897) under Antonio Conselheiro (Cunha, 1944) and the

"Holy War" in the Contestado (1912) under the "monk" José Maria (Queiroz, 1957) bear the marks of messianism. These native leaders attracted large groups of fanatic followers who projected their social discontent into endeavors of reorganizing society in the symbolic image of some sort of terrestrial paradise. The rebellion of Canudos erupted in the arid backlands of northeastern Brazil, and the "Holy War" infested the sparsely settled and underdeveloped hinterland of Santa Catarina.

Both movements, as countless minor ones which for their strictly parochial character caused no concern on the national level, were obviously irreconcilable to the authority and the teachings of the Roman Catholic church. In fact, they challenged that authority exactly on those points which the bishop of Bahia expounded in a circular letter advising the priests of the Canudos region that their parishioners be forbidden to hear the preachings of Antonio Conselheiro.

Seeing that in the Catholic church the holy mission of indoctrinating the people belongs only to the ministers of religion, it follows that a layman, whoever he may be, and however well instructed and virtuous, does not have the authority to exercise that right. (Cunha, 1944: 137.)

Among the religious movements of northeastern Brazil there was one which began inconspicuously enough with peaceful attempts to alleviate the fate of the *sertanejos* (inhabitants of the arid interior) stricken by the devastating drought of 1877. The name of the movement is linked to the town of Joazeiro in the state of Ceará, and the controversial personality of its parish priest, Father Cicero Romão Batista.

To stabilize the life of thousands of seminomadic *sertanejos* and to combat effectively the *cangaço*, or banditry fostered and exploited by local politicians, Father Cicero attracted the displaced and the migrants and taught them agricultural skills and handicrafts, along with the moral rules and religious beliefs of Catholicism. He spent a considerable part of his own income to alleviate the shortage of water; he recruited labor for public works sponsored by the Federal Government and acted as a personal mediator in numerous and violent family feuds caused by the traditional way in which political activities were pursued in northeastern Brazil. Eventually, as mayor of Joazeiro, Father Cicero ensured the rule of justice, at least temporarily, and achieved in 1911 a reconciliation of all local politicians. Under his leadership, Joazerio developed from a hamlet to a town of 30,000, and the surrounding countryside became one of the most productive agricultural regions of the state. But the town grew also into a center of religious pilgrimage, and the church which Father Cicero erected with the help of the people became a famous shrine. Over the years he acquired the reputation of a thaumaturge whose miracles attracted countless pilgrims who wished to partake of his miraculous powers (Bartolomeu, 1923).

It seems that the blind devotion and absolute obedience of the masses induced Father Cicero to take an increasingly active and highly disturbing part in state politics. His excommunication from the church further accelerated his career of a rebel who openly defied the authority of the government and converted the town of Joazeiro into a "state within the state." At this juncture, the continuous flow of pilgrims was reinforced by numerous *cangaceiros* whose devotion was divided between Father Cicero and the prospect of violence and plunder. The people of Joazeiro fortified the town and defeated a police force sent out to capture it. This easy victory marked the beginning of a rebellion during which the fanatics of Joazeiro conquered and looted many towns and finally marched upon Fortaleza, the state capital (1913–14). The intervention of the federal army and the procalamation of the state of siege eventually prevented the fanatics from taking over the state government. Although Father Cicero did not personally participate in these violent events, his almost legendary power served as a legitimizing device to bandits and politicians alike (Lourenço Filho, 1959:99–145).

Such religious movements seem to prove two things: Far from being apathetic and submissive, the marginal masses demonstrated their ability to organize themselves in their own fashion and thus to defy the tutelary aspects of the established social order, particularly the salvation monopoly of the Catholic church and the privileged status of its clergy. Neither one of the two major rebellions deliberately antagonized the Church—very few such movements do—but defiance is obviously implicit in any attempt to assume authority of which the Church is believed to be the sole legitimate holder.

The occurrence of deviant religious movements, developing out of a long tradition of messianism, shows that nonconformity did not begin with the emergence of Protestantism, nor did it remain within the confines of Protestant denominationalism. The parallel development of large Spiritualist sects and the transformation of syncretic African-Catholic cults, embodied in Macumba, Candomblé, and Xangô centers, into the more sophisticated version of the Umbanda bear additional witness to the vitality of a nonconformist strand in Brazilian society.

No major religious movement comparable to that of Canudos or the *Guerra Santa* has come to the attention of the Chilean chroniclers. Implicit dissent and the manifest desire to express belief in supernatural forces not sanctioned by the church have not extended beyond local *animita* cult centers under self-appointed guardians where the people worship the souls of persons who died a violent death, to local miracle healers and the various forms of deviation from the official credo such as those pointed out by Emile Pin, S. J. (1963: 31, 62, 65).

9

The Catholic Church and Social Control

✤ The pattern of religious deviance, however, cannot be fully understood as an expression of rebellion against traditional society. The position of the Catholic church in the power structure of Brazilian and Chilean society seems to have considerable bearing on the problem under scrutiny. And this brings us to the second qualification referring to the effectiveness of the church as a factor of social control.

It was pointed out earlier that, as a rule, Latin Americans do not hesitate to classify themselves as Catholics but that this does not ordinarily mean acceptance of the responsibilities implied by church membership. The most recent available census data reveal, for example, that 93.5 percent of all Brazilians (1950) and 92.9 percent of all Chileans (1952) declared themselves Catholics. If, however, Catholicism is measured by actual participation as required by church law, entirely different figures have been reported. According to a Chilean priest, "if 10 percent of the parishioners attend mass on Sunday the parish is rated as a "good" and if 20 percent of all parishioners fulfill their Easter duties—the minimum required by the Catholic church—the parish is rated as 'very good.'" (Muñoz Ramires, 1956: 14–15.) In Chile, regular Sunday mass attendance is reported to vary between 3.5 and 33 percent (Pin, 1963: 15). The average attendance at Sunday mass in Brazil amounts to only 10 percent (Coleman, 1958: 31). There are of course considerable regional variations, but whatever the figures may be in any particular locality or country they invariably represent only a minority of those who, by baptism and self-classification, may be regarded as Roman Catholics.

The largest percentages of "nonpracticing" Catholics are probably found among the peasantry, which elsewhere would be regarded as the stanchest element in the Catholic Church. It has been shown by such authors as Robert Redfield, George M. Foster, John Gillin, Charles Wagley, Donald Pierson, and many others including myself that the Latin American peasantry is not irreligious nor antireligious. Much on the contrary, its culture is saturated with religious beliefs and practices reflecting intimate and rather pragmatic relationships to all sorts of events and life crises that the individual feels he cannot control except by recourse to the supernatural. The core institution of Latin American "folk Catholicism" is undoubtedly the cult of the saints. All other institutions, particularly the brotherhoods, novenas, fiestas, pilgrimages, and street processions revolve around the cult of the saints, the nature of which often clashes with official Catholic doctrine. In prevalent folk belief, the saints are promoted to *de facto* deities that can bestow benefits and mete out punishments at will. A veritable folk pantheon was created which includes the second and third person of the Trinity. "Saint" Bom Jesus and the Holy Spirit (o "Divino") are typically thought of as particularly powerful saints and worshipped accordingly, while "God" becomes a rather abstract entity without specific functions. The statues of popular saints, such as the Virgin Mary, Saint Anthony, or Saint Benedict, are worshipped as if each effigy represented a separate supernatural being. According to Pin (1963:62)

Each Virgin is believed to be a distinct saint. If there are several statues of the Virgin in the same church, many faithful imagine that the effigies represent different personages. A priest who in obedience to his bishop does not permit more than one statue of the Virgin in his parish stirs up a small scandal. His parishioners say that he is cruel with those "so harshly punished little virgins."

A saint is usually approached by the institutionalized device of the "compact." People promise to light a candle, to dance in the saint's honor, to contribute gifts to his fiesta, to perform prayers or a pilgrimage to his shrine—always in exchange for a good crop, a husband, a lost object, protection against witchcraft, or the curing of a disease that may have befallen relatives, crops, or domestic animals. There is the general belief that one cannot successfully deal with environmental forces and influences or with the hidden evils of man and beast without the aid of the saints. Pregnancy, birth, marriage, sickness and death, travels and moving into a new house, the sowing and harvesting of crops are special occasions calling for supernatural protection that only particular saints can afford. Nonfulfillment of a promise entails punitive sanctions by the saint. Any failure on his part is not usually accepted with resignation, but rather resented, and sometimes physical punishment is inflicted upon his effigy.

Folk Catholicism contains many elements of pure magic. Mere physical contact with the effigy of a saint is often regarded as an effective act of propitiation or as protection against potential danger. Recited backwards, the Lord's prayer is sometimes believed to "close the body" against bullets. A prayer written on a piece of paper and swallowed by a person who has been bitten by a venomous snake renders the poison ineffective.

Brazilian and Chilean peasants live, one might say, in an enchanted world of evil spirits, magical powers, and powerful saints. The numerous shrines and images spell the promise of miracles, and many contain the crude testimonials of "actual" miracles: abandoned crutches, waxen limbs, and other material tokens of gratitude for cures performed by the saint.

The Catholic church is very much aware of the many distortions, misinterpretations, and adaptations current among the rural populations. "The Latin American people," writes a Jesuit, "constantly fear bad luck and ask religion and its rituals for protection. Here also lies the explanation of a certain passivity, and a perpetual supplication for miracles, the liberating intervention." (Pin, 1963:30.) The expectation of "liberating interventions" by the supernatural may in fact be regarded as a focal value of folk Catholicism and its influence upon the recent development of various sects emphasizing thaumaturgy or the direct intervention of the supernatural in human affairs seems to suggest, as we shall see, cultural continuity between Folk Catholicism and such groups as the Spiritualists, Umbanda, and the Pentecostal sects.

Far from being an exhaustive description of folk-Catholicism, the foregoing remarks are intended to show the extent to which the life of the peasantry is permeated with religious belief and ritual. Invocations of the supernatural in the form of preventive, protective, or productive rites accompany even minor events and actions; the evil eye, the werewolf, black magic, and a host of indigenous demons constitute permanent menaces calling for ritual defense or counter-magic. Brazilian and Chilean peasant culture is thus, in the fullest possible sense, a *sacred* culture over which the church has little control. Handicapped by a chronic scarcity of priests, the Church holds a rather peripheral position so far as the peasantry is concerned. Most rural parishes cover enormous areas with a widely scattered population and numerous chapels or "preaching points" served only by one or two priests at intervals from several weeks to several months or even years. And whenever a parish happens to be vacant—a rather common situation—the people may not see a priest for several years. Under such conditions, the priest becomes a kind of circuit rider whose time is completely taken up with baptizing infants, celebrating masses, and marrying couples who have been living together anyway. There is neither time nor opportunity for religious instruction. Whatever orthodox practice of Catholicism there may be, it is merely peripheral to the practice of folk Catholicism. At any rate, one may safely conclude that, as a rule, the peasantry is largely controlled by religion, but very little by the Roman Catholic church.

The fact that Latin American peasant culture has been classified as "sacred" does not imply that urban civilization is to be regarded as homogeneously "secular." In view of the fact that the working class of the cities is, to a very large extent, of recent rural extraction, one would hardly expect a solution of continuity with rural traditions. Though weakened, these are very much alive. The cult of the saints has its inveterate adherents, curers and sorcerers attract large clienteles, and African cult centers are found in all major cities of Brazil.

Patron saints are honored with fiestas preserving much of their original spontaneity and exhuberance. The participants tend to use them as the rural people do, heedless of ecclesiastic norms and teachings. "In Valdivia [Chile], four thousand people participate in the fiesta, two thousand in the procession . . . four hundred in the various masses and fifty-three take communion. Many people enter church during mass to offer their gifts and leave." (Pin, 1963:62.)

The mass means little, but a good relationship with a saint means a great deal. The attitude implied by the following observation (Pin, 1963:62) might be expected to exist among peasants rather than among the lower classes of Valdivia:

The devotees of the saints are scandalized when they see the priests taking away the money deposited in the poor box near the statues. They accuse the clergy of robbing the saints. In another place, the faithful burn the money they wish to offer a saint to prevent it from being stolen.

There are unmistakable indications that secularization has affected the middle and upper classes of urban Latin America to a far greater extent than the working class, in spite of the continued presence of the Catholic church. Secularism among these classes, particularly among the intelligentsia, is more than a growing indifference in religious matters, more than awareness of alleged incongruences between the "obscurantist" teachings of the church and "scientific progress." Secularism has been traced back to the weaknesses of the colonial church and to the "ecclesiastical chaos" that accompanied political emancipation in Latin America.

There seems to be a general consensus that the patronage system accounts for most of the adversities that have troubled the Catholic church during the last century and a half. The rights of royal patronage, bestowed upon the kings of Portugal and Spain, included the privilege of nominating candidates to vacant esslesiastical offices of any importance. The crown was also entitled to collect the tithes which the members of the church were expected to pay. "The Church thus became a tax-supported institution, in the same category with other civic institutions that financially depended on the state for their existence." (Coleman, 1958:7.) In other words, the patronage system actually meant interposition of the Iberian governments between the national churches and the Vatican. The American states claimed to be the legitimate heirs of the patronage system. Coleman (1958:15) went on to note that

Under the pretext that the right of patronage was inherent in the right of sovereignty (which of course it was not, although it might be in the exercise of sovereignty when granted by the Pope, as it was to Ferdinand and Isabella), the national governments attempted to set up a system of patronage and national vicariate much more injurious to the rights of the Church than the former system of royal patronage. The innovations of the French revolution in the ecclesiastical sphere were readily copied as each petty *caudillo* attempted to use the Church in his own way to further his political ambitions. A series of reforms, from the erection of new dioceses and the appointment of patriotic candidates to changes in the liturgy and disciplines of the Church, were attempted. Most of these offended even elementary ideas of ecclesiastical jurisdiction.

The ensuing struggle between the Vatican and the Latin American states spelled disaster for the Spanish American church.

With the exile or flight of most of the thirty-five bishops and archbishops, and the major religious superiors of the Orders (most of whom were Spanish and were presumed to be royalists, which often they were not), the leadership of the Church came to an abrupt end. Religious communities lost their superiors, and their property was nationalized. The morale of each community was wrecked by the inevitable political division of royalists or republicans, peninsulars or *Americanos*. The secular clergy was equally affected and reduced by at least fifty percent of its strength. There was no chance of replacing them since seminaries were nationalized as part of the universities, and entrance requirements of an impossible nature were imposed by the civil government. [Coleman, 1958:15.]

In contrast to Spanish America, Brazil settled the problem of church-state relationships in a peaceful manner. The Vatican decided to tolerate the patronage whose rights henceforward rested in the person of the emperor. The bulk of the Brazilian clergy was decidedly nationalistic and assumed a leading role in the building of a comparatively liberal and tolerant society. Indeed, being Masons, the Catholic clerics who were members of the Constituent Assembly proved to be even more liberal than their lay colleagues (Mecham, 1934:311). The absence of conflict between church and state (except for a few incidents), however, does not mean that the effects of state tutelage on the church were less detrimental in Brazil than in Spanish America. The elite of the secular clergy lined up with the imperial government against the religious orders whose wealth contrasted sharply to the relative poverty of the seculars and who "were ultramontane in sympathy and foreign in composition and control." (Mecham, 1934: 312.) Thus, under the reign of Dom Pedro I (1828) the creation of new religious orders or associations was prohibited, and drastic restrictions were imposed upon the existing ones. Entry and residence of foreign friars were no longer permitted, and those who obeyed superiors residing outside Brazil were expelled. Two orders, the Benedictines and the Carmelites, were prohibited from accepting new members. Whenever a religious order became extinct, its property was confiscated by the state (Mecham, 1934:313).

Such measures were not, as in some Spanish American countries, inspired by anticlericalism, but by the desire, shared by the emperor, the bishops, and the papal internuncio, to reform the "decadent" religious orders (Mecham, 1934:314). By the middle of the nineteenth century, state tutelage was so firmly established that the emperor could present his nominations "to all benefices and dignities independent of the advice and counsel of the prelates, as was the custom before." (Mecham, 1934:314.)

There is little doubt that the patronage system had the most deleterious effects upon the discipline of the clergy whose members were widely accused of "immorality" and "ignorance." Far from stemming the tide of anticlericalism among the urban population, the clergy rather precipitated it, while the Vatican was unable to interfere. Finally, in 1889 the empire was overthrown and Brazil became a republic. In 1890 the patronage system was abolished and Church and state separated. Now Rome was free to initiate a vast reform movement, but to such an extent had the Brazilian clergy been decimated and demoralized that a massive import of European priests was deemed necessary to rebuild the educational system, to reorganize parishes, seminaries and convents. (The expulsion of the Jesuit order in 1756 had been the first fatal blow to the existing educational system.) It seems noteworthy that particularly the members of the religious orders who came to Brazil regarded themselves as missionaries prepared to reconvert the people to the kind of orthodox Catholicism from which they had been alienated.

One major obstacle to the changes envisioned by the church was the image of the Catholic priest that had come to prevail in the mind of most Brazilians. At best, the priest was, and still is, regarded "as a mere functionary, a 'sacramentarian' performing spiritual acts for fees." (Considine, 1958:216.) Less charitable minds depict him as a cheat or a fanatic inclined to exploit the credulousness of the people and to violate the rules of celibacy. In fact, male celibacy seems so completely at variance with the Latin American sex mores and the conventional attributes of manhood that a celibate is commonly believed to be either abnormal or a hypocrite. Small wonder then that the priest is frequently ridiculed and his authority questioned. Latin American anticlericalism is not so much directed against the church as an institution as against the moral authority of the clergy to impose and to enforce ecclesiastical law. This applies to Brazil as well as to Spanish America. A recent survey of the religious practices and attitudes toward the church on the part of urban workers in three towns of central Chile reported that 77 percent of the interviewed were "in one or other way opposed to priests and the priesthood," but 47 percent believed the Catholic church to be the "true church" and 68 percent were nominal Catholics (Considine, 1958:141).

Quoting from an inquiry on the situation of the Catholic church in Valdivia (southern Chile), Emile Pin (1963:65) reported the following observations:

Far from being respected and recognized as an instrument of God, the priest is treated with suspicion, like a strange being.

The priest is believed to be a member of a class other than that of the workers, for he does not live with them and does not maintain any contact with them.

To them (the workers) the Church is something totally alien. It is not a position of hostility, but of practically ignoring its existence.

The Church is something for the rich and the women.

The Catholic Church is in a disadvantagious position in comparison with the Evangelical churches in so far as the worker identifies himself with the ministers and Evangelical churches rather than with the [Catholic] church and the Catholic priests.

Very few believe in the chastity of the priest. According to the majority, the priest is a businessman who uses the things of God to make money.

The question whether or to what extent anticlericalism is correlated with social class can only be answered in a very general way. Some of the interviewers who carried out the aforementioned survey felt that the Church does not reach the worker, who tends to regard it as something alien to his concerns. In fact, in Chile (as in other Spanish American countries) the traditional alliance between the landholding "aristocracy" and the Catholic church marked Catholicism as the religion of the rich. Muñoz Ramires (1956:29) writes

The upper class and certain selected groups of the middle class constitute what might be called official Catholicism that shines and is very much in evidence all over Chile. However, the people and a large part of the middle class . . . live out a life which is as obscure and despised as that of the remotest provinces. . . . While the upper class had priests even to teach (their children) mathematics and geography, the poor often were in want of somebody to explain them the catechism.

Although the association between the Catholic church and the upper strata of Brazilian society lacks perhaps the characteristics of a political alliance, the native clergy tends to gravitate within the orbit of the more prosperous sectors of the society, while the brunt of the pastoral and missionary work among the rural and urban masses is apt to be borne by the foreign clergy. But in Brazil, too, the children of the upper strata are often taught algebra and Latin by Catholic priests, while numerous rural parishes remain vacant for lack of clergy. The situation in the two countries differs in so far as anticlericalism is perhaps less pronounced in the middle and upper classes of Chile, while there is no indication of such class differentials in Brazil. Moreover, in Brazil there is no clerical bulwark comparable with the conservative party which encompasses most of landholding upper class of Chile.

Although Latin American anticlericalism is fundamentally a reaction against the generalized deterioration of the Catholic church under the patronage system it has doubtlessly been reinforced by a continuous flow of various philosophical ideas and principles sailing under such labels as "liberalism," "positivism," "marxism," and "materialism," which were eagerly accepted by the intelligentsia and enshrined in universities, Masonic lodges, political parties, and institutions of higher learning.

Furthermore, anticlericalism is an attitude of the Latin American male rather than of the female. At the critical age of sixteen, a young man tends to throw overboard what religious instruction he may have received and to join the peer group in its derision of the priesthood and submission to church rules, while the young woman, following the example of her mother, is likely to remain a faithful and devout member of the church. This, most Brazilian men believe, is as it should be, for "religion is women's business" and regarded as an effective control of female behavior.

The nominal Catholic in Latin America tends to consider membership in the church a birthright rather than a position to be achieved by complying with doctrine and church law. He refuses to be "pushed around by priests," and on the rare occasions when he decides to participate in some religious activity he does so without assuming future commitments of any kind. Full submission to priestly authority and minute fulfillment of religious duties are left to the *carolas* and *beatas,* as devout men and women are contemptuously called in Brazil. Reporting on the nature of Latin American Catholicism, Coleman (1958: 4) refers to certain "terms of contradiction" which suggest adaptations and reinterpretations of Catholic principles to meet accepted values and attitudes of the predominant culture.

Together with the deepest Catholic piety and devotion to the Blessed Virgin our sympathetic visitor witnesses no real regard for the Mass and the sacraments. An almost fanatical concern for the Sacrament of Baptism, he finds, is joined to a profoundly cynical view of the Sacrament of Matrimony. A visitor's final conclusion is that, whatever may be the tradition of this Catholicism, it reflects no real grasp of fundamental Catholic principles and suppositions.

There is some doubt whether such selective attitudes toward the Catholic creed can be changed merely by providing more adequate religious instruction. Inherent in the structure of the Catholic church there is a persistent demand for indoctrination and regimentation, unquestioning acceptance of priestly authority, and submission to church law. And this demand for unconditional surrender to the church (or any other institution, be it secular or sacred) sharply contrasts to one of the most deeply ingrained traits of the Latin American way of life—the right to question abstract rules meant to cover a wide range of personal situations or events. *Rules are made to serve man, not man indiscriminately to serve rules.* To obey or disobey ecclesiastical law establishing basic requirements for effective church membership is not simply a matter of instruction but of personal choice. "I have seen" writes Father Gustave Weigel (1958:421), an American Jesuit, "Latin American boys who entered into almost estatic converse with Christ after Communion, though they skipped all parts of the Mass, other than Communion itself. Nor did this profound ecstasy make them models of moral endeavor." On numerous occasions we recorded similar selective attitudes among practicing Catholics to whom particular religious experiences meant more than minute observance of rules, even if failure to observe them implied commission of a "mortal sin."

Men rather than institutions appeal to Latin Americans. This preference is clearly expressed in the prevailing attitudes toward the clergy. If the priest is a good man he will surely have a large following; he may, as Father Cicero of Joazeiro (northeastern Brazil) did, become a great thaumaturge and exercise a tremendous influence upon the community. But if the priest fails to live up to the expectations of the people, the dignity of the institution he serves does not save the parish from deterioration. The exercise of authority is a ticklish matter in Latin America. Depending on circumstances and personal qualities, it may induce submission or rebellion, and the right to rebel against authority, whatever its source, is considered inalienable by most Latin Americans.

The question about the viability of Protestantism as a form of social organization apparently has two distinct aspects. One bears on the alleged rigidity of the traditional social structure and its ability to prevent the spontaneous generation of social movements among the middle and lower social strata. It has been shown that neither society was institutionally equipped or closely enough integrated to prevent the occurrence of such movements.

The other aspect of the question concerns the capability of concerted action on the part of the lower strata, as well as the incentives for generating such actions. So far as religious movements go—and we are only concerned with these—reference was made to the eruptions of messianism among the marginal populations of the Brazilian hinterland; to the organized Afro-Catholic cult centers, many of which evolved into the nationwide Umbanda movement; and to the equally nationwide Spiritualist sects which, as Umbanda and its less sophisticated predecessors, emerged among the lower strata of the Brazilian cities. They all bear witness to the organizational capability of the masses, both rural and urban, and contradict the conventional image of apathy and conformism which allegedly prevents them from engaging spontaneously in organizational activities. In fact, none of these movements had, as Protestantism did, the benefit of foreign assistance. They were purely domestic and entirely spontaneous.

The people embarking upon the course of religious deviance were obviously motivated by the desire to correct what they perceived to be shortcomings of the traditional social order. Their unsophisticated ideologies reflect the image of a "better" society which the "fanatics" of Canudos and others actually attempted to put into practice.

In view of these facts, the moderate success of the early Protestant missions seems to derive from and to thrive on the weaknesses of the traditional social order. There can be no reasonable doubt about the existence of a middle stratum whose members, individually or in groups, could, if they chose to do so, initiate or join religious movements that were, both in ideology and structure, incompatible with the prevailing paternalistic tutelage system. There was, furthermore, a large marginal population, in overt or covert rebellion against the established social order, quite capable of generating movements of its own and fundamentally receptive to messianic ideologies that were in accord with folk tradition and translated their desire for a "better" society into concerted action.

10
The Viability of the Protestant Ethic

The normative content of American Protestantism, as taught by the early missionaries and shaped into tradition by the native clergy of the major denominations, imposed a series of severe restrictions upon personal behavior which are usually subsumed under the rubric of "Protestant ethic." These norms demanded strictest personal honesty, dedication to work, thrift, and abstention from "worldly pleasures" and "vices" concretely defined as premarital and extramarital sex, alcohol, tobacco, and certain other pleasurable experiences believed to be sinful in themselves or conducive to the commitment of sins.

Thus strict avoidance of such "worldly" forms of entertainment as theatrical performances, movies, gambling, and social dancing has traditionally been expected of the members of Protestant congregations. Likewise, exposure of the human body (on the beach, for example) and anything that might emphasize its sensual appeal, such as the use of cosmetics or decolleté dresses, are held to be incompatible with Protestant morals. These norms were "real" in the sense that the different denominations made serious efforts to convert them into actual behavior, and once they were recognized as "Protestant behavior" by the vigilant and critical non-Protestant sector of a community, the congregations really had to watch their step to live up to expectations. We are concerned here however, with the question of compatibility with traditional mores and morals.

At this point, the stereotype of the "corrupt," "indolent," "shiftless," and "easy-going" Latin may come to mind. Or one may dwell on the conventional macroscopic view of the Latin American economic systems, which were built with little regard for stability.

Most countries specialized in the production of commercial crops or raw materials from which high profits could be secured in the world market. Viewed in retrospect, the boom periods, characteristic of most Latin American economies, including those of Brazil and Chile, resemble large-scale gambling adventures; they were almost completely geared to the all-absorbing interest in immediate gains from single crops, hugh profits were drained off into conspicuous consumption, and general unconcern for the future exposed the countries to the price fluctuations of the world market. Economic depressions tended to assume the proportions of national catastrophes, leaving in their wake a depleted treasury, a bankrupt upper class, and a starving mass of unemployed or unpaid laborers. This "boom and bust" attitude, common throughout Latin America, has been defined by Wagley (1953:7) as a

desire to "get rich quickly," to make a strike by speculation, manipulation, or gambling, and to take a high profit while the taking is good before price levels crumble. Few Latin American businessmen are interested in a stable business built up over a number of years and based on a small margin of profit. Middle-class urbanites do not look forward to a comfortable old age by saving a little bit each year; instead they hope for a lucky break—to win at the lottery, a special favor from an important government official, or another windfall.

The desire "to get rich quickly" finds its strongest and most obvious expression in the extent to which gambling is rampant throughout Latin America. Whether practiced in the legal form of lotteries, betting on horse races, or in the various illegal but generally tolerated forms of card games and betting on animals or soccer games, gambling is invariably a branch of the economy, and thousands of individuals live on it, from the prosperous concessionaries of state-owned lotteries and jockey clubs down to the middle-class owners of booking establishments and the ragged street peddlers of lottery tickets. Ordinarily no one is criticized for the fact that he gambles or lives on gambling. A bookery establishment is no less respectable than a butcher's shop or a grocery store, and lotteries are widely used to provide funds for charitable and even educational institutions. In fact, the University of Concepción, Chile, runs a lottery that provides most of its income.

The unqualified acceptance of the preceding interpretation of Latin American economic behavior would, however, be tantamount to the fantastic notion that an economy can operate on the basis of speculation, manipulation, and gambling alone. The economic development of Brazil and Chile in recent decades cannot, by any stretch of imagination, be attributed to any one of those processes. Speculation and gambling cannot possibly play more than a marginal role in the basic economic processes, nor are such processes conceivable without adherence to rules of conduct socially recognized as moral, or without "dedication to work."

One wonders about the validity of such statements as the following by Weigel (1953:421), an observer of Chilean society:

By and large the American believes that life is for work, with the work occasionally interrupted with leisure so that further work may be more efficient. The Latin American thinks that life is for leisure, interrupted occasionally with work so that leisure itself is possible.

A long and intimate acquaintance with Latin America is apt to raise serious doubts about rashly generalized statements concerning certain phases of the values of that society. The qualifications one often wishes to make refer not only to regional differences but, above all, to the largely unexplored class differences. Leisure derived from lack of incentive or opportunity should be carefully distinguished from leisure as a deliberately cultivated ideal and attitude. The latter may in fact be regarded as a status symbol of the traditional upper class and those who endeavor to imitate its style of life. The former seems to be characteristic of the lower classes which are basically uncommitted to some of the predominant values of the upper strata.

The evidence supporting this statement is seen in recent changes that provided opportunities as well as incentives to a continuous stream of rural migrants flowing to the cities of Latin America. For example, the rapid transformation of São Paulo into a modern metropolis and important industrial center was accomplished by a labor force which had lain idle in the underdeveloped northeast and other areas of Brazil. As skillful and efficient construction workers, these migrants are now erecting hundreds of skyscrapers and factories, and when given a chance they even work on through the weekends to earn the higher wages paid for overtime.

While most members of the so-called aristocracy preferred their leisurely way of life to the stress and strain of industrial entrepreneurship (which fell to more ambitious immigrants from Europe and Asia), the lower classes proved much more amenable to the change of pace imposed by an emerging industrial culture. Brasília, the new capital, was built in record time by a migrant labor force recruited in the northeastern and central states. And the same sort of people are now building, with amazing speed and the aid of modern machinery, the new highways designed to link Brasília with the Amazon Basin.

The Protestant churches capitalized on existing "virtues" by strongly sanctioning them and thus promoting them to focal values of their emerging subculture. Such emphasis obviously precluded the pattern of tolerance characteristic of Brazilian or Chilean communities. Protestant morality considerably narrowed the range of permissible behavior and its corresponding institutional projections. Traditionally, a man could be a hard worker *and* regular purchaser of lottery tickets; conscientious discharge of family duties was not believed to be inconsistent with sporadic visits to taverns or brothels. To become a Protestant meant, among other things, to learn that such forms of behavior were morally irreconcilable with each other and had to be purged of their inconsistencies. And of course no community should tolerate the institutions that facilitated such behavior, although usually it lay not within the power of the Protestant congregations to eradicate institutionalized prostitution, gambling, dancing, or drinking.

At first glance, thrift seems incompatible, not only with the alleged shiftlessness and improvidence of the "Latin," but with his poverty as well. Actually, the *caixas econômicas* or *cajas de ahorro* (savings banks) appear to be extremely popular, particularly in Brazil where they cover most parts of the country with a dense network of branch offices. Since the subject has aroused little interest among the students of Latin American culture, the example of Cunha, a mountain municipio of São Paulo, may not come amiss. The region produces none of the big commercial crops, its mestizo peasants know little about modern agricultural techniques, but twenty years ago there was already a branch office of the state savings bank (Caixa Econômica Estadual) in the town of Cunha. While the big farmers resorted to the local branch of a bank, the *sitiantes* or smaller farmers took their savings to the Caixa Econômica. In fact, the total number of depositors had grown from 387 in 1930 to 895 in 1945 (Willems, 1961: 119). This may not be a very impressive total for a population of nearly 25,000, but at least it shows that among "old-stock" Brazilians thrift is not an unknown virtue. The municipio of Cunha is not exceptional in any sense, and similar cases could easily be discovered all over southern Brazil.

The aforementioned reduction of the range of permissible behavior suggests however that cultural incompatibilities do exist between the Protestant ethic and traditional Latin American mores. In fact, the prohibition of "worldly pleasures" in the sense defined above obviously clashes with the hedonistic values of the native societies. An initial qualification seems to be in order at this point. Uninhibited gratification of the senses appears to be essentially a prerogative of the male. So far as unincumbered enjoyment of sex is concerned, this cleavage has been known as the "double standard of the sex morals." Although the downright puritanical rules restricting female behavior in traditional Latin American society have been considerably relaxed in recent decades, drinking and gambling would still be regarded as unseemly for respectable women, while premarital or extramarital sex is almost as sternly sanctioned as it was in the past. Most Latin American males would probably agree that the Protestant model of asceticism admirably fits their concept of correct female behavior, and since most women have actually internalized these rules designed by a strongly androcentric society, *their* traditional way of life does not seem to be incompatible with the Protestant ethic.

The double standard is viable, however, only on the basis of a sharply drawn line of demarcation between "decent women" who live up to the puritanical code of behavior and those who are accessible for sexual enjoyment. The latter category includes not just prostitutes but also those women who enter a temporary union with a married man willing to assume economic responsibilities for them and the children they may have together. Traditionally, the line of demarcation between these two recognized categories loses some of its sharpness as one moves from the upper and middle classes to the lower classes. Recent changes, particularly in urban society, seem to be working toward a gradual blurring of the border line in all classes, apparently more so in Chile than in Brazil. Unfortunately, too little is known about these changes to warrant more than a tentative statement.

Iberian patriarchalism provides the double standard by which sex behavior is judged. The male role is centered around a set of values that may be called the "virility complex." The Latin American male adolescent learns that regular sexual intercourse is not only a physical necessity but also an essential attribute of manhood. Male chastity is ridiculed and suspected as a suggestion of sexual impotence. The male thus learns to build up his self-esteem largely in terms of sexual prowess. Although he readily assumes the economic responsibilities of married life, marriage is not expected to prevent him from having extramarital sex experiences.

On the other hand, the role of the female is centered around a cluster of values that may be characterized as the "virginity complex." Such institutional arrangements as early segregation of the sexes, chaperonage, and family-controlled courtship are regarded as component traits of the virginity complex. If an unmarried woman is known to have indulged in sexual experience, her chances of finding a husband are remote. Merely to be seen in the company of different men under circumstances suggesting intimacy may be extremely damaging to a girl's reputation. The same set of controls and sanctions continues to be operative in the life of a married woman. Exactly as before marriage, her behavior is under strict surveillance. She must refrain from any contact that, from the standpoint of a jealous husband, may be interpreted as an interference with his sexual monopoly. In other words, she must strictly avoid all those situations in which a man could find opportunity to make advances to her if he wanted to. The often violent way in which fathers or brothers react if the honor of a daughter or sister has been polluted is comparable to the intemperate sanctions a deceived husband is likely to inflict upon an unfaithful wife (Willems, 1953: 340–41).

Brazil and Chile resemble each other to such a degree that the following remarks translated from Pin (1963:73) would apply to any Brazilian town of comparable size and structure:

In Valdivia the following norms seem to be currently acceptable to the common people: Men may engage in fornication as they wish, as long as it does not do any harm to their homes; men have to take advantage of every opportunity if they do not want to be taken for perverts. To keep a concubine is too expensive, so that it is better to frequent prostitutes or to take advantage of accessible girls, especially of those who work in the factories and are believed to be always available. The sons are allowed to do whatever they want as soon as they are economically independent. Married women have to remain loyal to their husbands. It is almost regarded as a feat to have had sexual intercourse with a married woman.

The ethical objective of proselytic Protestantism was of course the elimination of the double standard, to outlaw premarital sex for men as well as women and to make the marriage vows binding for *both* sexes. In comparison to these restrictions other "vices" and expressions of *mundanismo* (worldliness) as defined earlier do not seem to be as deeply anchored in traditional patterns of behavior and may consequently be regarded as relatively minor problems, the only exception being perhaps drinking in Chile. Given the confrontation of two conflicting value systems and their corresponding ways of behavior, exactly what determined the acceptance, by many Brazilians and Chileans, of a moral code whose norms stand in such flagrant contrast to deeply ingrained traditional behavior?

The attempt to disseminate Protestantism by sheer proselytic effort —there are other forms of diffusion—is of course a history of acceptance *and* rejection. There are many communities in either country where Protestantism failed in spite of reiterated missionizing, or where it never attracted more than a handful of followers. More than one precarious foothold was subsequently lost because the local Protestants, yielding to continuing pressure, either deserted the new faith or the community, or both.

But swift acceptance of the Protestant faith by a comparatively large number of people did not always imply submission to its ethical norms, as the foundation of a substantial Presbyterian congregation in Constitución, Chile, shows. As reported by McLean (1954: 63–64), a local convert wrote at the turn of the century

I have given much thought to the question as to whether or not there really is a church in Constitución, because one does not see anything of that foundation, of those living stones, of those pillars that separate the church of Christ from the worldly society. Lying, drunkenness, profanation of the Sabbath prevail in almost all of its members and, nevertheless, one must not exercise evangelical discipline, for, in this case, in order to be consistent, it would be necessary to discipline everybody.

An extremely high rate of internal migration, particularly in Brazil, has contributed both, to the dissemination *and* to the weakening of Protestantism. One of the possible alternatives to dissemination by proselytism appears to be diffusion by migration which has been indeed a major factor of geographic expansion of most denominations. Many of our informants nevertheless voiced their skepticism about single individuals or families moving to localities that have no organized church life—where newcomers do not endear themselves to the community by implanting or furthering religious dissent.

These remarks of course do not answer the previous question; they are merely intended to prevent the impression that the history of the Protestant denominations in Brazil and Chile has been an unbroken chain of success. It seems quite safe to assume that in the process of having to choose between the Protestant faith and some traditional attitude toward religion, the number of people who decided to reject Protestantism has been much higher than that of those who accepted its conflicting value orientation. But even acceptance by a minority has to be explained.

Students of messianic or mystical movements in northeastern Brazil have pointed to their emphasis on asceticism. Reports on the religious uprisings of Juazeiro, (Lourenço Filho), Caldeirão (Duarte), Pau de Colher (Duarte), and Jeremoabo (Wagley), in addition to the major movements mentioned before, stress the stern demands the leaders made upon the morality of their followers. To join the sect of Pau de Colher, one was required to pay all his debts, to live a family life strictly in accordance with Catholic norms, to abstain from "vices," and to avoid all external signs of vanity (Duarte: 1963: 46–47). The leader of Jeremoabo "demanded of his followers rigid adherence to Catholicism, hard work, and abstinence from alcohol and tobacco." (Wagley, 1963: 246.)

These spontaneous manifestations of asceticism at the level of folk Catholicism are mentioned here merely to show that at least one marginal sector of Brazilian society has shown the capability of adopting such forms of behavior. Now the northeast has not been particularly receptive to Protestant proselytism, and the assumption of some kind of "cultural bridge" between the mystical asceticism of the northeast and Protestant puritanism does not seem to be a promising approach, especially in view of the fact that few if any cases of autochthonous asceticism have been reported from the southern regions where Protestantism has been most successful.

At any rate, the religious movements of the northeast suggest that whenever the message of a leader is perceived as relevant and meaningful by a group of underprivileged people, the adoption of ascetic patterns of behavior may be regarded as a necessary price to pay for the solution of problems which by traditional standards appear to be insoluble. In other words, the acceptance of asceticism ought to be interpreted in terms of the sociocultural context in which it occurs. If we compare the religious movements of the northeast with the emergence of the Protestant churches and sects, two characteristics seem to be common to all of them: The followers constitute part of an underprivileged mass of people whose socioeconomic situation has made them susceptible to the message of a religious leader. The message invariably contains the promise of a "better" life. Such betterment invariably requires immediate changes part and parcel of which are the ascetic ways of life.

An initially amorphous aggregate of followers enters a phase of organizational activity in the course of which a congregation or (as in the northeast) a community takes shape that is significantly different from, or even diametrically opposed to the surrounding society whose ills and evils it proposes to overcome. Carried by emotional exaltation and messianic expectations, eager to proclaim the rebirth of the self by engaging in forms of behavior intended to repudiate the weaknesses and sins of one's former life, the followers of such movements are often capable of astonishing feats. In a loosely integrated and unstable society they perform miracles of communal co-operation such as the fanatics of Caldeirão in the northeastern state of Ceará:

Within a short period of time, due to their religious ideal and work pattern following the system of mutual aid, the region, which has been considered as uninhabitable, was totally reclaimed, and developed a system of dams, wells, and cisterns, and the production of vegetables and animals sufficed to feed the group. [Duarte: 1963:43.]

Social cohesion and self-denial are maintained by a system of sanctions which in extreme cases, such as the movement of Pau de Colher, may culminate in the death penalty inflicted upon those who "turned into beasts," i.e., relapsed into "sinful" behavior. It is in this context of high-powered morale, carismatic leadership, messianic expectations and tight communal integration that ascetic behavior acquires meaning and worthwhileness. There is no intention here to overemphasize the affinity of the messianic movements of northeastern Brazil with the Protestant churches and sects. The comparison is meant merely to convey the idea that the acceptance of puritanical mode of conduct, far from being unique to Protestantism, has precedents as well as parallels in folklike religious movements, and that the sets of organizational circumstances in which such modes of behavior may emerge, resemble each other to a rather significant extent.

A rather obvious difference, however, should not be overlooked at this point. The acceptance of asceticism by both northeastern *sertanejos* and Protestants seems to be an integral part of a set of self-induced changes, yet the conditions leading to these changes suggest a major difference: The messianic movements of the northeast are responses to unchanging structural maladaptations of the traditional society, and the ultimate failure or suppression of all such movements seem to be reflections of structural rigidity of that society. The emergence and dissemination of various Protestant denominations however seems related to changing aspects of the traditional social structure and their ultimate success and permanency seem to be functionally related to fundamental sociocultural changes. Unlike the asceticism of the *sertanejo*, Protestant puritanism draws some of its meaning and worthwhileness from those changes. But this is no more than a hypothesis to be tested in another chapter.

PART III

Sociocultural Change and the Development of
Protestantism

11
Changing Conditions of Protestant Growth

It was suggested in a previous chapter that the development of Protestantism in Brazil and Chile occurred in a period characterized by major sociocultural changes and that the rapidly increasing membership of some churches and sects might be interpreted as a function of those changes. We hope to show in the present chapter that the development of Protestantism into a mass movement has been concomitant with certain changes in the social structure and value system of the two societies under scrutiny and that the largest concentrations of Protestants are now found in communities and areas most drastically affected by these changes.

The assumption that the growth of Protestantism may be regarded as a function of recent sociocultural change does not rule out, of course, the hypothesis that Protestantism in turn may become an *agent* of sociocultural change. In fact, we hope to show that acceptance of Protestant values tends to reinforce and give direction to certain changes in a fashion which appears to be quite consistent with the general trend of sociocultural evolution in Latin America. In other words, acceptance of Protestantism carries unmistakable rewards, it has a distinct "survival value" in a society suffering the pains of rapid industrialization and urbanization.

Recent change in Latin America is often viewed as a sudden leap out of the darkness of a colonial past. One easily forgets that the social history of the nineteenth century bears witness to a variety of major and minor changes that doubtlessly prepared the field for the more radical transformations of the twentieth century. For example, foreign immigration into Brazil which began in 1819 had truly revolutionary effects upon the traditional agrarian structure of the south, for it accelerated the development of the rural middle class. Thousands of European immigrants to Brazil and Chile were Protestants —something that would have been inconceivable in colonial Brazil or Chile. Nor would Protestant clergymen and missionaries have been admitted by the colonial authorities whose zeal in excluding heretics seems comparable only to the watchfulness that port authorities nowadays exhibit toward carriers of contagious diseases. Thus the arrival of the first Anglican, Congregational, Presbyterian, Baptist, and Methodist missionaries, the profuse distribution of Bibles and religious tracts by colporters, the preaching of the Gospel in public, and the founding of the first Protestant congregations composed of converts from Catholicism—these and similar events were possible only in a climate of changing social attitudes characterized by uncertainties and restlessness, by the weakening of social controls that for three centuries had effectively prevented the forces of the Protestant Reformation from penetrating the monolithic societies of Latin America.

This is not to say that Brazilian or Chilean society of the nineteenth century was particularly favorable to the religious and ethical reforms intended by the Protestant missionaries. Continuing contact between Protestant missionaries and Latin American communities produced the kind of conflict which might be expected when sharply contrasting value systems are brought into confrontation. Organized attempts to change deep-rooted religious beliefs and practices could not fail to arouse antagonism, resentment, and open hostility. One ought to bear in mind that Latin American society had absorbed Roman Catholicism so thoroughly that to many it had acquired a symbolic meaning above and beyond its religious content. This explains the somewhat surprising fact that many Latin Americans who were nominal Catholics at best arose in arms against the "Protestant peril" in defense of religious unity, which to many had become the equivalent of cultural unity. They identified Catholicism with their traditional way of life which they felt was threatened by an exotic doctrine seemingly incompatible with and inadaptable to their own value system. Of course, prejudice and legal discrimination against religious "heresy" were part and parcel of the colonial heritage, and by conceding an institutional monopoly to the Catholic church, a considerable portion of that heritage was perpetuated by the republics.

Nothing, however, would be farther from the truth than the idea of a solid wall of religious intolerance. Not only were there considerable differences from country to country, but within some of the republics the predominant attitude toward Protestantism was often marked by inconsistencies. Article 5 of the constitution of the Brazilian empire, for example, recognized Roman Catholicism as the religion of the state. The same article, however, contains a proclamation of religious freedom, qualified nevertheless by the stipulation that non-Catholic cults were to be practiced in buildings which by their external form could not be identified as churches. There were other legal restrictions deriving mainly from the fact that only Catholic parish priests could perform valid marriage ceremonies, which automatically branded Protestant marriages as concubinage and their offspring as illegitimate. The first Protestants to be affected by these discriminatory laws were the German Lutheran immigrants who, since 1824, had settled in southern Brazil. They too were the first to insist on liberalizing the law, and they thus prepared the field for a more tolerant attitude toward differing religious creeds.

Numerous observers who traveled in imperial Brazil reported manifestations of tolerance as well as intolerance. In a rather famous statement, made in 1845, the Reverend D. P. Kidder (Kidder and Fletcher, 1866:143), wrote,

that there is not a Roman Catholic country on the globe where there prevails a greater degree of toleration or a greater liberality of feeling toward Protestants. I will here state, that in all my residence and travels in Brazil in the character of a Protestant missionary, I never received the slightest opposition or indignity from the people. As might have been expected, a few of the priests made all the opposition they could; but the circumstance that they were unable to excite the people showed how little influence they possessed. On the other hand, perhaps quite as many of the clergy, and those of the most respectable in the empire, manifested toward us and our work both favor and friendship. From them, as well as from the intelligent laity, did we often hear the severest reprehension of abuses that were tolerated in the religious system and practices of the country, and sincere regrets that no more spirituality pervaded the public mind.

Not all Protestant missionaries were received as well as Dr. Kidder. The history of the Presbyterian, Methodist, and Baptist missions in Brazil reports frequent instances of strong opposition, even physical aggressions, to which evangelists and colporters were exposed (Mesquita, 1940:56, 100, 133, 137, 217, 270, 287; Ferreira, 1959:157; Buyers, 1945:416). It would seem that local reactions to Protestant proselytism varied so radically as to make generalizations almost impossible. The establishment of organized churches often had disintegrating effects on the community whose members refused to accept the *crentes* (as the Protestants are usually called) as equals. The way in which conversion affected the social status of the Protestants in the community was aptly described by Hugh C. Tucker (1902:203–264). Reporting on his own experiences as a colporter at the close of the nineteenth century, this missionary wrote as follows:

Another fact also that militates greatly against the native colporter and his work is the contempt in which converts from Romanism are held by the masses generally. Many think it is all right for the foreigner who was born and brought up in the Protestant faith to follow that way and even engage in the active work of propagating his religion. But for a native Brazilian, who was brought up a Roman Catholic to apostatize and become a Protestant is intolerable; such are held in great disdain, and by some are considered unworthy of respect. It is difficult for the foreigner to realize fully the position in which the native convert is placed when he abandons the religion of his country and of his ancestors. Rome's assumption of the claim to be the only true Church with an infallible head, a regular and uninterrupted transmission of ministerial authority through bishops and priests, and an elaborate form of ceremonial worship has through centuries maintained a firm hold upon the minds of the masses. Many religious rites and ceremonies have become social customs, inseparable from the real social life of the people. For one to abandon these is in a great measure to ostracise himself from his people.

It was in Brazil rather than in Chile that anti-Protestantism tended to express itself through the language of nationalism. José Felicio dos Santos wrote in 1921.

Protestantism is detested by our best people, even outside the Catholic milieu. It is not only the enemy of our traditions, not only of the traditions of our fatherland, but also of the traditions of our race. In the history of Brazil Protestantism only appears associated with the elements of disgrace, spoliation, devastation, and ruins. [Cit. ap. Rossi, 1938:23.]

And Antonio Torres's imputation of political intentions was repeated in more or less vituperative language by many Brazilians who had little or no interest in any kind of organized religion including the Catholic church:

The North Americans furtively continue their policy of expansion among ourselves, and, at the same time, of our defamation among themselves. . . . It is not necessary to be a Catholic in order to assist the Church in its nationalistic mission. It suffices to be a Brazilian and a patriot. . . . To defend the Catholic church means to defend Brazil. [Rossi, 1938:24.]

Still in 1938 a Jesuit priest expressed a similar point of view in a more sophisticated language:

The Protestant churches, outside their early and dishonorable manifestations only emerge on the National scene after the spirit of *brasilidade* of our people had taken shape, and with their propaganda they have raised the doubts and apprehensions of many students of our realities. The Catholic church however emerges in the very beginning of Brazilian life, and it is under its protection, under the activity of the secular and regular clergy that the history of Brazil unfolds as more than a few historians, who are not suspect of being friends of the Church, sincerely stated. Therefore, if we did not have motives of a superior order—which would be absurd—a sane and well understood patriotism would suffice to induce the Brazilians to lend prestige and to support the activities of the Catholic church. [Rossi, 1938: 173.]

The Protestants had thus to face the frequently repeated charge that their way of life was incompatible with Brazilian traditions, and, still worse, that they were mercenaries or dupes of a foreign political ideology. It was left to them to dispel these suspicions and to prove themselves good citizens. One way of doing this was emancipation from the tutelage of American mission boards and the formation of autonomous national churches.

During the first half of the nineteenth century Chile was rather adamant in her refusal to tolerate any form of religious worship except Roman Catholicism. Article 10 of the constitution of 1822 stipulated that

the religion of the state is the Roman Apostolic Catholic to the exclusion of any other; its protection, preservation, purity, and inviolability is one of the first duties of the chiefs of the state, as it is [the duty] of the inhabitants of the territory to respect and venerate it, no matter what their private opinions are.

At any rate, the same charter (article 221) assures the citizenry that their thoughts and manifestations thereof are not punishable providing they do not contain "calumnies, insults or instigations to crime."

Juan de Egaña's treatise on religious liberty deeply impressed public opinion during the period of political emancipation, not only in Chile, but in most Spanish American republics. Egaña opposed religious liberty on three grounds:

A large number of religions in a single state leads to irreligion, which is the tendency of our century. Two religions in a state lead to a struggle which eventually will result in the destruction of the state or of one of the religious parties. Religious uniformity is the most effective means of consolidating the tranquillity of the populace.

Egaña did not want "to punish opinions," yet he suggested that "temples be refused to other cults and that those engaged in proclaiming them be forced to leave." (Donoso, 1946: 183–184.)

As in Brazil, the first Protestant congregations on Chilean soil were founded by foreign residents and German immigrants. Their toleration served as precedents and kept religious controversy in a state of flux. When in the second half of the nineteenth century Methodist, Presbyterian, Baptist, and Anglican missionaries began to preach their creeds they found support as well as opposition (Donoso, 1946: 188ff.; Arms, 1923:31). "But after inaugurating her independent career as one of the most intolerant of the Catholic governments of South America, Chile has become in recent years one of the most liberal nations in matters of religion." (Mecham, 1934:246.) In 1865, an amendment to the constitution was enacted liberalizing the practice of non-Catholic cults. It also "permitted dissenters to establish and maintain private schools to teach their children the doctrines of their religion." (Vergara, 1962:39.) In 1884, the Law of the Civil Register was enacted depriving the Catholic priests of the prerogative to administer the records of vital statistics which were entrusted to civil functionaries. The union of the state and church, however, was dissolved only by the constitution of 1925.

In 1885, a Protestant group received legal recognition, whereby those who professed the Reformed church religion according to the doctrines of the Holy Scriptures, might promote primary and secondary instruction according to modern methods and practice, and propagate the worship of their beliefs obedient to the law of the land. (Mecham, 1934:262–263.)

In spite of all tolerance—or indifference as some prefer—in matters of religion, the struggle of the Protestant churches for social recognition has been harder and less successful than in Brazil. The traditional loyalty which the upper social strata, particularly the landholding "aristocracy," feel for the Catholic church has made it virtually impossible for the proselytic Protestant churches to gain followers among the members of that class. And from the standpoint of the status-seeking historical churches, the overwhelming success of the

Pentecostal movement has been a distinct drawback. Although the unorthodox and completely unsophisticated forms of proselytism practiced by the Pentecostal sects have attracted thousands of followers among the lower classes, they have also generated ridicule and contempt in the Chilean society at large. The disdainful designation *canuto* has gained wide currency and is often indiscriminately applied to *all* Protestants. The popular definition *los canutos son los locos que gritan en la calle* (the *canutos* are the crazy ones who shout in the street) obviously expresses derision and the desire to ostracise such dubious elements from middle-class respectability.

There is of course nothing unusual about the social ostracism inflicted upon those who accept a radical innovation, especially if they happen to belong, as most Protestant converts do, to the underprivileged classes of a rigidly stratified society. The dividing effects which the new creed had upon the community were emphasized by the fact that its ethical corollaries indeed conflicted with cherished social customs. Social ostracism as well as the moral obligation to disobey customs taken for granted by the community at large, led to general withdrawal of the Protestants from what they branded as mundanismo, and the organization of tightly integrated bodies of believers who sought to compensate structural isolation with internal cohesion and the fullest possible participation in group affairs.

The early history of Protestantism clearly reflects reluctance and opposition of the recipient societies as they were confronted with the new faith. The Brazilian Baptist church, for example, which eventually became one of the most successful of the historical churches, was founded in 1882 (Crabtree, 1937:54). After seven years of considerable missionary effort in various parts of the country, it had nine local churches with a total membership of 312 (Crabtree, 1937:82). Ten years later there were only 784 Baptists in the entire country (Crabtree, 1937:119). Crabtree's description of the vicissitudes of early evangelical endeavor suggests tenaciousness and moral stamina on the part of the missionaries rather than impressive success. In 1862 the first Presbyterian congregation was established in Rio de Janeiro. By 1869 there were six churches with a total membership of 279. After forty-three years of incessant proselytism and a major schism there were fourteen thousand Presbyterians in Brazil (Ferreira II, 1960:92). In the same year (1905) the Methodist Church, which had begun its missionary efforts in 1836 (Read, 1965:181), reported a membership of six thousand.

Although very few reliable figures are available, Protestant missions seemingly encountered even greater difficulties in Chile. At the turn of the century, the Presbyterian Church which had been established in 1863 counted approximately five hundred members "in full communion." By 1954 the total membership was 2,078—certainly not a very impressive growth for seven decades of evangelical endeavor (McLean, 1954:72–73; Vergara, 1962:41). The Methodist Church in Chile never fully recovered from the schism of 1909 which carried away most of its followers including one of its most respected leaders. The minutes of the fifty-eighth Annual Conference of the Methodist Church in 1958 reported a total of 4,581 communicant members "or slightly less" than the official figure of 1957. More successful than either Methodists or Presbyterians, the Baptists counted 7,205 members in 1958 (La Voz Bautista, 1959:12). Moore traced the Baptist movement in Chile back to German immigrants who settled in 1888 near Victoria, then a typical frontier community. During the first decades, very few people were converted to the new creed. By 1920, six years after the Foreign Mission Board of the Southern Baptist Convention of the United States had decided to subsidize the Chilean Baptists, these merely consisted of "a few scattered congregations mostly around Temuco, with little training, no institutional work, not a single church house, school, or pastor's home." (Moore, MS:16–17.) The same author pointed out in 1959 that besides the seven thousand members of the Chilean Baptist Convention there were "as many or more scattered among two or three other missions or conventions, plus many thousands of people who, if forced to name themselves, would call themselves Baptists." (Moore, MS:17.) Even if Moore's estimate of a Baptist constituency of fifty thousand seems too high, many more Chileans were no doubt attracted by the Baptists than by the other historical churches. What appears to be more relevant in the present context, however, is the fact that *growth on a large scale began only after 1930*, when the rate of social change picked up momentum and the traditional culture began to crack under the strain of the great depression, industrialization, and population increase.

The assumption of a functional relationship between sociocultural change and the growth of Protestantism seems even more viable with regard to the development of the Pentecostal sects. In Chile, Pentecostalism emerged from a schism in the Methodist Church that took place in 1909. In Brazil it was a Swedish missionary who in 1910 founded the Assembly of God, and in the same year an Italian missionary, who had been a member of the Presbyterian church in Chicago, established the Christian Congregation of Brazil. Since the Pentecostals have shown a biblical reluctance in counting their followers, almost no figures are available on early developments, but for about two decades their proselytic effort seems to have caused little concern to the historical churches. A survey on Brazil, published in 1932, stated that only 9.5 percent of the Brazilian Protestants, excluding the communities of German origin, belonged to Pentecostal bodies (Braga and Grubb, 1932:71). It seems that after 1930 the Pentecostal movement gained momentum, both in Brazil and Chile. The Christian Congregation of Brazil reported 17,761 baptisms between 1935 and 1940 (Francescon, 1958:25). This figure however has been dwarfed by recent increases. According to Read, the Christian Congregation had, in 1940, 50,223 communicant members. During the next two decades this figure grew fivefold and reached 264,020 in 1962. Using the Institute of Church Growth formula ("active communicant members times two equals community"), total membership came close to 600,000 persons in 1962 (Read, 1965:28). With regard to the Assembly of God, Read (1965:120) reports a growth from 14,000 in 1930 to 702,750 in 1962. It is not entirely clear, however, whether these figures include only communicant members or the "total community."

The growth of the historical churches in Brazil has been considerable since 1930. In 1935 the Brazilian Baptist Convention reported 43,306 members (Mesquita, 1940:349). In 1958 total membership had climbed to 163,859, and in 1961 it was reported to be 186,595 (O Estatista, 1960:7, No. 1). The Presbyterian Church of Brazil has maintained the second place so far as membership growth among the historical churches is concerned. From 55,468 communicants in 1946 it grew to 88,154 in 1958 and to 103,000 in 1963 (Read, 1965:113). The Methodist Church of Brazil has grown at a considerably slower rate. Its membership of 6,000 in 1905 climbed to 30,060 in 1941

(Buyers, 1945:435), reached 44,453 in 1958, and 52,998 in 1962 (Read, 1965:183).

Unfortunately, figures on religious affiliation in Brazil and Chile, as in most other countries of Latin America, can only be considered as approximations. So far as Protestant denominations are concerned, official census figures reflect, not only congenital weaknesses of governmental inquiries, but also inconsistencies in the way of reporting denominational membership. Some churches count only their communicants, while others include minors. Information supplied by denominational authorities responding to inquiries of entities such as the Evangelical Confederation of Brazil varies from careful membership counts to mere estimates. A major attempt to provide statistical information on the development of Protestantism in Latin America was made by Father Damboriena. Unfortunately, his figures are not consistent, neither with each other nor with official census counts. Comparing the total number of Protestants according to his Table 4, with the totals of Tables 23 and 24, for 1957, one wonders about the following discrepancies (Damboriena, 1962: 17, 53, 63):

PROTESTANTISM IN CHILE AND BRAZIL (1957)

	Table 4	Tables 23 and 24
Brazil	1,755,929	2,080,982
Chile	370,428	582,151

The source quoted by Damboriena claims a total of 4,071,643 Brazilian Protestants for 1961, while the official figure for the same year amounts to less than half of that number (Instituto Brasileiro de Geografia e Estatistica [I.B.G.E.], Anuario Estatístico, 1963). The latter figure is certainly far too low, while the former one, based upon information supplied by the different denominations, suffers from rather generous estimates in which some of the sects seem to indulge.

Official census data on religious affiliation were sporadic in the past, but beginning in 1940 they have been consistently included in the national censuses. The first count of Protestants carried out in 1890 reported a total of 143,743, or one percent of the entire population of Brazil. In view of the relatively slow development of the proselytic churches, one may assume that the majority of these Protestants was composed of members of the German Evangelical churches. After a gap of half a century, the census of 1940 reported 1,074,857 Protestants representing 2.61 percent of the Brazilian people. Ten years later, according to the census of 1950, there were 1,741,430 Evangelicals in Brazil, and the percentage on the total population has grown to 3.35 (*Conselho Nacional de Estatística*, 1953: 1). The Evangelical Confederation of Brazil reported a total of 2,697,273 Protestants for 1958. If we assume that the population of Brazil had grown to 66,-000,000 in the same year, then 4.1 percent of all Brazilians were affiliated with some Protestant church.

Estatística do Culto Protestant do Brazil, an annual census of Brazilian Protestantism since 1955 (I.B.G.E., 1956, 1960) reports an increase from 1,405,347 Protestants in 1955 to 1,897,611 in 1960, a gain of 35 percent in five years. Though incomplete, these figures are nevertheless indicative of a growth rate more than double that of the general population.

For the year 1961 Taylor and Coggins (1961: 5) reported a total of 1,763,142 "church members," and the figure of 3,394,673 constituting the "Protestant Community" in Brazil. There is no reason to assume that these data are more accurate than those of *Estatística do Culto Protestante do Brazil*.

Statistical information on the development of Pentecostalism in Chile is unavailable or vague. Census data concerning the growth of Chilean Protestantism in general (Table VI) suggest that large-scale expansion of the sects began after 1930. Between 1954 and 1960 the congregations of the Iglesia Metodista Pentecostal grew from 615 to 804, and those of the Iglesia Evangelica Pentecostal from 494 to 611. Vergara thinks that in 1960 the former must have had more than 200,-000 members and the latter about 150,000 (Vergara, 1962:121–122). These figures do not include, of course, the membership of the numerous Pentecostal congregations independent of either institution. Drawing on undisclosed sources, Vergara (1962: 247) refers to a total of 2,317 "Pentecostal groups" with a joint membership of 459,040. Although lower than Damboriena's figure of half a million (1962:63), Vergara's estimate surpasses the total number of Protestants reported by the census of 1960 (Table VI).

All these figures apparently refer to the "total Protestant community," including minors and perhaps those who attend religious services without being communicants. Interestingly enough, Taylor and

Coggins report a "Protestant community" of 403,140 in 1961, a figure considerably lower than Vergara's total of 564,536 and somewhat below the census figure of 411,530 (Taylor and Coggins, 1962: VII). Actually, Vergara thinks that another 10 percent should be added to the preceding total, raising it to 620,000 (Vergara, 1962:248).

In a recent paper on the "Protestant Expansion in Chile," Cristián Lalive d'Epinay (1966:26–27) found the official census data "extraordinary enough to overcome the temptation to raise them further." Commenting on the development of Chilean Protestantism in general, he writes as follows:

In 1920 there were 55,000 Protestants in Chile, 17,000 of whom were aliens. In the following period the increase is small, almost exactly proportional to the population increase, and in 1930 only three out of every 200 persons are Protestants. Now the explosion begins: The annual growth rate rises from 1.46 percent between 1920 and 1930, to 6.45 percent during the following decade, and to 6.60 percent at the present time. It is surprising that from 1930 to 1960 the annual growth rate should have remained constant: Every 10 or 11 years the number of Protestants doubles, and today, after 30 years of expansion, 11 out of every 200 persons are Protestants.

12

The Ecology of Protestantism in Brazil

✣ In both countries, the membership of the different Evangelical bodies began to augment, at an increasingly faster rate, since 1930. This development runs roughly parallel with the changes that affected the culture of both societies. Parallelism however, does not necessarily indicate relationship. The assumption of a functional relationship between sociocultural change and expansion of Protestantism will gain in validity if it can be shown that the areas most strongly affected by certain changes are also those of the heaviest concentration of Protestants, and that, conversely, in those which have remained relatively untouched by particular changes, diffusion of Protestant creeds has made comparatively little progress.

To examine the relative position of Protestantism in the five geographical regions into which Brazil is conventionallly divided, *Estatística do Culto Protestante do Brasil* offered the only available chance for regional comparisons. This census is far from complete, but it presents at least the results from 1,600, or approximately two thirds of all Brazilian *municipios*. The last available data refer to 1960.

Table VII shows that 61.5 percent of all Brazilian Protestants are located in southern Brazil, the population of which corresponds to only 35 percent of the total population. The most glaring discrepancy between the number of Protestants and relative population is found in the northeast, which contains 22.1 percent of the total population but only 9.2 percent of all Brazilian Protestants. The seven states of the northeast constitute an area of high population density which has remained relatively unaffected by recent sociocultural changes and exhibits a profound attachment to its historical traditions. Of the three major areas, the south has doubtlessly been the focal area of all major changes, leaving the more heterogeneous east somewhat in the middle between conflicting tendencies. North and center-west represent little, either in population density or number of Protestants, but it should be noted that in both areas Protestantism fares relatively better than in the northeast. This is understandable, for neither region is firmly committed to the value system and the type of social stratification that have acted as impediments to changes in the northeast.

Within this context, the position of proselytic Protestantism in the south is less impressive than the figures seem to indicate. It ought to be borne in mind that a very large proportion of all southern Protestants belongs to the nonproselytic churches of German provenience. It would be absurd to assume a relationship between this type of Protestantism and recent changes, for the existence of German Protestantism preceded these changes by almost a century. The southern state that has been undergoing the most rapid and far-reaching transformations is of course São Paulo. Within its confines, the occurrence of German Lutheranism is limited to a few congregations which represent an exceedingly small proportion of the total Protestant constituency of this state. Its 400,936 Evangelical citizens constitute 21.2 percent of all Brazilian Protestants, while its population represents only 18.1 percent of the Brazilian people.

If we take the most rapidly changing states of the east and south, after eliminating the two southernmost states of Rio Grande do Sul and Santa Catarina with large populations of German Lutheran stock, a contiguous region composed of six states remains: Minas Gerais, Espírito Santo, Rio de Janeiro, Guanabara, São Paulo, and Paraná. Culturally speaking, the two remaining states of the east, Bahia and Sergipe, should be classified with the northeast because they resemble this area more than their southern neighbors. By thus partitioning the East among the Northeast and the South we create two major areas which in spite of their internal differentiation may be considered as subcultures. In fact, the northeast has always been regarded as such, and so has the south, while the intervening states were sometimes classified as "Industrial Brazil" or "Industrial States of the Center" (Wagley, 1948: 460; Azevedo, 1959: 161 ff.). If industrialization and its attendant changes are selected as criteria of classification, it is of course inconsistent to exclude the deep south as some authors do. We are thus inclined to regard the aforementioned six states plus Santa Catarina and Rio Grande do Sul as one major culture area of Brazil. Only the predominant characteristics of their Protestant population make it necessary to exclude the latter two states from the present comparison.

The area thus limited was inhabited, according to the census of 1960, by 35, 334, 195 people representing 44.4 percent of Brazil's total population. In 1960, 936,902 members of Protestant churches were recorded in this area. (I.B.G.E. *Estatística do Culto Protestant do Brasil.* 1960) This amounts to 49.4 percent of Brazil's total Protestant population.

On the other hand, the rectified northeast now including Bahia and Sergipe had a population of 22,428,873, 221,480 of whom declared themselves to be Protestants. This means that, while 31.6 percent of all Brazilians inhabited the northeast (in 1960), its Protestants amounted to only 11.6 percent of the total Protestant population of the country.

To measure recent developments of Brazilian Protestantism the figures for 1956 and 1960 were compared. In the latter year, there were 356,583, or 28.9 percent more Protestants than in 1956. Examining the four previously defined culture areas, absolute as well as percentage increases show variations in accordance with the characteristics of each area (See Table IX). At first glance, the gain made by the south may seem comparatively small, but if the state of São

Paulo is isolated from the rest of the area it becomes at once obvious that diffusion of the different Protestant creeds has been far more extensive in this state than anywhere else in Brazil. In four years the number of Protestants increased by 157,653, or 64.8 percent.

Although the figures concerning north and center-west represent relatively little in the total picture of Brazilian Protestantism, the growth rates referring to these two areas are much higher than those of all others. Since there were comparatively few Protestants to begin with, a substantial increase is of course reflected in high percentages. The increase itself is not surprising, mainly because commitment to traditional values appears to be weak in either region. Especially center-west may be considered a vast frontier, but also the north seems to have entered a new phase of economic development.

The assumption that the diffusion of Protestantism has been roughly parallel to the processes of industrialization and urbanization, and that the largest concentrations of proselytically minded Protestants are found in areas where these processes have been most intensive, is supported by figures concerning the growth of the industrial labor force and its distribution within Brazil. Table X shows that between 1920 and 1940 the number of industrial workers almost trebled and that in 1960 it was almost twice as high as in 1940. The dominant position of the area previously labeled "south" is obvious from Table XI. In 1920 the industrial workers of that area represented 66.7 percent of the total industrial labor force of Brazil. In 1940 that percentage had risen to 69.2, and in 1950 it reached 70.8. Figures for 1960 are not yet available.

Within the area, the state of São Paulo maintained a clearly dominant position. In 1920 the number of industrial workers in São Paulo did not exceed 30.5 percent of the Brazilian labor force. In subsequent decades this percentage climbed steadily. It reached 34.9 percent in 1940, 41.2 percent in 1950, and 45.2 percent in 1960.

The obvious correspondence of Protestant concentrations and areas of pronounced sociocultural change—in general, southern Brazil and more specifically the state of São Paulo—is suspectible of further testing. Somewhat detailed information is available on São Paulo which has been divided into twenty-three "ecological areas" (Lopes, 1957: 81 ff.), characterized primarily by geographical and cultural facts such as economic production, occupations, urbanization, and educational achievements (see maps). Each ecological area has its distinct historical tradition of land occupation and use; in each the social structure shows signs of being intimately associated with a particular economic system, responsive or unresponsive to changes that bypassed some areas and deeply affected others.

The census on Protestants of 1960 refers to 372 *municipios* out of a total of 504. No Protestant congregations seem to exist in some *municipios*, while others failed to report their Protestant population. Although further information is unavailable, one may safely assume that the total number of Protestants in the state of São Paulo is substantially higher than the figures indicate.

Immediately obvious from Table XII is the dominant position of Zona Industrial, a region that includes the metropolitan area of São Paulo City, all surrounding satellite cities, except Santos, as well as other more or less industrialized *municipios* forming a contiguous belt around the state capital. This area accounts for 233,175 or 58.1 percent of the Protestant population of the state, while the population of Zona Industrial amounts to 46.0 percent of the total population of the state.

Zona Industrial and especially its core, the metropolitan area of São Paulo, is doubtlessly undergoing faster and more radical changes than any other part of Brazil. Although there is no other concentration of Protestants in the state comparable to that of Zona Industrial, there are nevertheless pronounced variations in the way in which the Protestant population is distributed. Comparison of three contiguous areas, Vale do Paraiba, Serra do Mar and Litoral, for example, shows that the latter had almost nine times as many Protestants in 1960 than did Serra do Mar, which in turn had about one fifth that of the Paraiba Valley. Again it seems possible to explain the major differences in terms of urbanization and industrialization. Santos and its metropolitan area account for 9,474 out of the 15,796 Protestants inhabiting the coastal region of São Paulo. Of the remaining 6,224, 1,116 live north of Santos and 5,108 to the south.

It happens that neither important cities nor large industries are found in the southern sector of the coastal regions, which could possibly explain this difference. The north however has a more tradition-bound society living in a state of geographical and cultural isolation which only very recently has begun to break down in some parts.

Certain sections of the southern coast are as isolated as the north, but there are at least two major foci of recent land occupation by migrant populations which are engaged in modern, commercial agriculture (rice, bananas, tea, mainly), totally different from the desultory subsistence agriculture that predominates in the north.

One of these areas consists of two *municipios*, Registro and Jacupiranga, where a few thousand Japanese immigrants developed modern tea farming and processing. The other area is composed of five *municipios* adjacent to a trunk railway linking Juquiá with the port of Santos. These two areas account for 80 percent of all Protestants located in the southern coastal regions.

The difference between the southern and northern coast of São Paulo raises the question whether urbanization and industrialization alone generate conditions favorable to the eclosion of Protestant movements. The most perfunctory glance at Table XII shows that it would be difficult to maintain such an assumption. Many of the twenty-three ecological regions have no large urban centers, yet considerable proportions of the people are Protestants. In fact, the occurrence of large Evangelical congregations in purely rural areas is by no means limited to the southern coast of São Paulo, while on the other hand there are numerous urban centers, particularly in northeastern Brazil, where Protestantism has made little headway.

Our initial hypothesis of a functional relationship between the expansion of Protestantism and general sociocultural changes should not be taken in the sense that these changes are exclusively related to urbanization and industrialization. They may and do occur in rural areas, although the modern Latin American city provides a setting which has proven particularly destructive to the traditional social structure. The predominant traits of this structure—familism and feudal paternalism with its built-in sanctions—are found in preindustrial cities as well as in vast rural areas. They may break down in both, and *they may never have existed at all in certain rural areas where a native peasantry was bypassed by the hacienda or plantation system.* A brief analysis of the Paraiba Valley and Serra do Mar will elucidate these statements.

One of the smallest percentages, .5, of São Paulo's Protestant population is found in the Serra do Mar. Its population density (16.5 per square kilometer in 1950) is higher than that of four other regions

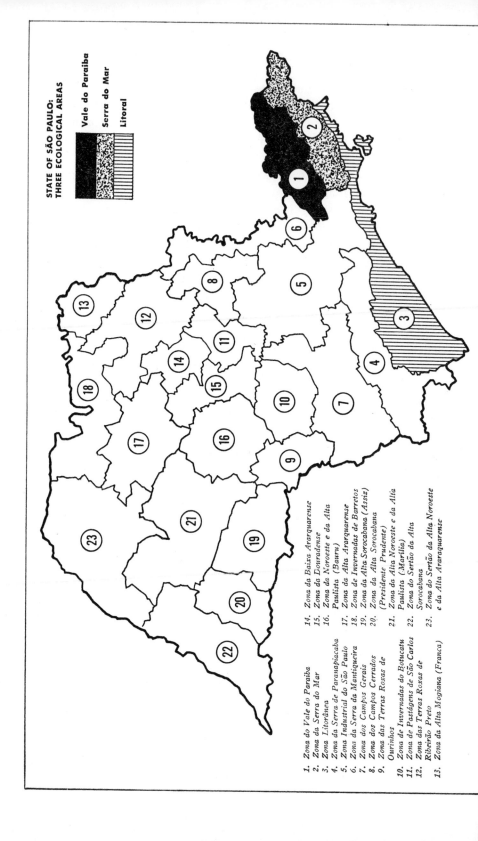

STATE OF SÃO PAULO:
THREE ECOLOGICAL AREAS

Vale do Paraiba
Serra do Mar
Litoral

1. Zona do Vale do Paraiba
2. Zona da Serra do Mar
3. Zona Litorânea
4. Zona da Serra de Paranapiacaba
5. Zona Industrial do São Paulo
6. Zona da Serra da Mantiqueira
7. Zona dos Campos Gerais
8. Zona dos Campos Cerrados
9. Zona das Terras Roxas de
   Ourinhos
10. Zona de Invernadas do Botucatu
11. Zona de Pastágens de São Carlos
12. Zona das Terras Roxas de
    Ribeirão Preto
13. Zona da Alta Mogiana (Franca)

14. Zona da Baixa Araraquarense
15. Zona da Douradense
16. Zona da Noroeste e da Alta
    Paulista (Bauru)
17. Zona da Alta Araraquarense
18. Zona de Invernadas de Barretos
19. Zona da Alta Sorocabana (Assis)
20. Zona da Alta Sorocabana
    (Presidente Prudente)
21. Zona da Alta Noroeste e da Alta
    Paulista (Marília)
22. Zona do Sertão da Alta
    Sorocabana
23. Zona do Sertão da Alta Noroeste
    e da Alta Araraquarense

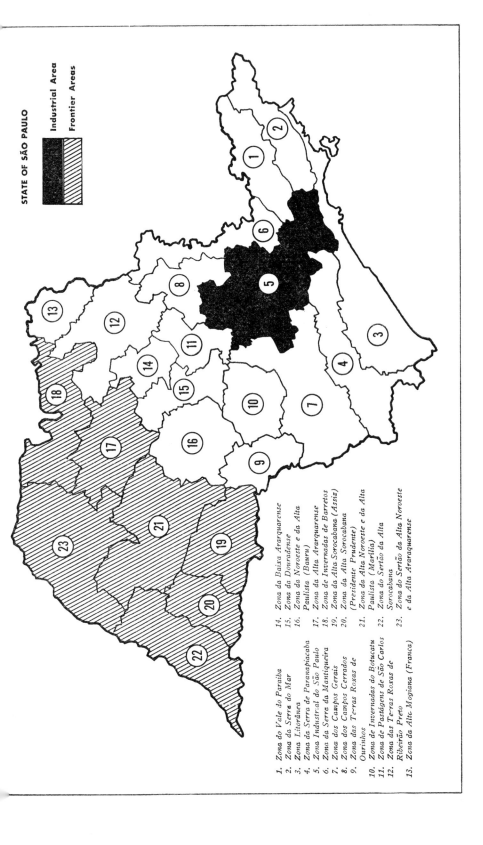

STATE OF SÃO PAULO

Industrial Area
Frontier Areas

1. Zona do Vale do Paraíba
2. Zona da Serra do Mar
3. Zona Litorânea
4. Zona da Serra de Paranapiacaba
5. Zona Industrial do São Paulo
6. Zona da Serra da Mantiqueira
7. Zona dos Campos Gerais
8. Zona dos Campos Cerrados
9. Zona das Terras Roxas de Ourinhos
10. Zona de Invernadas do Botucatu
11. Zona de Pastagens de São Carlos
12. Zona das Terras Roxas de Ribeirão Preto
13. Zona da Alta Mogiana (Franca)

14. Zona da Baixa Araraquarense
15. Zona da Douradense
16. Zona da Noroeste e da Alta Paulista (Bauru)
17. Zona da Alta Araraquarense
18. Zona de Invernadas de Barretos
19. Zona da Alta Sorocabana (Assiz)
20. Zona da Alta Sorocabana (Presidente Prudente)
21. Zona da Alta Noroeste e da Alta Paulista (Marília)
22. Zona do Sertão da Alta Sorocabana
23. Zona do Sertão da Alta Noroeste e da Alta Araraquarense

which have several times as many Protestants as the Serra do Mar. Until recently, geographical and cultural isolation has kept outside influences to a minimum, but like the northern coast of the state, Serra do Mar has been exposed to Protestant proselytism, for most *municipios* have Protestant congregations, and the foundation of most of these antedates recent "progress" in the form of highways, bus lines, electricity and the like. Decisive, however, seems to be the fact that all *municipios* except one belonged, until about fifty years ago, to the oldest coffee-producing area of the state.

In other words, the social structure of Serra do Mar was shaped by the hacienda system, and when coffee agriculture disappeared and the region became one of the poorest of the state, the old structure persisted by sheer inertia. The more enterprising people left the region, and the ones who did not want to or could not leave it showed little desire for change. The individual continued to live within the confines of the traditional kinship group, unwilling or unable to do things that would have been severely criticized by his numerous blood relatives, in-laws and *compadres*. Although devalued, their land holdings still provided a centripetal force which held most of the kindred together. And the landless *agregados* (peons), the tenant farmers, and share croppers continued to expect guidance and material support from the landholders, and these in turn took their power position and paternalistic responsibilities for granted.

This situation poses, according to numerous members of the Brazilian Protestant clergy, an almost unsurmountable barrier to proselytic endeavors. Regardless of the position of the Catholic church in the individual community, Catholicism is felt to be an integral part of the traditional way of life. Yet there is a notable deviation from this regional pattern. Cunha the only *municipio* of the Serra do Mar, which for climatic reasons never belonged to the coffee-producing sector of the region, accounts for 1,274 or 68.4 percent of all Protestants in the Serra do Mar.

The existence of a Protestant community in this *municipio*, which was until recently part of one of the most isolated regions in the state and whose people showed a profound attachment to traditional forms of behavior (Willems, 1961), raises an important theoretical problem. *It would seem that, under particular conditions, diffusion of Protestantism (and perhaps other forms of religious dissent) may occur in a traditionalistic rural setting without being preceded by changes in other sectors of the culture.* This, however, is a hypothesis to be explored in another chapter.

The Paraiba Valley, the third of the ecological regions under scrutiny, constituted the core of a coffee-growing area of which the Serra do Mar was hardly more than the southeastern fringe. In a manner of speaking, the valley served as a route by which coffee agriculture entered the state of São Paulo. When it reached the valley in the early nineteenth century, the local society had already been shaped by a previous plantation cycle during which sugar cane was the big commercial crop. Thus the traditions of a feudal past could be resumed with renewed vigor. In contrast to the Serra do Mar, however, the Paraiba Valley soon became the main line of communication and transportation between Rio de Janeiro and São Paulo. A number of important towns developed where the urban residences of an opulent aristocracy of hacienda owners were located. Many of these belonged to the nobility of the Second Empire, and for several decades Taubaté, the largest town of the valley, overshadowed the state capital in size and political power.

Toward the end of the nineteenth century, coffee agriculture began to decline rapidly. The old plantations were exhausted, and coffee could be produced elsewhere at lesser cost. By the time of World War I the whole region was thoroughly impoverished, but the unprecedented expansion of two metropolitan areas, São Paulo and Rio de Janeiro, soon reversed the trend. Transportation facilities, abundant electric power, and cheap labor began to attract numerous industries, and new commercial crops such as rice and potatoes transformed the Paraiba Valley into one of the most advanced agricultural areas of São Paulo. Under the impact of these changes, the rigid social structure of the past began to crumble, industrial entrepreneurs supplanted the landed aristocracy, a new middle class of businessmen, professional people, and white-collar workers arose, and numerous migrants from the surrounding rural areas formed a rapidly increasing industrial proletariat.

The historical Protestant churches had already gained a foothold in some towns of the Paraiba Valley by the turn of the century, but their chances to expand were limited by the usual strictures of a tightly woven society. In spite of a considerable population density (45.9 per square kilometer in 1950) the historical churches numbered only 3,010 members in 1960, while the Pentecostal sects reported a membership of 6,381. In the Serra do Mar the proportion between the two groups was almost exactly the opposite. The historical churches reported a membership of 1,496, while the Pentecostal sects had not been able to recruit more than 366 members. The structural differences between these two regions could hardly find a more eloquent expression. Needless to say, Pentecostalism sprang up *pari passu* with the intensification of social change during the last two decades.

In comparison with the Paraiba Valley, the coastal region shows a lesser disproportion between Pentecostals and historical Protestants. On the coast, 41.3 percent of all Protestants belong to the historical churches, while in the Paraiba Valley these represent only 32.3 percent of the total. Of course, the coastal society, despite the archaism of its way of life, was not molded by the hacienda system and was consequently unhampered by its attendant strictures. On the other hand, Pentecostalism found its strongholds in the most urbanized areas of the two regions, where society had reached its greatest fluidity and where the historical churches held less appeal to the lower classes than the Pentecostal sects.

Dearth of information rules out a detailed analysis of all twenty-three ecological areas of São Paulo. But on the whole, in the "older" regions the Protestant population appears to be relatively smaller than in the newly settled areas of the state.

Beginning in the last quarter of the nineteenth century the settlement of a vast frontier composed of areas 16 through 23 (see map), gradually gained momentum and reached its peak between the two world wars. In the westernmost parts this process is still going on, while the areas which received the bulk of their settlers in the earlier decades of this century have changed already from the amorphousness of a frontier society to the more organized though highly dynamic society which in 1952 produced 64 percent of all coffee, 83 percent of all cotton and (in 1953) 47 percent of all cattle raised within the state of São Paulo (Lopes, 1957:148).

During a decade of field research, the geographer Pierre Monbeig encountered none of the structural rigidities characteristic of the tradition-bound agrarian society prevalent in "older" areas. Migrants from many parts of Brazil and numerous Japanese immigrants were found to be in the process of social ascent. Many settlers who never before had been landowners became proprietors of *sítios* (medium-sized holdings) or even *fazendas*. On the other hand, the critical conditions of the coffee market had forced many estate owners to divide their holdings and sell them in smaller plots. Furthermore, many proprietors of uncultivated tracts of land found it profitable to sell them piecemeal to new settlers.

Along with the development of agriculture and cattle raising new towns emerged and became, often within an incredibly short time, important urban centers (Monbeig, 1952: 69, 146, 192, 322).

There were usually enough Protestants among the new settlers of the frontier area to establish initial congregations. And, naturally, the amorphousness and instability of the frontier society favored proselytic initiatives, particularly those of the Pentecostal sects.

The development of Protestantism in these eight ecological areas as indicated on Table XII shows expected and unexpected internal variations of considerable magnitude. Unexpected is, so far as the proportions of Protestants are concerned, the difference between Alta Sorocabana (19, 20, 22) and all other zones except 18. Given the frontier character of all these zones, now or in the recent past, especially of those preceded by the adjectives *Alto* or *Sertão*, the differentials of Table XII are difficult to explain. In fact, available information seems insufficient to support any hypothesis one may want to propose on the nature of these differences. Expected however is the fact that at least some of these areas should have comparatively large proportions of the state's Protestant population. In fact, in areas 21 and 23 these proportions are the highest outside Zona Industrial. Particularly relevant in the present context seems to be No. 23 with its extraordinary increase rate of 170.4 percent. This is perhaps the region that has preserved more frontier characteristics than any other part of São Paulo.

Our assumption that these recently settled areas are characterized by a changing society derives from the fact that their population is composed of migrants from many different subcultures of Brazil, as well as from different European and Asiatic nations. They left behind communities of rigid structure with set value systems that failed to satisfy their aspirations for a "better life." Their cultural heterogeneity and their differing aspirations prevent them from building replicas of their native communities. The new regions of São Paulo are structurally as different from the old ones as, *mustatis mutandis,* the frontier society of the American West was different from the Victorian society of New England. So far as Protestantism is concerned, it ought to be borne in mind that large contingents of Protestants were already among the first settlers of the São Paulo frontier. Thus Protestantism has been from the very beginning an integral part of most pioneer settlements, while the older regions had to be "penetrated" by sheer proselitizing effort.

The heavy concentration of Protestants in the frontier regions and in Zona Industrial seems to derive, to some degree at least, from the fact that they tend to be among the first to recognize the economic advantages accruing from migrations to areas that promise superior agricultural conditions or better paying jobs. The missionaries and pastors of the historical churches we had opportunity to interview were unanimous about these migratory tendencies, and Emile Léonard reported quite a few instances of old established Presbyterian congregations which in 1948 had already lost a considerable proportion of their members to interregional migrations (Léonard, 1952: 455).

It has already been pointed out that the development of Protestantism in Brazil cannot be understood simply as a function of urbanization and industrialization, although the foregoing data clearly indicate urban conditions are to be considered as the breeding ground par excellence of religious dissent. The cities as well as the rural frontier of the south are relatively free from the strictures of the traditional social order. The new class structure is the product of the considerable social mobility; neither the feudal loyalties characteristic of the hacienda system nor the more subtle controls of the kinship group find much chance to survive in the impersonal and atomistic society of the city and the rural frontier. If a man wishes to join a group of religious dissenters he may do so without feeling impeded by what his family and *compadres* may have to say about his decision. Nor will he feel constrained by the opinion his *patrão* may have of the *crentes.* In fact, his new boss may already have discovered that he is getting his money's worth from Protestant rather than non-Protestant labor.

If the preceding macroscopic approach disclosed significant differences between changing and relatively stable regional cultures, and their impact on religious dissent, a microscopic approach may be more appropriate to scrutinize intraregional differences. As there are stable enclaves within the rapidly changing subculture of São Paulo, relatively high rates of change may be found in such communities of highly traditional regions as northeastern Brazil.

Sertão Novo, located on the São Francisco river in the state of Pernambuco, constitutes a case of rapid change with obvious effects on the diffusion of Protestant creeds. In 1952, the town of Sertão Novo had a population of about 600 living in approximately 200 houses. Eight years later, an economic resurgence of considerable proportions had swelled the town population to 5,000 distributed over 2,800 dwellings (Eduardo, MS:4).

The first attempt to introduce Protestantism in Sertão Novo goes back to 1935 when a newcomer founded a Baptist congregation of three people. The founder was not only a migrant but a skilled artisan belonging to the lower ranks of the local middle class. His proselytic zeal attracted two members of "traditional" families, but otherwise the meetings held in his home and his indefatigable evangelism eventually aroused enough hostility to make him leave town. Before leaving, however, he converted the owner of a small farm who was to become the leader of the local dissenters. The small congregation met in a farmhouse, and after a series of unsuccessful attempts to rent a vacant building in town a church was erected on the rural property of the leader. In 1952 the rural congregation of Sertão Novo had 127 communicants, while no more than twenty townspeople had accepted the new faith. Since all these townspeople belonged to influential families they were in a strong enough position to resist the pressures of the community and the Catholic priest. But the congregation did not have a permanent minister, and religious services were rather infrequent. Among the increasing flow of migrants, however, there were Baptists from other municipios, and by 1956 the congregation had its own pastor. As the urban population of Sertão Novo increased, opposition to the Protestants crumbled away. In 1958, the new Baptist church was dedicated with virtually no opposition from the Catholics. Yet the growth of the Baptist congregation lagged far behind the increased rate of the population. In 1960 the urban church had fifty-seven communicants, and the membership of the rural church had grown to 143.

A minister of the Assembly of God who in 1958 had established himself in town attracted 145 members of the lower class, most of whom were migrants from surrounding municipios. But because of the effort of a Catholic missionary the Pentecostal congregation had shrunk to 30 or 40 in 1960 (Eduardo MS:9).

In sheer numbers, Sertão Novo represents little in the annals of Brazilian Protestantism. Its lack of success compared with similar communities farther south may be said to reflect the traditional tone of the regional culture of which even the migrants were integral parts. The circumstances under which religious dissent entered the community seem highly significant, however. The original founder was a member of the lower middle class, and almost all converts joining the Baptist congregation belonged to "traditional" families. It seems that the Baptist congregation was allowed to survive because of the social composition of its membership. Likewise, the rural congregation owes its establishment and survival to the fact that the founder and leader was a member of the landowning rural middle class. It was in *his* house and, later, in a temple erected on *his* land that the converts found a haven secure enough to make survival and modest expansion possible.

Two conditions seem to be responsible for the weakening of opposition to Protestantism in Sertão Novo. The large number of immigrants, who by 1960 outweighed the original population eight to one, atomized the social structure of the town and made organized resistance difficult, if not impossible. Secondly, a shift of the cultural focus, from sacred to more secular values, in the form of sudden technological and economic development dampened religious zeal and created an atmosphere of restraint and relative indifference.

The two groups became reconciled, and the tensions of many years virtually ceased to exist. In 1960, the relationships between the Baptist minister and the priest were respectful and cordial as indicated, for example, by the invitation tended by the former to the latter, to visit the Protestant temple. [Eduardo, MS:9.]

As in many other communities, religious pluralism had become a permanent fixture of the local culture, in spite of its conservative traditions.

13
Internal Migration and the Growth of Protestantism in Brazil

❖ Freedom from traditional forms of constraint may help carry out a decision, but it does not, of course, motivate anybody to join a Protestant or any other church. If migration removes certain traditional controls, anchored in the social structure, it also takes the migrant away from his "personal community," namely "the group of people on whom he can rely for support and approval." (Henry, 1958: 827.) Regardless of the economic situation in which a person may find himself, his personal community provides a social identity and a sense of security of which the migrant to the city or a new frontier feels deprived. In a number of instances, one of which was described before, we were able to observe the effectiveness of the paternalistic hacienda system as a source of personal security.

But there is no intention here of suggesting that the migrants are foolishly abandoning an institution still capable of solving all problems of personal welfare. On the contrary, the exodus from the hacienda has been caused, to a very large extent, by the inadequacies of its decaying structure. Though exceptions are quite common, the hacienda is no longer capable of providing the kind of security it once provided.

Nevertheless, the shock accompanying the transition to an individualized urban or frontier society is extremely severe, as we shall see farther on. The migrant reacts to the new situation by seeking, mostly by trial and error, a group of people with whom he may identify and in whose midst he may find emotional affinity. Among the alternatives open to him, one of the most readily accessible is the Protestant sect.

We do not wish to discuss at this point the question of whether or in what way the sect actually satisfies the migrant's keenly felt need for a new personal community. The foregoing remarks are merely intended to point out that the disintegration of the traditional social structure and the problems arising therefrom are directly related to internal migration. In fact, the sort of internal migration that concerns us here seems inconceivable without major social changes and the concomitant problems of adjustment to a different social order as represented by the industrial city and the frontier community. Heavy concentrations of migrants in areas where the Evangelical churches and sects have recruited most of their followers strongly suggest that Protestantism is indeed a reaction to changes in the traditional way of life.

The history of both Brazil and Chile reports numerous cases of internal migration. The mining of copper and nitrates in Chile, of gold and diamonds in Brazil, the coffee agriculture in São Paulo, the rubber boom in the Amazon Basin, and cocoa farming in Bahia attracted many thousands of laborers, but all these migrations were relatively minor events compared with the exodus from the Brazilian northeast as well as from the states of Minas Gerais, Bahia, and Rio de Janeiro. Higgins (1963: 202–203) reports,

In 1940, 3.4 million Brazilians were living in states other than those in which they were born. By 1950 the figure had reached 5.2 million. The internal migrants constituted 8.5 percent of the total population in 1940 and 10.3 percent in 1950. These figures suggest that the Brazilian population is one of the most mobile in the world.

Interstate migration before 1940 had already led to massive population losses in northeastern and eastern Brazil. According to the census of 1940 the northeast showed a migration deficit of 365,045, while in the east it reached a total of 484,965. The greatest losers were the states of Minas Gerais (582,520), Bahia (233,668), Rio de Janeiro (229,146), Ceará (115,751), and Pernambuco (112,962). The state of São Paulo on the other hand gained 495,162, the Federal District (now Guanabara) 551,300, Paraná 150,598, and Goiás 119,466 migrants (Silva, 1963: 44).

Between 1940 and 1950, the Federal District (Guanabara) gained 392,829 and the state of São Paulo 665,200 additional inhabitants from internal migrations (Silva, 1963: 61). In 1951 alone, 194,074 Brazilians migrated to the state of São Paulo (Silva 1963: 62).

The fact that the states of Bahia, Minas Gerais, and Rio de Janeiro were the heaviest losers through internal migration seems particularly significant. Higgins (1963: 203) continues,

These states were not those with the worst conditions, where the "push" was strongest, but those nearest the expanding industrial centers where the "pull" was most apparent. The states with the largest positive balance of movement have been those which have achieved highest rates of economic development. São Paulo and Guanabara are the leading industrial centers, Paraná and Goiás are purely agricultural. Thus internal migration is not only rural-urban but also rural-rural. The migrant labor force seeks employment and higher wages in industrial cities and also new lands not yet occupied.

Internal migration of course contributed to the rapid growth of most Brazilian cities, especially the state capitals. The estimated number of residents from other states who migrated to São Paulo City between 1940 and 1950 was 524,043, or 23.8 percent of its total population in 1950. The corresponding figure for the Federal District was 392,829, or 16.5 percent of its 1950 population (Silva, 1963: 78).

The extent to which the Protestant congregations of the most urbanized areas and the rural frontiers are actually composed of migrants from other parts of Brazil is not known. In such areas as northern Paraná, one of the most extensive and successful rural frontiers of contemporary Brazil, the overwhelming majority of the population consists of migrants, and so do of course the Protestant congregations. One may assume that particularly in the cities, such as São Paulo and its industrial satellites, the sects have attracted large numbers of rural migrants. At least the newcomers among these can easily be identified by their clothes, their posture, their behavior in city traffic, the way the women carry their infants and suckle them wherever they happen to be, and their speech pattern. Large proportions of such people were often observed at mass gatherings in revival tents, temples, and in or near buildings where charity was dispensed by sectarian institutions or spiritual solace was offered by miracle workers. Manuel de Melo, leader of a Pentecostal sect named Brazil for Christ, attracted huge crowds. There were, patiently waiting in the street, several hundred people who betrayed their recent rural origin beyond any doubt. In 1963, three years after our initial observations, the crowd besetting the small center of the sect, located in downtown São Paulo, had grown considerably, and so had the squalor of its components, most of whom were obviously migrants from the northeast, Bahia, and Minas Gerais.

Three facts seem relevant in the present context:

1. A continuous flow of migrants proceeded from regions known for their archaic social structure.

2. The bulk of these migrants settled in the most urbanized and industrialized areas of São Paulo and Guanabara, as well as in the agricultural frontier zones of Paraná, São Paulo, and Goiás.

3. The cultural distance between the regions of origin and those in which the migrants chose to settle may be considered maximal within the range of subcultural patterns characterizing Brazil.

Assuming that the need for personal adjustment, as well as the magnitude of such adjustment, is directly proportional to the cultural distance between the region of origin and the region of settlement, the process of rebuilding a viable personal community among the migrants may be expected to be difficult. In view of such difficulties, one may further expect the migrants to join proselytizing groups such as the Protestant sects and churches equipped to provide a new social identity, relative emotional security, and even a measure of material assistance to their members. Although we are unable to corraborate this statement with statistical evidence, it may be assumed that the concentration of Protestants and migrants in the same areas is more than mere coincidence.

14

The Ecology of Protestantism in Chile.

✤ The most recent figures on the distribution of Protestants in Chile are those of the national census of 1960. The breakdown by provinces, arranged in a geographical order from north to south, shows the bulk of the Protestant population to be located in the most urbanized and industrialized provinces of the country. Santiago, Valparaiso, and Concepción account for 48.1 percent of all Chilean Protestants (Table XVIb). This figure is almost equal to the proportion (48.7) the population of these three provinces represents within the total population of Chile.

Table XVIb also shows that the proportion of Protestants residing in these three provinces increased from roughly one third in 1920 to almost one half of the total Protestant population in 1960. Each of the three provinces, however, suggests a somewhat different trend. The proportion of the Chilean Protestant population living in Valparaiso dropped from 14.2 percent in 1920 to 6.4 percent in 1960, while in Concepción the corresponding figures show exactly the opposite trend. The proportion of Protestants living in Santiago has risen from 13.4 percent in 1920 to 26 percent in 1960, but there seems to be a significant difference between Santiago and Concepción. The percentage of the Protestant population residing in Concepción has been consistently higher than the proportion of the general population of that area, while in Santiago this proportion tends to develop in the opposite direction. Further scrutiny of table XVI also shows that the proportion obtaining in Concepción roughly applies, in varying degrees, to that part of southern Chile called La Frontera, the frontier. In fact, eight provinces of southern Chile harbored, in 1960, no less than 48.2 percent of the total Protestant population, while only 30.1 percent of all Chileans inhabited that area.

The relative strength of southern Protestantism is also reflected in the figures of table XVIa. Only in the eight aforementioned provinces did the percentage of Protestants significantly surpass the national average of 5.6 percent.

If the industrial province of Concepción is eliminated from the area under scrutiny, the remaining seven provinces still account for 32.5 percent of all Chilean Protestants but for only 20.6 percent of the total population.

Although the available data are not adequate for a thorough analysis of the ecological distribution of Chilean Protestantism, it seems that two sets of conditions have to be taken into account:

First, there seems to be a relationship between the concentration of Protestants and industrialization. The most industrialized provinces—Santiago, Valparaiso, and Concepción—which in 1960 harbored 71.3 percent of the Chilean industrial labor force, accounted for almost half of the country's Protestants. Taking each of these three provinces separately, there seems to be a rough parallel between the growth of the labor force and the degree of Protestant concentration. Between 1916 and 1952 the increase of the industrial labor force in Concepción amounted to 960 percent, in Santiago it was 830 percent, and in Valparaiso only 390 percent. Between 1952 and 1960 Concepción again occupied first place, Santiago followed, and in Valparaiso there was no increase at all. Between 1920 and 1960 the proportion of Chilean Protestants concentrated in Concepción rose from 4.6 percent to 15.7 percent, in Santiago it grew from 13.4 percent to 26.0 percent, and in Valparaiso it decreased from 14.1 percent to 6.4 percent.

Thus, within each of the three provinces, the dynamics of the Protestant movement obey different rhythms: Concepción has achieved predominance and Valparaiso has lost the dominant position it once had. Santiago is still the province with the largest Protestant population in the country, but the proportion of the general population it holds has grown faster than its share of the Protestant population, while in Concepción the opposite is true. But in all three provinces Protestantism has grown considerably, particularly since 1942, as the ratios of table XVIa indicate.

If urbanization is considered a separate process—which of course it is not in the present context—it seems to move roughly parallel to the rise of Protestantism, at least since 1930. The two decades between 1940 and 1960 mark the largest gain in both urban growth and dissemination of Protestantism (Appendix Tables XVIc and XVId). The city of Concepción with its five satellite towns appears to lead with regard to both, Protestantization and urbanization. Santiago follows, and the decline of Valparaiso as a major area of Protestant concentration is perhaps related to its relatively moderate urban growth. Unfortunately, available census data on Protestantism refer to provinces only. Consequently, it is impossible to determine the exact proportion of Protestants living in the *cities* of Concepción, Santiago, and Valparaiso.

Santiago, Valparaiso, and Concepción have also been the main target areas of a rapidly growing flow of internal migrants. Between 1940 and 1952, 259,184 migrants settled in the province of Santiago, 11,814 in Valparaiso, and 33,285 in Concepción (Instituto de Economia, 1959: 54). In 1959 it appeared that approximately 630,000 residents of Greater Santiago had been born outside the metropolitan area. This means that 36 percent of the population of the nation's capital consisted of migrants from other provinces. No recent figures for Valparaiso and Concepción are available, but one may safely assume that, at least in Concepción, the proportion of migrants to the native-born population has greatly increased since 1952.

Secondly, in contrast to the aforementioned areas, the seven southern provinces accounting for 32.6 percent of all Chilean Protestants are neither industrialized nor heavily urbanized. The highest percentage of Protestants—14.9 percent in 1960—is found in Arauco, perhaps the most rural of the seven provinces, yet up to 1930 Protestantism was almost nonexistent in Arauco. A similar situation prevailed in Bio-Bio: the Evangelical minority was still negligible in 1930, but in both provinces the percentages doubled between 1952 and 1960 (Table XVIa). On the other hand, five provinces already had substantial Protestant communities in 1920, and in a few of these—Malleco, Cautin, Valdivia, and Osorno—the 1960 ratios lie considerably above the national average of 5.6 percent. In fact, for many years Cautin was called "the capital" of Chilean Protestantism, a position which it has not been able to maintain, as Appendix Tables XVI and XVIa indicate.

If neither the presence nor the absence of early Protestant nuclei seems to have much bearing on recent developments, a long tradition of ethnic and religious pluralism in southern Chile may have something to do with Protestantization. Most of Chile's Indian population lives in that area, and since the middle of the nineteenth century there has been a small Protestant minority of German extraction. Actually, the German Evangelical Church, like the German Lutheran churches in Brazil, has never developed missionary activities of any description. Its total membership does not exceed 25,000 (Taylor and Coggins, 1961: 81), and if, according to Vergara (1962: 33), the majority of these German-Chileans do not participate in church activities at all, it is difficult to see how the Lutherans could have spurred a major religious movement in southern Chile. Besides, in some of the southern provinces, such as Arauco, Bio-Bio, and Malleco, the Lutheran church is virtually nonexistent. It is conceivable, however, that because of the presence of a Lutheran minority an early model of religious pluralism was set up which may have some bearing on the ulterior expansion of Protestantism in a few provinces. "Accustomed to live side by side with persons of different creeds, people were perhaps more tolerant and, consequently, more receptive to the 'new' Gospel." (d'Epinay, 1965–66:32.)

Another hypothesis, however, appears more promising. The provinces of Aurauco, Bio-Bio, Malleco, and Cautín are usually classified as La Frontera, and as in certain regions of Brazil frontier conditions may have considerable bearing on the dissemination of Protestantism. Since our field work was mostly concerned with Cautín, the core of La Frontera, the following description is limited to that province, but many of its traits, *mutatis mutandis,* are found in most parts of continental Chile south of the Bio-Bio River.

Like the rest of La Frontera, Cautín is predominantly rural. In 1954, only, 2,346 persons were employed in its few industrial establishments, (Krause, 1956:97), and Temuco, the capital with a population of 74,-700 in 1960, is no more than a service center for the surrounding rural area. Nevertheless, Temuco has been one of the most successful centers of evangelization in Chile. Most prominent among the historical bodies is the Baptist church with seven churches and a *colegio* which in 1959 had an enrolment of 350 students. The Christian and Missionary Alliance made Temuco its national headquarters where it maintains a school for missionaries, a modern publishing house, and eight primary schools scattered over a large rural area. An Anglican mission has been working in the Temuco area since 1895. It has approached the rural people, particularly the Mapuche Indians, through schools and medical services, and it now operates twenty-five small rural churches and two hospitals. Furthermore, there have been, for approximately half a century, a Methodist congregation with its own school and a growing community of Seventh Day Adventists which also maintains a publishing center. The three main Pentecostal bodies are of course represented in Temuco and so are a number of smaller sects. A total of thirty-three Protestant churches were located within the city limits. Other towns in Cautín, such as Lautaro, Nueva Imperial, Loncoche, Villarica, and Pucón, play similar but minor roles as centers of diffusion of various evangelical creeds. The success of so much proselytism is reflected by the fact that in 1952, 13.9 percent of the population of Cautín claimed to be Protestant, a figure which more than trebled the national average of 4 percent.

The conditions under which the Protestant churches originated and developed in the province of Cautín are not unlike those we encountered in certain areas of Brazil. Temuco was founded in 1881 as a military establishment in order to pacify the Mapuche Indians, who resisted the Spanish and Chilean *conquistadores* longer than any other

South American tribe. In other words, the "history" of the region began when the "civilized" areas of Chile had already been molded by the prevailing hacienda system. *Cautín was definitely a frontier area and remained so until the turn of the century.* Land was plentiful and could easily be taken away from the Mapuche who, after the first onslaught of the new settlers, were confined to reservations. By Chilean standards, an unusually large proportion of the land was divided into small and medium-sized farms. In fact, in 1956 the number of farms measuring from 0.1 to 100 hectares was estimated at 66,519, occupying a little less than one third of the total farming area of the province (Stagno, 1956:114). Only fifty-four latifundia with more than 2,000 hectares each, were reported in 1955. These totaled about 13 percent of the agricultural area of Cautín (Stagno, 1956:112–113).

It seems safe to conclude that small and medium-sized holdings prevail in Cautin, and that, emerging out of frontier conditions, its social organization has not been exposed to the restrictive controls of the hacienda system to the same degree as that of many other provinces. Furthermore, for a number of circumstances which considerations of space make it impossible to describe in detail here, land ownership has been remarkably unstable in Cautín. Stagno (1965:111) writes,

The percentage of landowners who succeeded in keeping their holdings through various generations (of the same family) is very small, agricultural property has been exposed to continuous change, division, and lease, and therefore failed to develop a *tradition* which is to be regarded as the principal condition of a solid system of agriculture.

A great deal of instability has been caused by excessive division of the land, and many holders of *minifundia* had to sell out and move to local towns where there was little demand for their services. As a matter of fact, a large proportion (probably one third) of the population of Temuco, the fourth largest city of Chile, was found to live in conditions that can only be considered appallingly poor, even by Latin American standards.

Since the not-too-distant frontier days, the province of Cautín has been wide open to missionary endeavor; freedom from traditional controls combined with the many hazards of an incipient society and followed by the continuing crisis of a stagnant economy are the basic factors that seem to account for the unusual success of Protestant proselytism. Also, the fact that approximately one fourth of the population of Cautín consists of Mapuche Indians appears to be of considerable importance in so far as the dissemination of Protestant creeds is concerned. A great deal of missionary effort, both Catholic and Protestant, has been invested in the conversion of the Mapuche, and a substantial proportion of the Indians belongs now to various Protestant churches.

In contrast to La Frontera and the industrialized areas of Chile, there are such provinces as Coquimbo, Aconcagua, and Colchagua, where Protestantism has so far failed to attract much of a following and where, even in 1960, the ratio of Protestants remains less than half the national average of 5.6 percent. In 1960, the Evangelical population of these three provinces amounted to only 3.5 percent of all Chilean Protestants, while the population constituted 8.4 percent of Chile's total population. It would seem that in these three provinces the changes affecting the traditional social order have been less intensive than elsewhere. So far as the extreme north is concerned, it seems quite possible that the fluctuations characterizing the Protestant population of that region reflect the vicissitudes of the mining industry over a period of four decades.

Attachment to traditional behavior, mainly the result of physical and cultural isolation, is also found in the archipelago of Chiloe. A recent study of the religious lore of Chiloe proved the persistence of Catholic folk traditions that have long since disappeared in most other parts of Chile (Acuña, 1956). In spite of the fact that Chiloe has never been affected by the hacienda system and its feudal components, its ratio of Protestants is still the smallest of all Chilean provinces (Table XVIa).

The findings of this chapter may be summarized as follows:

In both countries the rapid diffusion of proselytic Protestantism, particularly of its Pentecostal versions, was found to be concomitant with the processes of urbanization and industrialization. In both countries the largest concentrations of Protestants are located in the most urbanized and industrialized areas, while in regions characterized by a continuing predominance of the traditional social order, the number of Protestants has remained comparatively small.

The temporal and spatial relationship between the development of Protestantism and the emergence of an industrial civilization in Brazil and Chile was interpreted as supporting evidence for the hypothesis that proselytic Protestantism indeed thrives under conditions of socio-cultural change. The conditions of sociocultural change and the attend-ant social problems, as they occur in the industrial cities of both coun-tries, are intensified by a large-scale rural-urban migration. The rapid increase of the Pentecostal sects seems to be related to the presence of numerous rural migrants.

In both countries proselytic Protestantism was also found to be relatively strong in areas which, in the recent past were, or are now, rural frontiers and consequently involved in processes of sociocul-tural change accompanying the appropriation of virgin land and the foundation of new communities composed of people from different subcultural or national background.

Protestantism has found some acceptance in rural areas where a native peasantry was allowed to develop unhampered by the feudal controls of the traditional class system. Since the data seemed incon-clusive, the finding was presented merely as a hypothesis to be tested in the following chapter.

15
Excursus on Protestantism in Traditional Society

✤ In a previous chapter, the existence of a rural middle class both in Brazil and Chile was put in evidence, and it was suggested that this class might have played a strategic role in the diffusion of Protes-tantism. Our brief survey of São Paulo and the relationships between the ecological areas of that state and the development of Protestantism yielded some data indicating that no matter how isolated and tradi-tion-bound a region is, it may be receptive to religious dissent provid-ing its social structure remained relatively unincumbered by the heri-tage of the traditional agrarian society.

The municipio of Cunha proved to be such a region. Located in the Serra do Mar where large-scale coffee agriculture impinged upon the social structure, Cunha constituted a rather marginal area whose altitude discouraged coffee farming. In 1960 the Protestants of this municipio constituted more than 68.3 percent of all Protestants of the Serra do Mar. Very few of them live in the town of Cunha whose familism and class structure differ little from those of the surrounding *municipios* which, at one time, were integral parts of an opulent coffee-growing area. But the gentry of Cunha has never been able to establish effective controls over the numerous farmers who inhabit the vast hinterland of the *municipio*. Ownership could easily be established since, until 1930, land had hardly any cash value.

Thus land ownership, combined with subsistence farming and little dependence on markets created a frugal, hard-working, and self-reliant peasantry. In 1950 there were in the municipio of Cunha 1,274 agricultural holdings covering an area of 86,508 hectares. Of these, 1,074 or 84.3 percent measured fewer than 100 hectares and occupied a total area of 32,683 hectares. This seems a remarkable fact in a country supposed to have no rural middle class.

Even more remarkable is the relatively small number of holdings of fewer than 10 hectares, of which there were only 226 representing 21 percent of all holdings under 100 hectares. Considering the extremely low value of the land, however, and the extensive nature of farming techniques, holdings of the 100- to 200-hectare category could by no means be classified as large. In 1950 there were 116 of these covering an area of 16,766 hectares. Only 86 *fazendas* or 6.8 percent of all holdings measured more than 200 hectares, and the area occupied by these amounted to 37,059 hectares or 42.8 percent of the total agricultural area of the *municipio* (I.B.G.E., 1955).

Cunha may thus be characterized essentially as a *municipio* with a strong rural middle class, and it was among the rural middle class that, by the turn of the century and long before any kind of major cultural change had touched the area, Brazilian Methodist missionaries succeeded in founding two purely rural congregations. The conversion of several hundred people seems to have passed almost unnoticed, or in any event it failed to elicit the sanctions which in more tightly knit communities are known to have prevented effectively the growth of heterodoxy.

In the town of Cunha, however, where the "old families" resided and class cleavages followed the hacienda pattern, attempts to evangelize the townspeople led to repeated outbreaks of violence against a handful of Protestant converts who typically belonged to the lower class. The leading townspeople, though very few of them were practicing Catholics, felt enough solidarity with the Roman church to encourage or at least to tolerate violent repudiation of Protestantism (Willems, 1961:90).

Evidence from Cunha thus seems to confirm our hypothesis that absence of the hacienda system and presence of a rural middle class create conditions under which religious dissent may develop. It should be emphasized that Protestantism never was embraced by more than a small minority of Cunhenses. In 1960 there were 1,274 Methodist in a municipio with a population close to 30,000. But to understand the strategic role of these Protestant congregations, two facts should be kept in mind: religious pluralism has been accepted by the people of Cunha as a matter of course, and Protestant out-migrants from Cunha have been feeding the Protestant congregations of other areas in the state of São Paulo, mainly those of the rapidly industrializing towns of the nearby Paraiba Valley.

Freedom from the strictures of the traditional agrarian society alone does not, however, fully explain the diffusion of Protestantism in Cunha. The absence of structural rigor is also manifest in the somewhat loose way in which the folk Catholicism of these peasant farmers is perpetuated. Since all Catholic traditions in this and similar cases are wholly oral and almost uncontrolled by any constituted authority adherence to orthodoxy can of course not be expected at all. Intensive field work in Cunha indeed revealed that local deviations depend on how the *sacristão,* the man in charge of the prayer services (*rezas, novenas*) perceives the church-controlled doctrine. His interpretations are accepted with obvious unconcern for orthodoxy.

There is a broad range of tolerance within which people discharge their religious obligations. Novelties may be accepted, especially if they present themselves under unusual circumstances that fit the people's concept of the supernatural. Every region has its tradition of saints, faith healers, and thaumaturges whose miraculous deeds quite often exercise considerable influence upon the religious behavior of the people. In fact, two occurrences in the recent history of Cunha bear witness to the eagerness with which the most unconventional events are accepted at face value.

During the revolution of 1932 a young man who had been "liberated" from the local jail let his blond hair grow, vested a white tunic, and presented himself to the people as the "returning Christ." He ordered the people to build a church in reparation for their sins. His numerous followers began to carry heavy rocks to the place where the church was to be erected. The brief episode ended when the police took the youth back to jail.

The second event refers to a faith healer who announced his own death and resurrection during Holy Week. He "died" and a large number of mourners accompanied his coffin to a previously determined locality. At night he left the coffin, and on Easter Sunday he returned to an expectant mass of faithful followers. Fearing acts of fanaticism, the local sheriff, who "was a Protestant and did not believe in those *bobagens* (foolishness)" arrested the miracle worker, but not without meeting some resistance among the followers of the resurrected "Christ" (Willems, 1961:140–141).

Occurrences of this sort not only reveal lack of sophistication but above all a constant readiness to accept, unhampered by doctrinal scruples, new religious experiences within a roughly hewn framework of Christian concepts. It would seem that under such conditions religious dissent finds ample chances to succeed, as indeed it did in a somewhat selective fashion when Methodism became a permanent part of the local peasant culture.

To subject our hypothesis to a further and perhaps more convincing test, a number of *municipios* in the state of Minas Gerais was selected, and it was attempted to show statistically that *municipios* with a relatively large Protestant population have a higher proportion of medium landholdings than do the *municipios* with small Protestant populations.

Minas Gerais was chosen because of all Brazilian states it has the largest number of medium landholdings (see Table II) and its Protestant population representing 7.3 percent of all Brazilian Protestants (in 1960) may be considered a sizable minority. Furthermore, Minas Gerais, without belonging to the typical plantation areas of the country, has shown a strong attachment to its cultural traditions. During the last decade, industrialization has begun to make a strong impact on certain areas, but these were excluded from our inquiry.

Using the returns for 1956 (*Estatística do Culto Protestante do Brasil*) a total of sixty-six "rural" *municipios* in different regions of the state was chosen. They are rural in the sense that in none did the urban population exceed 30 percent of the total. In fact, in most cases the urban population did not even surpass 20 percent, and the term "urban" should be considered a statistical rather than a cultural category.

These sixty-six *municipios* were divided into two groups, those with Protestant populations of five hundred or more and those with fifty or fewer Protestants. Concentrations of five hundred or more Protestants in any single municipio were considered "high," concentrations of fifty or fewer were considered "low." There were twenty-nine municipios of the first type and thirty-seven of the second type.

The landholdings were divided into three categories—small, medium and large. Farms with fewer than ten hectares were classified as small, those measuring from ten to fewer than one hundred hectares were considered medium, and all those with one hundred or more hectares were classified as large. This classification is of course open to criticism. It could be said, for example, that holdings with more than five, but fewer than ten hectares are not really small in the sense of *minifúndios,* or that holdings with 150 or even 200 hectares are a far cry from the large estates in the sense of *latifúndios.* If our concept of the medium holding is thus perhaps somewhat narrow, it seems less vulnerable to criticism than if it had been extended either way. In the area under scrutiny, holdings of more than ten but fewer than one hundred may safely be ranked as middle-sized.

While figures on Protestantism refer to 1956, data on the size of landholdings were taken from the agricultural census of 1950. It was assumed that during the intervening years no significant change affected the distribution of land in Minas Gerais.

Table XVII shows that our hypothesis is indeed borne out by the facts. In the twenty-nine municipios with a relatively high ratio of Protestants 65.9 percent of all landholdings belonged to the medium category. In the thirty-seven *municipios* with relatively small Protestant congregations, this figure amounted to only 51.4 percent. A test of the null hypothesis that the proportion of medium landholdings is equal in the two groups of *municipios* resulted in the rejection of the null hypothesis at the .01 level of significance (Walker and Lev, 1953: 77–78).

Our assumption that the size of the landholdings appears, to a significant degree, correlated with religious affiliation is further corroborated by a comparison of the proportions of small and large farms in the two groups of municipios. In the twenty-nine municipios with large Protestant populations only 12.8 percent of the holdings are small and 21.2 percent are large, while in the thirty-seven municipios with few Protestants the small holdings represent 19.5 percent and the large holdings 29.9 percent of the total number of farms.

Application of the proportion test resulted in the rejection of two other null hypotheses at the .01 level, namely, that the proportion of small landholdings is equal in the two groups of counties. Regarding the relation of size of landholdings and concentration of Protestantism in Minas Gerais, we may now accept as tenable the following hypotheses: the proportion of medium landholdings is positively associated with a high concentration of Protestants; the proportion of small landholdings is negatively associated with a high concentration of Protestants; the proportion of large landholdings is negatively associated with a high concentration of Protestants.

It seems easier to prove *that* these associations exist than to explain cogently *why* they exist. In Cunha, freedom from controls traditionally exercised by the landed upper class and the Roman Catholic church made it possible for a few hundred families to embrace the Protestant faith. No comparable body of data is available to extend our own findings in Cunha to the sixty-six municipios of Minas Gerais. But whatever information there is seems to suggest that similar conditions prevail in many municipios of that neighboring state, as indeed they predominate in many communities all over the country.

Maintenance of the traditional social order is predicated upon the power position of the landowning upper class. Wherever that position is curtailed by a relatively numerous rural middle class, deviations from established norms including religious dissent are bound to occur, particularly if, as so frequently happens, the Catholic church is powerless to prevent such deviations. This situation most likely affects the urban as well as the rural sectors of the regional society.

Pressures and sanctions brought to bear on merchants, civil servants, and professional people tend to be ineffective where political parties have to compromise with a large Protestant constituency, where families are divided into Catholic and Protestant branches, and where it appears profitable to seek the patronage of several hundred or thousand Protestant farmers whose purchasing power has some weight within the economic structure of the *municipio*.

Why is the proportion of small landholdings negatively associated with a high concentration of Protestants? The small landholder, particularly the owner of a *minifundium* of fewer than five hectares, usually gravitates within the orbit of one or several large estates. Seldom does the land produce enough to free its owner or operator from the necessity to seek seasonal employment on a large nearby *fazenda*. Sharecroppers are of course more dependent than owners, but even the owner can rarely afford to make decisions at variance with the wishes of his seasonal employers. More often than not, the old feudal loyalties that prevail between patrón and peón also apply to the relationship between *fazendeiros* and small landholders. It seems important at this point to stress the difference between this segment of Brazilian rural society and its urban counterpart, the industrial working class. While the latter plays an extremely active role in the diffusion of religious dissent, the former is kept in line by the traditional ties that bind him to the rural upper class.

The existing negative association of large landholdings with high concentrations of Protestants may of course be expected. In Brazil, as everywhere else in Latin America, the owners of the big landed estates constitute the bulwark of the traditional social order and its symbols. Catholicism, if only in name, is one of these symbolic values to which this class, perhaps more than any other, appears to be deeply committed.

Minas Gerais is probably not very different from other "traditional" areas of Brazil where middle-sized landownings occur with relative frequency and the diffusion of Protestantism is meeting with moderate success. In no way, however, do the present findings affect our hypothesis that a high growth of Protestantism is concomitant with the occurrence of major culture change.

Unfortunately, no statistical data are available to extend the foregoing inquiry to certain areas of Chile.

Following is a list of *municipios* of Minas Gerais with relatively large Protestant congregations (1956):

Municipios	Number of Protestants	Municipios	Number of Protestants
Aimorés	2,332	Lajinha	1,993
Cabo Verde	542	Lambarí	515
Carangola	1,213	Manhuaçú	1,182
Caratinga	3,537	Manhumirím	1,044
Cataguases	622	Muriaé	1,483
Conselheiro Pena	2,104	Mutúm	1,991
Coronel Fabriciano	579	Paracatú	627
Espera Feliz	2,424	Patos de Minas	1,258
Frutal	1,097	Presidente	
Galiléia	623	Olegário	693
Governador		Resplendor	5,395
Valladares	4,366	Santa Margarida	777
Inhapím	1,712	Tarumirím	848
Ipanema	833	Teófilo Otoni	2,700
Itueta	2,388	Tumiritinga	706
Ituiutaba	906		

Municipios of Minas Gerais with relatively small Protestant congregations may be listed as follows:

Municipios	Number of Protestants	Municipios	Number of Protestants
Almenara	39	Jesuânia	32
Andrelândia	13	Ladainha	18
Ataléia	29	Lima Duarte	27
Betím	10	Matias Barbosa	24
Bom Sucesso	48	Monte Sião	41
Bueno Brandão	44	Pedra Azul	23
Buenópolis	44	Pedro Leopoldo	8
Campo Florido	14	Pitanguí	18
Carandaí	44	Pratápolis	40
Carlos Chagas	46	Ribeirão Vermelho	28
Congonhas	14	Rio Novo	19
Coqueiral	15	Santa Rita de	
Coromandel	22	Jacutinga	15
Curvelo	47	Santa Vitória	23
Eloi Mendes	6	São Francisco	25
Guaraní	19	Teixeiras	15
Iguatama	29	Tiros	9
Itabira	6	Virgínia	7
Itaguara	14	Volta Grande	36

PART IV

Adaptations and Selections: The National Churches
and Pentecostal Sects Emerge

16
Schisms and Nationalism

✤ Earlier in this volume we made clear that we are concerned with three kinds of changes regarding Protestantism: changes in the value system and social structure that created conditions favorable to a rapid expansion of different Protestant creeds; changes that these creeds or their organizational concomitants underwent in contact with the cultures of Brazil and Chile; finally, changes that the acceptance and diffusion of a Protestant way of life imparted to the native cultures. The second of these changes will be examined in some detail in the present chapter.

It is often observed that cultural elements cannot be transferred from one context of patterned behavior to another without some major or minor adjustments in structure or content. Such changes, one is told, are necessary or inevitable, for the new element must fit an existing set of institutions and values. The assumption is of course that the behavioral implications of the new element are at variance with well established patterns of the recipient culture. If there is no conflict, the transfer may occur with no changes at all. This however is clearly not the case with the introduction of Protestantism in Latin America. The main points of conflicts were shown in a previous chapter, and one can hardly escape the impression that they bear on a series of discrepancies in religious doctrine and moral behavior. Acceptance and dissemination of the new values and attitudes are consummated facts, but at what expense to the purity of the doctrine and their accepted institutional expressions? What, if any, modifications were necessary or "just occurred" in order to adjust Protestantism to the Brazilian and Chilean way of life? If Protestantism emerged out of the intricate processes of transfer without losing its identity, one is forced to conclude that it affected the native cultures more than it was affected by them. In other words, the scrutiny of possible changes undergone by Protestantism itself points to the impact it may have upon the way of life of those who embraced it.

The crises of transfer which Protestantism underwent in Brazil and Chile are reflected by a series of phenomena such as temporary rejection, the deterioration of new congregations after some initial success, clashes between missionaries and congregations or between foreign missionaries and native clergy, the emergence of factions within ecclesiastical bodies advocating conflicting points of view about almost any conceivable matter; but none seems to be a more eloquent expression of cultural incompatibilities than the schism. This is not to say that all schisms arise from cultural conflicts, but those that erupted during the formative period of the Protestant churches usually did spring from differences between the cultural background of the American (or sometimes European) sponsors or missionaries and that of the native congregations. Historical records sometimes represent such rifts as "personal incompatibilities" between leading clergymen, which of course they were, but usually one detects cultural involvements underlying what seem to be mere personal differences. Nor does it matter, of course, whether a schism was caused by motives that seem trifling in retrospect. Cultural commitments are often of a transient nature, and once they belong to the past it is difficult to comprehend the sway they held over historical decisions.

Most schisms in the Protestant churches of Brazil and Chile seem to be directly or indirectly related to "nationalism." This term covers a variety of things, especially in connection with the activities of foreign missionaries and the foundation of institutions dependent upon higher ecclesiastical authorities in the United States or Europe. Manifestations of nationalism rank all the way from criticism of foreign missions and missionaries to internal differences in which the "natives line up against" the foreigners.

Probably right from the very beginning the American churches recognized the need for recruiting a native clergy which sooner or later would have to be invested with sufficient authority to direct church affairs in an autonomous fashion. It was assumed that at some point in the development of a new church the "natives" would have "matured" enough to "take over." One may expect natives and foreigners to disagree sometimes about *when* exactly church development had reached the point of maturation. The verdict of "too early" from the standpoint of an American mission board might appear an undue and arbitrary postponement from the viewpoint of indigenous church leaders. This apparently was the situation of the Presbyterian Church in Brazil which by the turn of the century had attracted a number of outstanding members of the intelligentsia. Their leading role in the struggle for emancipation from foreign authority eventually produced the schism of 1903 and the foundation of the Independent Presbyterian Church of Brazil. The controversies that caused the rift were centered around two problems: the role which the schools were supposed to assume in the diffusion and consolidation of the church and the so-called "Masonic question" (*questão de maçonaria*).

The *colégios* which the Presbyterian and other Evangelical churches had established in Brazil were soon recognized by many citizens as the most progressive and effective educational institutions of the country. Originally conceived as instruments of evangelization, they were interpreted by certain sectors of the native society as institutions of progressive secular education, a field in which Latin America was obviously lagging. Thousands of Brazilians thus received a secondary education of an advanced type, and though only relatively few were converted, most remained lifelong friends and protectors of their schools. Some orthodox members of the native Presbyterian clergy however preferred plain evangelization and parochial schools to institutions whose effectiveness as means of diffusing the Gospel seemed doubtful (Léonard: 1951:195). Defining the conflict of values inherent in this controversy, Léonard (1951:195) wrote,

North American Protestantism, generally of a more pragmatic than theological nature, easily identifies religious truth with the obligations or manifestations of a civilization which it calls Christian. The primordial importance which the missionaries and the *Board* afforded to instruction and the *colégios* constituted an expression to of that tendency.

Many, but by no means all, members of the Brazilian clergy shared this preference. These conflicting value orientations are, in a somewhat more comprehensive contest, those between "American pragmatism" and "Latin American humanism" identified with a strong emphasis on theology. Léonard (1951:180) continues,

In a general way, the young and very much intellectualistic Latin churches were disappointed by the pragmatism and theological weakness of a certain North American ministry; they reacted through a complex of intellectual superiority to what they felt was a complex of ethnic superiority on the part of the missionaries.

The *questão de maçonaria* arose from the opposition of a group of orthodox Brazilian Presbyterians who perceived a basic incompatibility between Freemasonry and Christianity. No true Christian, they affirmed, could possibly be associated with a Masonic lodge. Masonic prayers did not mention Christ and consequently they were not Christian prayers; the Great Architect was not identical with the Trinity, and the theory of regeneration through masonic morality failed to take cognizance of the workings of the Holy Spirit (Léonard, 1951:198). In fact, within the context of Latin American culture, Freemasonry, correctly or incorrectly, seems to denote antagonism or hostility to Christianity and Christian churches, an association which is certainly nonexistent in the United States. Thus the new Independent Presbyterian Church became an anti-Masonic denomination. In retrospect, these arguments apparently served as catalysts that precipitated the process of emancipation of the Brazilian churches including the main body of the Presbyterian church from which the Independent Presbyterians seceded in 1903.

The schisms that plagued the Protestant churches in Brazil and Chile (and perhaps all schisms) seem to fall into two categories. There are numerous instances of rifts that are organizational rather than doctrinal in nature. Although value conflicts or controversies about minor points of doctrine may be instrumental in the process of separation, the schism produces a new sect or church whose theological and ethical tenets do not substantially differ from those of the mother church. The schism in the Brazilian Presbyterian church seems to be a case in point. Repudiation of foreign tutelage or of any kind of higher ecclesiastical authority, as in churches with a radical congregational constitution, may lead to separation and "multiplication by scissiparity." In this connection, Léonard (1952:153) referred to the seven Baptist churches of Bahia, six of which were originated by schisms, which in no way affected the common doctrinal tenets.

Almost all major Protestant denominations, historical or not, have given origin to separate bodies that usually carry on the name of the mother church preceded or followed by such adjectives as "independent," "free," or "national," indicating emancipation from some restrictive authority, foreign or domestic.

The schism that ruptured the Baptist church in Brazil in 1923 was obviously a rebellion against the American tutelage. In a "manifest" which the dissenting congregation and pastors presented to the

Brazilian Baptist Convention, the reasons are expounded with great candor.

We do not believe that the Gospel extirpates from the Brazilian heart the love of his fatherland and its concerns, the vital interest in national problems, something which this same Gospel does not do in other lands. We believe even less that the Gospel must always come under the cover of the particular dispositions of this or that race. We have come to think that exactly the same Gospel which in England is adapted to the British and assumes Saxonic characteristics, can do the same in Brazil by imparting purely Brazilian approaches and characteristics to our work. Even here in Brazil, the methods adopted in Rio de Janeiro are not always appropriate in Recife or Bahia and vice-versa. Let us live then within the liberty which the Gospel establishes. On the other hand, everything or almost everything here differs from the United States, and the religious conditions of the Brazilian people . . . demand that we change our ecclesiastical policy. The ultramontanes spread the rumor that we "sold" ourselves to the United States. We know how silly, illogical, and unfair that campaign is, but unfortunately some workers act as if the United States were our Holy Apostolic See.

Is it not a shame that after forty years of missionary work in Brazil, the denomination should not have succeeded in producing a man able enough to be the editor of the *Jornal Batista?* In so many years these prodigious workers (the missionaries) have not yet discovered a Brazilian able to use his own language better than a foreigner? . . . And thus many other positions in the economic system of the denomination are held by foreigners. . . . Why were the property rights of institutions which supposedly belong to the Brazilian Baptist Convention, *colégios,* seminaries, a publishing house and even the temples, transferred to the Commission in Richmond or to its representative? The Brazilian denomination as represented by the Convention, does not even own a single tile. . . . [Léonard, 1951:428.]

Wounded political sensibilities are expressed in the following passage of the Manifest:

The missionaries demonstrated that they do not know how to work without assuming control of everything. They deny us the right to direct our work by withdrawing spiritual and financial support which they could lend to this Convention at the precise moment when it decides to assume control over the work of evangelization. They only pay in order to control, for according to one of them, the one who pays gives the orders!

Our beloved brethren, the missionaries, are not convinced that we are able to govern ourselves. . . . This is the idea of the American Government with regard to the Cubans, the Filipinos, and, in part, to almost all the peoples of Central and South America. . . . Is the Brazilian Baptist people inferior to other peoples? . . . For how long do the missionaries want to have us under their tutelage as if we were children? . . . Their mission here consists of helping us to develop the work, but not to direct it perpetually as if they did not intend intelligently and sincerely to develop the national forces by providing opportunity to direct and to serve. [Léonard, 1951:424.]

The Baptist Manifest spells out most of the grievances that have at one time or another led to internal dissent or schismatic movements in the Protestant churches of Brazil and Chile. Some of its passages clearly discern the cultural conditioning of missionary activities, something the American churches learned only after a long period of trial and error.

The other kind of schism represents a radical departure from the supernaturalism and doctrinal system of the mother church. Whatever organizational changes there are, they rather derive from subversive approaches to the supernatural and from doctrinal accretions or modifications; in brief, the new group of believers most likely bears the structural marks of the *sect* rather than the *church*. The Independent Presbyterian Church of Brazil never was a sect, but the Methodist Pentecostal Church of Chile most certainly was, perhaps still is, a sect, and the schism of 1909 that originated it surely belongs to the second category.

A sect is a schismatic group springing from, and developing in opposition to, an organized church and becoming independent of it. Finding its authority in what it regards as a truer understanding of the scriptures or of primitive Christianity, it sustains a critical attitude toward the parent institution and, indeed, toward the patterns of contemporary culture in general; and seeks in detachment a more positive realization of the Christian life. [Ferm, ed., 1959:699.]

The occurrences which eventually resulted in a sectarian movement were quite consistent with the orientation of the parent body. The Chilean Methodist Episcopal Church had preserved, to a considerable degree, the revivalist character of the frontier period, as expressed in the following passage:

No element in the Wesleyan heritage was more wholeheartedly accepted and more faithfully declared than the emphasis on religion as experience. It was this that gave the untrained itinerant preachers confidence and boldness, that clothed their message with power, and that constituted the secret of their hold upon the masses. It made religion a tangible thing, readily understandable by all, that could be put to the test by daily living. In his own consciousness the seeker could find the certitude of his pardon, adoption and sonship in the family of God. [Barclay: 1950:301-302.]

It was precisely during a revival in the Methodist temple of Valparaiso that "extraordinary manifestations" occurred which the most exalted faithful interpreted as "possession" (*tomada*) or "baptism by the Holy Spirit." These "manifestations" were apparently preceded by long hours of fast, repentance, and prayer. As the religious services continued, an increasing number of participants showed signs of great emotional stress or disturbance, there were the sounds of

laughter, weeping, shouting, and chanting"; some people talked in tongues or had visions, some fell in ectasy and "felt themselves removed to some other place—to heaven, paradise, some beautiful fields, combined with various experiences—they talked with the Lord, with angels and with the devil. . . . Those who underwent such experiences felt great pleasure (*gozaban mucho*), and usually were much changed and full of the spirit of worship, prayer and love. [Hoover, 1948:33.]

The American missionary Hoover who witnessed these phenomena from the very beginning described the experiences of many of his parishioners who underwent such "seizures by the Spirit." There is not the shadow of a doubt that, no matter what a person might hear, see, smell, or otherwise feel, *it had an overwhelming appeal to the senses.* Within the Pentecostal vocabulary, the term *gozo* recurs with great frequency. It means enjoyment, pleasure, or gratification, and always refers to the sensuous experiences that accompany the *tomadas del Espirito*. The possessed had visions of "celestial beauty," they saw Elysian landscapes of extraordinary luminosity, God and the angels spoke to them, or they heard "heavenly music." External expressions of the emotional thrill they seemed to experience were faints, convulsions, laughter, weeping, verbal ejaculations, inarticulate shouts, chanting, dancing, and "speaking in tongues."

After recovering from the *tomadas*, the subjects reportedly experienced a feeling of "profound happiness" and a strong impulse to communicate their experience to the world. Men, women, and children

felt impelled to go onto the streets and to preach aloud, to seek their friends and neighbors, and to travel to other localities with the sole purpose of making people repent and of letting them know through their testimony that such a sublime experience was a privilege now accessible to everybody, exactly as it was at the time of the apostles. [Hoover, 1948:43.]

The revival of Valparaíso was followed by similar events among the Methodist congregations of Santiago, and before long the church was in turmoil. "Orderly" services were seemingly impossible, and many were taken by such a frenzy that the opposition of the more sober elements, including the church authorities was overridden. On one or two occasions the police were called to intervene in the service which apparently tended to engulf the congregation in what seemed complete emotional chaos.

Among those who were feeling the full impact of the *tomadas* there was of course no intention to secede from the church. Hoover himself saw nothing in these events but a revival of the genuine Christian spirit, but the church authorities took a different view. Officially, the "events of Valparaíso" were interpreted as "hallucinations," as "outbursts of madness" and the *tomadas* were compared with "epileptic seizures" (*El Heraldo Evangélico*, 1909). In other words, the American missionaries who were in full control of the Chilean Methodist Church condemned the incipient Pentecostal movement in the strongest possible terms, which of course antagonized the "fanatics," as they were called, who were acting out of the unshakable conviction that their experiences were genuine. The irreconcilable attitude assumed by the church authorities and their more sophisticated followers finally led to the expulsion of the "fanatics" who proceeded to establish three different congregations. A group of dissenters from the Second Methodist Church of Santiago was the first one to organize itself as an independent congregation under the name of Second Methodist Pentecostal Church (Segunda Iglesia Metodista Pentecostal). It was followed by the First Methodist Pentecostal Church which seceded from the First Methodist Church of Santiago, and finally in 1910 Hoover, the "soul of the movement," organized the Pentecostal congregation in Valparaiso. (There seems to be some doubt as to whether, in the beginning, there were two or three Pentecostal congregations. See Vergara, 1962:113–114.)

These three initial congregations, under the superintendency of Hoover, adopted the name Iglesia Metodista Nacional. Intensive proselytism during the following two decades accomplished three things:

From a strictly local movement the new sect developed into a national institution with ramifications in most provinces. In 1929 there were "at least 22 organized churches, and every one of these had various congregations in different districts and localities, some controlling as many as ten." (Vergara, 1962:117.)

The new sect recruited its membership among the lower classes of the country.

A native leadership emerged solely on the basis of successful missionizing.

In 1932, the Iglesia Metodista Nacional split into two separate bodies, the Iglesia Metodista Pentecostal under Manuel Umaña, and the Iglesia Evangelica Pentecostal under Hoover. It seems that the intense nationalism of Umaña and his followers (*nada con los estranjeros*) was adroitly used to legitimatize the rift, although the rival sect, after the death of Hoover, became as indigenous in its social composition, leadership, and attitudes as the parent institution.

The schisms of 1909 and 1932 served as precedents and models for a whole series of secessions which utilized the organizational schism as a device of expansion rather than of mere dissent. Each of the two sects that resulted from the schism of 1932 generated in turn a number of autonomous Pentecostal bodies of greatly varying size and geographical distribution. The following two tables were compiled from Vergara's survey (1962:153–180).

The preceding enumeration does not cover, as Vergara points out, many small Pentecostal groups of independent rather than schismatic origin. The number of secessions as well as the dates at which they occurred suggest the existence of a pattern, a "continuing instability" which, in all likelihood, has already added to, or subtracted from, the list presented in 1962. Most of these schisms originated in personal rivalries and rifts, dissatisfaction with certain leaders, administrative policies, and the like. In other words, the schisms were organizational rather than doctrinal. In fact, by attending the services of these many groups, by listening to their prayers, hymns, and sermons, one would hardly reach the conclusion that they constitute discrete sects.

The native vigor of the Chilean Pentecostal movement did not discourage foreign sects of the same persuasion from establishing missions in various parts of the country. In 1942, the General Council of the Assemblies of God in Springfield, Missouri, sent its first missionaries to Chile, while Swedish evangelists representing the Autonomous Assemblies of God had already begun to make converts in

OFFSHOOTS OF THE IGLESIA METODISTA PENTECOSTAL (1962)

Name of sect	Year of Founding	Membership	Geographical distribution
Iglesia Evangélica de los Hermanos	1925	Small	Mostly in Santiago and Valparaíso
Ejército Evangélico de Chile	1933(?)	5,000(?)	From Santiago to Valdivia
Ejército Evangélico Nacional	1942	No information	From Santiago to Llanquihue
Movimiento Evangélico Nacional	1960	No information	
Iglesia Misionera de Cristo	1947	900(?)	Mostly Santiago
Corporación Evangélica de Vitacura	1933	8,000–10,000	From Santiago to Puerto Montt
Iglesia Pentecostal de Chile	1942		From Antofagasta to Valdivia
Iglesia Evangélica Metodista Pentecostal Reunida en el Nombre de Jesus	1950	60,000(?)	Mostly from Rancagua to Temuco
Misión Cristiana, Iglesia Evangélica Pentecostal	1953		
Iglesia Pentecostal de Chile Austral			Southern Chile
Iglesia Evangélica Cristiana	1936		Mostly Santiago
Iglesia Pentecostal Apostólica	1938	Small	Santiago and Antofagasta(?)
Misión Cristiana Apostólica	1938	200	Mostly Santiago
Iglesia Evangélica El Pesebre Humilde de Cristo	1943(?)	Very small	Santiago and Curicó
Iglesia de Cristo Evangélica Nacional	1946(?)	100	Santiago

OFFSHOOTS OF THE IGLESIA EVANGÉLICA PENTECOSTAL (1962)

Name of sect	Year of Founding	Membership	Geographical distribution
Iglesia de Dios Pentecostal	1951	60,000–70,000	From Copiapó to Puerto Montt
Misión Iglesia Pentecostal	1952	Small	Mostly Santiago
Corporación Evangélica Pentecostal	1956	15,000(?)	Concepción and Malleco
Iglesia Cristiana de la Fe Apostolica	1932	60(?)	
Iglesia Cristiana Ganada con su Sangre	1936	8(?)	
Iglesia Evangélica de Nueva Jerusalem		70(?)	Concepción

1937. Since 1945, the International Church of the Foursquare Gospel has attracted a number of followers, and the Church of God—of North American origin as is the preceding one—has been active since 1950 (Vergara, 1962: 175–180). Although recent figures are not available, there is little doubt that these four Pentecostal groups together represent no more than an exceedingly small proportion of the Chilean Pentecostal movement.

One may be inclined to see in this process of fragmentation nothing but the natural consequence of a complete freedom of conscience which entitles the Protestant to seek the truth wherever he thinks he will find it. It seems, however, that this trend has been reinforced by rather specific patterns of Latin American social organization, namely *caudillism* and *rebellion against authority*. The situation was further complicated by the attempt to transfer the espiscopal organization of the Methodist Church to the Iglesia Metodista Pentecostal. In fact, the title "bishop" was bestowed upon Manuel Umaña, but none of the dissenting Pentecostal sects went as far as the schismatics of 1909, although in some cases their leaders wield a degree of authority that one does not find in any of the historical churches.

So far as we were able to determine, most conflicts within the Pentecostal bodies have been caused by an inherent structural inconsistency. On the one hand, the sectarian character of these groups emphasizes, surely as a reaction against the Catholic tradition, the primacy of the laity, especially in all aspects concerning proselytism and development. On the other hand, the successful leader who has received more than an ordinary share of graces from the Holy Spirit is easily held in awe by the faithful. His voice is respected as the voice of God, and if he can add to his other endowments the reputation of a miracle worker, a successful healer perhaps, there is no limit to the reverence with which he is surrounded by his followers. Thus two opposing principles are operative in the Pentecostal sects, one "democratic" and the other "authoritarian." They clash as soon as rival leaders with similar divine endowments arise and accuse the ones in power of misusing their authority or, as they sometimes put it, of "antidemocratic behavior." If the rival is able to sway enough followers, the split occurs and a new sect is born. There is much bitterness during the conflict, and such words as "caudillo" and "cacique" are freely used, but little of it seems to remain once the secession has taken place.

A handbill distributed by the Iglesia de Dios Pentecostal voiced its criticism of the Iglesia Metodista Pentecostal by contrasting the virtues of W. C. Hoover to the attitudes of some of his successors:

Hoover gave all his life and fortune to the Work. He wore out the shoes given to him by his relatives in his search for the lost sheep, and he said: "The pastor is but the most humble, obedient and submissive member of the church." Nowadays there are those who do not limit themselves to the uncontrolled spending of their churches' money, but they make themselves caciques, dictators of the faithful and they goad those who may reproach their conduct. He [Hoover] taught how to sing the hymns harmoniously without instruments that made them lose their sacred originality. He did not accept birthday gifts and offerings, but he censured those who did, for he considered this as a sign of ego worship contrary to the teachings of the Word. He did not accept errors such as "the Holy Ghost told me so" for not being in accord with the teachings of the Bible. Numerous errors result from this fact: "They prophetize a vision of their own heart" (Jer. 23:16). He did not do anything to impede the manifestations (i.e., seizure of the Spirit), yet he did not anything either to cause them. Neither instruments nor stylized *glorias a Dios* [glory to God]. He corrected the error of calling *pastora* [feminine form of *pastor*] the wife of the pastor. This was the first superintendent of this Work: any error which nowadays one notices in those churches is not to be attributed to him, but to the men who, forgetful of the Word, put their trickeries, ambitions, pomposities, prejudices above the sacred leadership of the Spirit of God.

During the annual conferences of two dissenting Pentecostal bodies, the Misión Iglesia Pentecostal and the Iglesia Pentecostal de Chile, the *caudillismo* of certain Pentecostal leaders was severely criticized. "The pastor," one critic remarked,

receives the tithes of the total membership including the *locales* [newly organized congregations without pastors of their own]; consequently he is not interested in conceding independence to these groups; much on the contrary, he organizes a great number of such *locales* until they constitute *pastorados* with three or four thousand members. This 'pastoral monopoly' generates actions and reactions which reflect the vices of ecclesiasticism and bring ruination to newly begun works [of evangelization]. This is why the *caudillos* select simple-minded men who lack the perspicacity to see through their manipulations, and this is why lay members who perceive their way of conducting church affairs, are expelled. This also explains the immovability of superintendents and bishops, the elimination of democratic procedure in the filling of positions, the negation of opportunities to lay members, and the exclusion of members and common citizens from the conferences and policy meetings. It further explains the effort to rule on economic matters without paying heed to the denunciations that some pastors have registered in their name temples and other properties. And this is why there comes a point when secession takes place. Usually the leader of such a movement shares the procedural secrets and never discuses them openly. When he is expelled from the group he in turn builds his own machine and the same cycle repeats itself again, namely the iniquitous exploitation of the credulity and good faith of the members.

One of the more candid expressions of religious caudillism may be seen in the pennant which was profusely distributed during the festivities celebrating the fiftieth anniversary of the Iglesia Metodista Pentecostal de Chile. In the center of the pennant there is a black terrestrial globe showing the outline of South America in lighter color. And out of the globe emerges the bust of bishop Manuel Umaña.

Many of our interviewees proudly remarked that this, after all, was a way of growing and conquering "Chile for Christ." One of our informants, a Methodist himself, invoked the image of cellular fission which in fact appears to define the process in a metaphorical fashion. In a number of cases an organizational schism occurred or was about to occur when individual congregations had reached a size that tended to destroy their effectiveness as primary groups or personal communities. In a crowd of several thousand, the individual begins to feel anonymous, the pastor becomes less and less accessible, and upstarts with good records as missionaries find ample opportunity to voice discontent and to recruit followers by offering the services which the pastor can no longer provide.

There are, as we shall see, other institutionalized mechanisms that sanction the ascent of new leaders in a rather unique way. At any rate, if the schism occurs, it does not necessarily weaken the parent institution for the Iglesia Metodista Pentecostal and the Iglesia Evangélica Pentecostal have weathered many rifts, but are still the largest sects in Chile. The split thus performs the function to recreate the social intimacy and the personal bonds among the faithful which Pentecostalism seems to require.

The organizational schism may indeed be considered conscious attempt to reinforce the sectarian character of the movement as a whole. This finding is validated by the fact that the principle of sectarianism has been formally recognized as the *élan vital* of the Pentecostal movements. Hoover who is generally accepted and revered as the father of Chilean Pentecostalism, stated it in his booklet, and his words have acquired an almost dogmatic validity to his followers. Actually, Hoover proffered the well-known argument that in the course of time the established churches lose their original "purity": more and more they tend to be ruled by human interests rather than by the "Word of God." New churches emerge because of the "decadence" and "infidelity" of the established ones. The oldest churches are generally the "most infidel, not to say the most corrupt ones." Hoover mentioned the Catholic, the Lutheran, and the Anglican churches as examples of decadence and corruption. And he recognizes the same influences in the Evangelical churches, although in his opinion the development has not yet reached the point of complete deviation.

The most sincere and fervent souls "however are unable to tolerate such a situation. They feel that God has called them to sever their ties with the 'contaminated' institution and to form a new church which, by its very nature, is a sect." The word sect he derives from *secare*, to cut, and the cut which the sect performs "separates the pure from the impure, the things of God from the things of the world." The future of the sect stands and falls with its capacity of keeping apart from worldliness which is identified with wealth, lust for power and prestige, "slackness of the soul," "moral debility," and vice (sex, tobacco, alcohol, gambling, dancing, theater).

Furthermore, Hoover (1948:106–118) condems the popular belief that "ignorance is the cause of vices and evil, and that a good education is necessary to develop a child into a good man." Much on the contrary, he points out,

the lawyers and the wealthy (who surely show no lack of education) are the ones who exploit the poor, who deny wages to the workingman, who defraud widows and orphans. . . . Educated men employ themselves in government offices and embezzle huge sums, in the Railway Company of the State, in the treasuries, in public works and in the stock market. Educated men are the ones who falsify money and checks and defraud firms, etc . . .

Thus the ignorant and the poor have a better chance to maintain the purity of original Christianity than the rich and well educated, provided they keep away from "worldliness" and abstain from vices.

The strongest possible emphasis on discontinuity between the converted and unconverted, the notion that the true Christian spirit implies aloofness from the things of the world to avoid "contamination," attest more than anything else the sectarian character of the Pentecostalist movement. It explains, for example, why the sects consistently refuse to join the ecumenical movement in Latin American Protestantism, for even the loosest association with other Protestant bodies is felt to be a threat to the purity of the sectarian spirit.

As we shall see, however, some leaders begin to understand that limited political involvements are useful, if not necessary, to vouchsafe the kind of religious freedom stipulated by the present constitution. The impermanence of Latin American constitutions explains the concern of the Protestant bodies for religious freedom. Constitutional guarantees per se are not felt to be sufficient. Political participation is increasingly emphasized to assure law enforcement and to prevent constitutional changes which could conceivably restrict the prevailing freedom of religion.

The preference expressed by Hoover for the poor, the ignorant, and uneducated gained wide and indisputable currency among the Chilean Pentecostal sects. The new creed became indeed a religion of the lower classes, and the sect leaders definitely wish to preserve it as such. Any kind of learning beyond mere literacy—the *crente* must of course read the Bible—is frowned upon, and educated members who show intellectual interests or ambitions are watched with considerable suspicion. A minor split which recently occurred in a provincial town of the Central Valley was originated by a small group of "educated" members of the Iglesia Metodista Pentecostal who attempted to open schools and to "promote the cultural development of the congregation." These attempts were thwarted by the local junta, and since the promoters refused to conform to the "authoritarianism" of the local pastors the split became inevitable.

Since all learning, except knowledge of the Bible, is held to be dangerous to the true faith, very few pastors have ever been exposed to the teachings of a theological institution. One of the most successful pastors of the Iglesia Metodista Pentecostal whose *circuito* (his own congregation plus the dependent locales) now has about four thousand members, told us that at the beginning of his career he had had a "revelation" that "ordered him to burn all books in his possession." He complied with the divine order and has not read a book since, except the Bible and Evangelical tracts. "Much knowledge extinguishes the Spirit" he added, and his view happens to coincide with that of Bishop Umaña.

17
Schisms and Nationalism: The Brazilian Pentecostal Sects

✠The Pentecostal creed was introduced in Brazil by foreign missionaries. The two largest and oldest sects, the Assembléia de Deus (Assembly of God) and the Congregação Cristã do Brasil (Christian Congregation of Brazil) were established almost simultaneously in 1910, the year in which the Chilean Pentecostals formally seceded from the Methodist Church. Neither of the founding missionaries was American, yet the Protestantism of both had a distinctly American background. Luis Francescon, the founder of the Christian Congregation, a native Italian and Catholic, was converted in Chicago and joined the First Italian Presbyterian Church in that city. Years afterward, he was, as he put it, "sealed with the gift of the Holy Spirit" and repeatedly received direct messages from the Lord who suggested that he dedicate his life to missionary work. Induced by a "sacred revelation," Luis Francescon chose Buenos Aires for his first proselytic endeavors. A few months later, again under "divine guidance" he went to São Paulo where the Italian community proved receptive to his preachings. At first the Christian Congregation was a sect for Italian immigrants because all services were conducted in the Italian language. Part of the Italian heritage may be seen in the extraordinary importance which this sect pays to music. Instrumental music is explicitly recognized as a means to "praise God," and whenever feasible, the congregations maintain an orchestra. In contrast to the folk music of the other Pentecostal sects, the music played by the orchestras of the Christian Congregation is more sophisticated and rather operatic in style. The special rules that regulate the constitution of orchestras determine, among many other details, that "the brethren musicians continue to study music, even after having been examined and admitted. If possible, they should take a teacher, or some other competent person."

Obviously, the Christian Congregation was specially adapted to the cultural heritage of the large Italian population of São Paulo. The Italians were rapidly being assimilated by Brazilian society, however, and among the younger generations there were very few who wished to be reminded of the national heritage of their parents or grandparents. Thus guided by opportunity and divine revelation the elders of the sect decided to drop the Italian language in 1935. This well-timed adjustment to a changing cultural situation not only assured survival of the sect but laid the foundations for an increasingly rapid expansion outside São Paulo City and the state of São Paulo.

The Assembléia de Deus was established by the Swedish missionary Daniel Berg in Belém do Pará where his preachings produced a split in the local Baptist congregation. Actually, prior to his "baptism by the Holy Spirit," Berg had been a Baptist, and the schism of Belém had been preceded by a similar split in Stockholm. The Pentecostal movement initiated in Brazil by Berg has had the continuing support of its parental organization in Sweden, and some Swedish missionaries are still active in various parts of the country.

A separate Pentecostal start could be traced back to the activities of two American missionaries of the Church of Christ. Under the emotional impact of a revival which took place in Alagoas, one of the northeastern states of Brazil, both became Pentecostals and joined the General Council of Assemblies of God in the United States. There is now an Assembléia de Deus Cruzada de Fé (Assembly of God, Crusade of Faith) under the leadership of Virgil Frank Smith, one of the two founders. It is related to Berg's organization through the National Convention of Assemblies of God.

The Assemblies of God in Brazil are, like some Pentecostal sects in Chile, divided into *ministérios*, the administration of which is strictly centralized and produces, in the words of an American missionary, a sort of "bishops and small popes." There is usually a *ministério* in each state capital, but large metropolitan areas have several *ministérios*. São Paulo City, for example, is divided into three *ministérios*, with congregations all over the state. One of these, the *ministério do Belenzinho* (named after the city district Belenzinho), comprises numerous congregations in São Paulo and Mato Grosso with a total membership of approximately 78,000. The *ministério do Ipiranga* seceded from the *ministério do Belenzinho* because the pastor refused to accept the authority of its leader. Missionaries and provisional pastors are on the payroll of the *ministérios* which collect regular offerings from all affiliated congregations. We were informed that the monthly salary of a high ranking pastor varied between 25,000 and 35,000 cruzeiros, an amount comparable to the income in the higher echelons of the civil service.

More radical versions of religious caudillism in Brazil are represented by a number of schismatic movements that were generated, according to the words of one of its leaders, by "the ecclesiastic machine of prepotent popes and the consequent loss of vitality and love."

Even more than in Chile, the Pentecostal churches in Brazil have attracted the masses by spectacular cures for the numerous illnesses that afflict the people. Any charismatic sect leader who shows unusual skill as a miracle healer is likely to draw large crowds. One of the most successful healers, an American missionary of the International Church of the Foursquare Gospel, gained many followers in São Paulo, and when in 1956 his sect sponsored a National Crusade of Evangelization, many Protestant groups joined this interdominational movement. The revival tent was (and still is) used very extensively for spontaneous gatherings of the Crusade which invaded most regions of Brazil. Apparently, the revivalist atmosphere of the Crusade caused many defections among the historical churches as well as the Assemblies of God, and a number of new Pentecostal sects emerged which are primarily concerned with the mediation of divine healing. The most conspicuous of these sects is probably the Igreja Evangélica Pentecostal Brasil para Cristo (Pentecostal Church Brazil for Christ) under Manoel de Mello, a markedly personalistic movement of considerable fluidity. Another issue of the Crusade, Miguel Elias, founded the Igreja Pentecostal do Avivamento Bíblico (Pentecostal Church of Biblical Revival) and more recently the Igreja Pentecostal Maravilha de Jesus (Pentecostal Church Miracle of Jesus).

There are at least seven or eight other Pentecostal sects that are continuously subdividing or changing their names. All these new sects use with more or less success the operational techniques of the Crusade, namely, the revival tent, the radio, and the Gospel of Immediate Salvation. The latter emphasizes that Jesus not only saves, but he saves *now* and *here* in this world. This means that salvation from sickness and the social evils of our time is available to the faithful. The combination of these three techniques has had almost revolutionary effects upon the methods of evangelizing which hitherto had been utilized. Religious broadcasts have since become standard procedure, not only in the new sects, but in the historical churches as well. The only religious body that has remained entirely aloof from such modernization is the Christian Congregation and, interestingly enough, without tent revivals, without broadcasts, without any sort of public exhibition at all, this sect has attracted more people than any other Protestant body in Brazil, except the Assembly of God.

The fact that foreign missionaries have played a conspicuous role in the diffusion of various Pentecostal creeds in Brazil has in no way affected the development of a rather stringent nationalism in most sects. The extremely loose structure of the Pentecostal bodies prevented foreign mission boards from exercising the sort of control that stimulated emancipatory movements among the historical churches. Furthermore, the home organizations were far too poor to afford major financial aid which could have led to economic dependence. Scores of Baptist, Methodist, and Presbyterian churches in Chile and Brazil were erected with the financial assistance of American mission boards, but we know of no Pentecostal temple built with American dollars.

Two differences between the Pentecostal sects in Chile and Brazil should be pointed out. First, the schism of 1909 and the subsequent expansion of Pentecostalism in Chile dealt an almost paralyzing blow to the historical churches, with the possible exception of the Baptists. It seems noteworthy that little effort has been made in recent years to compete with the Pentecostal missionaries who seek to attract the masses by preaching, praying, and singing in the streets and public squares. The Pentecostals inherited these methods from the earlier missionaries and developed them in a way now felt to be "undignified" by a clergy which has grown in sophistication and class consciousness. No such change occurred in Brazil. The historical churches continue to grow slowly in spite of Pentecostal competition, and evangelization in public places, although sparingly employed, carries little social stigma in Brazil.

Secondly, the leaders of Brazilian Pentecostalism show more sophistication and familiarity with the use of such mass media as press and radio than do their Chilean brethren. The few Pentecostal tracts and periodicals that have been published in Chile reflect a rather modest degree of literacy, while the Pentecostal movement in Brazil has produced an impressive literature of its own. Emilio Condé of the Assembly of God is the author of at least half a dozen books. Many sect leaders are gifted writers who publish abundantly in periodicals and religious tracts that may be bought at newspaper stands and, in such cities as São Paulo and Rio de Janeiro, in specialized bookstores. Bishop Eurico Mattos Coutinho, a former Presbyterian who became the founder and leader of a Pentecostal sect, wrote down revelations he received from the Holy Spirit and published them in a volume of considerable literary quality. Again, the only exception is found in the Christian Congregation which condemns, as a matter of principle, all public utterances as manifestations of human vanity. It should be added, however, that the interest in learning and formal education which the Pentecostal sects have shown so far seems to be limited, as in Chile, to the three Rs and, in a few isolated instances, to trade school courses. The sources of sophistication shown by many leaders do not lie within the confines of their sects but in institutions of higher learning, frequently in Protestant seminaries which they attended before becoming sect leaders. (Read, 1965:165–166).

18

Protestantism and the Lower-Class Culture

✛The rapid expansion of the Pentecostal sects, especially in comparison with the historical Protestant churches, justifies the assumption that these sects meet certain needs, or perhaps correspond to certain aspirations of the people exposed to the brunt of cultural change which they neither control nor understand. In the preceding chapter, it was shown that the development of Protestantism, particularly since 1930 or thereabout, is related to internal migration and concomitant changes in the social structure and that these changes made it necessary to attempt a restructuring of primary group relations in which the migrant can find his lost identity. The Protestant congregation with its strong accent on intimate co-operation, personal responsibility, mutual as well as self-help, provides opportunity for the individual whose personal community has been destroyed, to "find himself."

Three aspects of this problem should probably be pointed out at this juncture. Above all, joining a Protestant congregation is by no means the only alternative open to those in search of a social identity. Competitive religious groups such as the various spiritualistic sects, the Umbanda (a fusion of African cult forms and spiritualistic beliefs) and a number of local African cult centers variously named *candomblé, macumba,* or *xangô* have attracted the masses in Brazil, and in both countries the social gospel of political radicalism has served as a rallying point for the masses. Conversion to Protestantism ranks as only one alternative among several, and there is of course a considerable amount of shifting from group to group. Official Brazilian computations, which are notoriously incomplete, report 66,335 exclusions from Protestant churches in 1956, 84,814 in 1957, and 116,975 in 1960 (*Estatística do culto Protestante* 1956:1, 1957:1). Our informants were virtually unanimous in that the turnover within the Pentecostal sects is particularly high.

Secondly, the search for a social identity can be fully appreciated only if the peculiar position of the lower classes is taken into account. In contrast to their highly articulate and well led counterparts in Europe and the United States, the lower classes of Chile and Brazil are only now emerging from a state of social anonymity. True enough, urbanization tends to accelerate the coming of age of the working class, but there is no longer any doubt that the cities of Chile and Brazil (as those of most other Latin American countries) were totally unprepared to handle the sudden influx of rural migrants and to adapt their obsolete administrative patterns to ecological and structural changes that had become inevitable. In the absence of responsible planning the newcomers settle wherever they find an empty space, build crude shelters with whatever materials they can lay hands on, and before long large clusters of such hovels cover hillsides, swampland, and any available ground surrounding the city proper in all directions. People live in indescribable squalor in these shantytowns. In the beginning there is neither electricity, running water, drainage, sewers, transportation, nor any of the other facilities that are taken for granted in the nearby city where most of the migrants work. Some improvements are usually introduced in the course of time, for many settlers are voters and some compensations have to be offered in return for their ballots. But such superficial improvements as electricity, bus lines, or paved streets fail to make habitable areas which by nature are unfit for human habitation. According to recent estimates, approximately half a million people live in the *favelas* of Rio de Janeiro. (The Brazilian Institute for Geography and Statistics defines a *favela* as follows: a minimum number of 50 buildings grouped together; predominance of huts and barracks of a typical rustic appearance, usually made of planks and galvanized sheets or similar material; unlicensed and uninspected buildings on lands of third parties or unknown owners; not included in the general network of sewerage, running water, lighting, and telephone; nonurbanized area, lacking proper division into streets, numbering, feeing, or rating system.)

Four hundred thousand more inhabit the *poblaciones callampas* (shantytowns) of Santiago. It is true that at least in Santiago great efforts have been made to ameliorate the living conditions of the lower classes, but a steady stream of new migrants has so far offset the gains. Nor does the squalor of the shantytowns exhaust the social problems of the underprivileged. Runaway inflation, both in Brazil and Chile, keeps the purchasing power of earnings at a substandard level, regardless of legal minimum wages and periodical increases. The rate of in-migration far exceeds the creation of new jobs, and thousands of newcomers are only marginally employed. The chances for upward mobility, even for those who are skilled and literate, are remote (Hutchinson, 1960). In 1960, the "social consequences of industrialization" were summed up as follows by the United Nations Department of Economics and Social Affairs (1961: 24):

Mere physical separation from kinsfolk and community of origin can deprive the individual of social identifications and of material and moral support

when these are most needed. "Anomie," the feeling of being lost and root-
less, family disintegration, lack of supervision of children, the formation
of delinquent gangs of youths, and collapse of personal morals sometimes
results—though by no means always. . . . It is demonstrably false from
evidence available today that a modern industrial society cannot have strong
and stable family and community bonds, once the new society is established.
But in the process of transition, of breakdown of old social forms and
creation of new ones, there is a particularly dangerous stage when attitudes
and behavior may be without anchors, controlled more by passing winds
of demagogy, fadism, or mob spirit than by established values of home
and community.

It is difficult indeed to avoid the impression that in Brazil and
Chile (as elsewhere in Latin America) the economy is run for the
benefit of the upper classes. The lower classes command attention
only as recipients of charity or as foci of actual or potential rebellion.
It would appear that the constant necessity to face problems of such
magnitude wears people down to the point that any kind of relief,
however futile or extravagant it may seem, is welcome, if only as a
means of temporary escape.

Thirdly, the attractions Pentecostalism holds for the underpriviliged
masses are multifarious and rather complex. The felt need to rebuild
a meaningful system of primary relations (the personal community)
in an atomized society may be satisfied, in some way at least, by the
Pentecostal sect as well as any other church or sect, provided it meets
certain organizational prerequisites which are found in the Catholic
parish organization only under exceptional circumstances.

Like other Protestant bodies, the Pentecostal sect offers "redemption"
from certain forms of habitual behavior which are defined as sinful
and therefore "degrading." According to many of our life histories, the
convert feels dissatisfaction with his way of life, even before conversion took place. Although previous religious and moral encultura-
tion may have contributed to those feelings, it became apparent that
several other factors played a decisive role in determining a radical
change of personal habits. In the first place, many of our informants
associated vice with sickness and conversion with health. A Pentecostal pastor in Chile told us about his unhappy youth which he had
spent in the "pursuit of sexual pleasures" and alcoholic excesses. Eventually he contracted a serious venereal disease which "no doctor was
able to cure." When he finally "accepted Christ," his ailment miracu-

lously disappeared and his health became excellent. "Before my conversion," another member of a Pentecostal sect confessed, "my wife was very sick, and I lived without God and hope. Now we all enjoy good health." A woman left her husband because she wanted to live a "purer and more Christian-like life." She was convinced that "vices are bad for the organism." Several interviewees affirmed that they "gained health through faith." A man confessed that before his conversion he had lived "in vice and sin." Now he was living a "much better and healthier life." A woman "accepted the Spirit" because she desperately wished "to cure her sick daughter," and conversion really solved her problem. One of our male informants told us that before his conversion "he had much sickness in his family" because he was not "living in the grace of God." The idea of a "rebirth" so often associated with religious conversion thus appears to contain a physiological component. The seat of the newly acquired moral virtues is a healthier organism, a point of no minor importance in countries where the morbidity rate continues to be very high among the underprivileged classes.

Furthermore, our life histories reveal a great deal of "unhappiness" with a life of "vice and sin," even if the person is *not* afflicted with physical maladies. The following excerpts may cast some light on this aspect of conversion.

H. A. L. MALE, AGE 78. Formerly rural laborer, now street peddler. Married. Never had any religion.

My wife attended services in the local Methodist temple and invited me to join. I refused because I was drunk almost every night. Once in a dream I saw God who invited me to go to church. I went and accepted Christ. I felt that the Lord had forgiven all my sins. When the services were over I felt relief, satisfaction and *gozo*. I gave up drinking and became a different person. Before my conversion I had a violent temper, but now I live in peace with my wife, my granddaughter and my neighbors. I have more self-confidence now, work regularly and make more money. We had a winter that was almost like summer, there was never any lack of bread. Not like before when there were days without any food at all.

Wants to learn to read and write, "to learn more about God and the Holy Scriptures."

E. G. G. FEMALE. AGE 18. SINGLE. Domestic servant. She liked the Gospel since she was a child.

Grandmother used to take me to a Pentecostal temple, but I had no energy to resist temptations. Afterwards I returned to church to repent but I always fell back into sin. One day I heard the voice of the Lord who told me that all my sins had been forgiven. My heart filled with *gozo* and I was seized by the Holy Spirit. I danced and heard soft voices singing exquisite melodies. I felt carried away to another place of wondrous beauty. When I recovered I found myself kneeling and praying in front of the altar. Immediately all temptations and anxieties ceased. I gave up painting my lips and curling my hair. My only desire is to work and to go to church. Once I fell sick with paratyphoid fever. Two weeks later, still very sick, I went to church and was again seized by the Spirit. An *hermana* who did not know of my sickness, also had a *tomada del Espiritu*, walked over to the place where I knelt and laid hands on my head. The same day I felt completely cured. When I was fourteen years old I had ear surgery and became almost deaf. After my conversion I took part in a *cadena de oración* (continuous prayer meeting of seven days). During one of these meetings an *hermano* laid hands on my head and gradually my hearing went back to normal.

C. C. T. FEMALE. SINGLE. AGE 21. Seamstress. She was a Catholic, but found that Catholicism "lacked foundations."

When I was sixteen I began to go to a Protestant church with my uncles, but remained indifferent during the first year. Suddenly, during a church service, I felt invaded by a great sadness and understood the presence of the Lord. I repented my sins and ceased to crave the distractions of the world. Never again did I go to a dance or to the movies. I only wish to work for the Gospel.

M. H. A. A. MALE. AGE 28. MARRIED. Soldier. Was educated in Catholic school, but "hypocrisy of priests" made him lose respect for church.

I began to attend church services in Valparaiso. I gave up smoking, drinking, gambling and relations with prostitutes, but did not become emotionally involved in this new religion until three years later when suddenly, in a Methodist church in Santiago, I felt a strange impulse which carried me to the altar. I was not aware of what I was doing; I had the impression of being alone in the church and felt the presence of God, a *gozo* I had never felt before. I wished to surrender my life to the Lord to serve him. I experienced a strong desire to shout and communicate what I was feeling to everybody. I felt forgiveness of my sins and profound relief.

M. is somewhat critical of the "lack of faith" and "the professional attitude" of pastors. What keeps him in church is "his hope for a revival."

M. C. A. FEMALE. AGE 63. WIDOW. Was seamstress, lives with son. Was Catholic, but never attended mass. Conversion to Protestant faith was gradual.

Invited by friends, I attended Methodist and Baptist services, but could not bring myself to get interested. Eventually I found a Methodist church whose services I liked. Frequently I asked God to cure my arthritis. One day I knelt in front of the altar, and when the hands of the preacher touched my head I felt a shiver running through my whole body, a strange sensation I had never had before. I felt no weight, exactly as if my feet were not touching the ground, and my nerves relaxed. I thought I was another person and for the first time in twenty years I raised my arms to heaven. I prayed for forgiveness, but I cannot recollect my words. A sensation of well-being and pleasure as never before invaded me completely. I wept with joy. During the next half hour my whole body kept shaking violently. Since then my life has been peaceful and contented. Now I can use my hands again. Every day I feel better, I don't take sedatives anymore, and my arms are improving, thank God.

G. A. FEMALE, AGE 63. MARRIED. She was an agricultural laborer. Husband who was construction worker, is now street peddler. Long ago she ceased to practice the Catholic religion because it failed to assuage her anxieties. Invited by a preacher she attended church services and was converted. "I felt a great relief, an inexplicable joy. The Lord had forgiven my sins. There is now peace in my soul. Before my conversion, I had a terrible temper. I smoked a great deal, but now I don't smoke anymore. I live in peace with my husband and the neighbors. To help my husband I work with satisfaction and joy." She is illiterate, but feels a strong desire to learn to read and write in order to "learn the word of God."

G. S. MALE. AGE 51. MARRIED. Repairs and sells shoes. Never practiced any religion at all. Was alcoholic and suffered from "anxieties." Approximately thirty years ago S. killed a man and was sentenced to death for first-degree murder.

When I arrived in prison, I was in a terrible fury. Like a maniac I shouted vengeance against everybody, members of my family, neighbors, the judge, the police, just about everybody. My only wish was to escape for a couple of days to take revenge. They called me *el loco*. After the first week or so, somebody gave me a Bible and I began to read. I also had some talks with another convict who had been converted in prison. Then one day I had a vision in plain daylight. Out of the corner of my cell walked a beautiful woman followed by an old man with a white beard and penetrating eyes. They walked all around the cell and disappeared in the same spot they had come from. My brother, the convict, said to me: "The angel of Jehovah is walking around. Be prepared to receive the baptism of the Lord." One day, some weeks later, when I felt desperate, I heard a voice: "All thy sins are forgiven . . . This is what the world has given thee . . . I shall pick thee up like a filthy rag and cleanse thee in my precious blood so that thou preach my Gospel in the streets." I felt a shiver and for the first time I bent my knees and prayed with all my soul. I changed completely, the prison seemed pleasant and my cell different. A profound feeling of peace and *gozo* never left me.

While G. S. was waiting to be executed, the prison was destroyed by an earthquake. Unlike most prisoners, S. made no attempt to escape but saved many inmates who had been buried under the debris. The Supreme Court commuted his sentence to 20 years, then to 15 and finally to 11 years. Since G. S. left prison he has devoted almost all of his free time to the preaching of the Gospel. He is now pastor of a Pentecostal congregation.

From these excerpts a pattern emerges which is borne out by a number (27) of other life histories and numerous interviews. All subjects expressed dissatisfaction with their way of life before conversion. "I drank a lot and was very unhappy." "I accepted the faith because I want to live a better life." "Before conversion I felt emptiness in life which only the church could fill." "I sought peace and happiness and was tired of vices." "Because of my vices we lived in poverty." (Now he owns a small factory.) "I drank so heavily that my wife deserted me, but I felt dissatisfied with my licentious life." "I joined the church because I had a revelation in a dream. Before I led a very disorderly life." "I was in search of something that would change my life of a drunkard." "Before conversion I had no religious ideals whatever; I was vain, egotistic and had terrible family problems." These are typical statements of Chilean converts who are now members of a variety of different churches and sects (Temuco and Concepción).

A typical problem encountered in life histories and interviews was what the subjects called *un genio tremendo*, a terrible temper. According to their own explanation they were possessed by irascible moods, usually accompanying or following heavy drinking. At the slightest provocation they would physically attack members of their own family, neighbors, or anybody who happened to rouse their anger. Others could not resist "temptations," indulged in illicit sex, alcohol, tobacco, smoking, malicious gossip, frequent altercations with family members and neighbors, or simply in "worldly pleasures." Many of them hated their spouse to the point of committing physical violence or entertaining thoughts of murder.

Conversion is invariably described in terms of a strong emotional experience that may or may not be accompanied by visions or miracles. At any rate, the subject feels great relief, happiness, joy or *gozo. All his sins are forgiven.* He is at peace with himself and the world. In fact, he has now more confidence and faith in himself and the world. He no longer craves worldly pleasures and often spends most or all of his free time in proselytic endeavors. Work which had often been drudgery before the conversion is now felt to be pleasurable, and some subjects indicate that their material situation has improved.

There is little doubt that the troubles preceding conversion were manifestations of personality disorders of varying intensity. Conversion, among other things, reflects aspiration to a "better life," to "peace and happiness." Exactly what this life looks like can easily be inferred from the actual behavior of Protestant converts from the lower ranges of the society. Surely enough, the convert sheds his "vices," but *as he does he carefully rids himself of forms of behavior which the society at large holds in disrepute.* Drunken bouts, tavern brawls, wife-beating, illegitimacy, neglect of children and a disorganized home life, personal appearance suggesting neglect and uncleanliness, failure to improve poor housing conditions, and similar traits are often held against the lower classes. One may say, they are identified with lower-class behavior and therefore looked upon with a mixture of moral indignation and amused contempt. It seems that the Protestant convert is particularly sensitive to such criticism, for henceforward he carefully avoids "disreputable" forms of behavior. He refrains from alcohol, his attitudes toward his family change, instead of violence there is now patience and the "desire to forgive." If he lives in concubinage he seeks to legalize his union; he begins to enjoy home life and, thanks to his newly acquired money-saving virtues, he is soon able to ameliorate somewhat the shanty he may be living in. The place is kept cleaner and so are the children. Maybe the husband buys a sewing machine for his wife and a bicycle for himself. In fact, the latter has become an exceedingly important factor in the propagation of the Pentecostal faith in Chile. A major aspiration of every *roto chileno* become Pentecostal is to purchase, at the earliest possible opportunity, a dark woolen suit, black or preferably dark blue, colors which, in his mind, symbolize middle-class status. On Saturday and Sunday afternoons one often meets, in the working class districts and *poblaciones* of Santiago, processions of hymn-singing bands of men and women. Invariably, the men are dressed in dark suits and whenever approached for information or a brief interview, they respond with grave dignity and solemn words befitting their new station. These sects very definitely convey an air of petit bourgeois respectability, dependent of course on strongest congregational cohesion and supernatural sanctions. *The desire to become respectable, that is, to adopt middle-class behavior, obviously plays no minor role as a determinant of conversion.*

19
The Religious Determinant

✠The preceding Chapters may have conveyed the impression that people join a Protestant denomination to rid themselves of anxieties, to recover from physical ailments, or to become socially respectable. It is true of course that "utilitarian" motives play an important role in determining conversion, but one should not lose sight of the fact that in both societies (as in the rest of Latin America) secularization has not yet made much headway among the lower social strata whose rural heritage is still fresh and saturated with a diffuse religiosity that makes no clear distinctions between the sacred and the secular.

A person practices religion to the extent that he approaches, in an institutionalized fashion, certain supernatural powers in which he has learned to believe, either to enlist their assistance or to prevent undesirable interference on their part in matters recognized as hazardous or uncontrollable by ordinary means. We may assume that human societies feel a "need for religion," insofar as religion seems to offer the solution for a variety of problems which—it is believed—cannot be solved otherwise. If the members of a society are allowed to choose among several different religious systems, preferences suggest functional differences of certain systems compared with others, not necessarily for the society as a whole, but for those segments that feel that the system of their choice is better adapted to their needs than any other system. Quite frequently a group refuses to commit itself exclusively to one system and prefers syncretism instead. The *animita* cult of Chile (an *animita* is a miniature chapel erected in a spot where a person has died a violent death, visited frequently by people who worship the soul of the dead and seek his assistance in situations of personal distress) combines elements of the Catholic cult of the saints with pre-Spanish elements. Umbanda and Spiritualism in Brazil are aso examples of such syncretic religious systems.

The question now arises why the religious approach offered by the Protestant sects was chosen by large segments of the lower classes of Chile and Brazil in preference to the traditional Catholic approach. If the Catholic church is ill-equipped to serve the religious needs of the masses, why does folk Catholicism with its unorthodox cult of the saints no longer meet these needs? In the first place, folk-Catholicism is predominantly a *rural* religion, adapted to the specific problems of a primitive peasantry. Folk-Catholicism is associated with crops and animals, with droughts and floods, with the evil spirits and demons of the jungle and the country crossroads. Life in an industrial city poses different problems believed to require a different approach to the supernatural. Basically unaltered are only the problems which accompany the life cycle of the individual, namely, birth, marriage, sickness, and death; and even these seem to gain a somewhat different significance in an urban setting. Secondly, the pantheon of saintly helpers is thought of, within the framework of folk Catholicism, as a *local* pantheon. Saints are not approached *in abstracto*, but one enters a compact with the Virgin of Lapa, Aparecida, Guadalupe, or any other of the many local variants that mediate more direct and satisfactory relationship between the saint and the worshipper. Furthermore, the cult is localized in so far as at least the principal saints have their particular shrine, usually a church or chapel where the material projection of their presence, an image or statue, instills a sense of immediacy and reality into the mind of the unsophisticated peasant seeking relief from distress. Migration to a distant city or a frontier region without religious tradition tends to alienate him from the saints, as it alienates him from the relatives, friends, and neighbors he left behind.

Finally, as indicated before, folk Catholicism, unlike church-controlled religion, is flexible and unorthodox. Although there are cases of fanaticism, always limited in space and time, it is basically tolerant and open to innovations. The miracle is probably the most frequent source of change within the framework of folk Catholicism. Christ or the Virgin appears to a person, the locale of the vision rapidly becomes a center of worship and the visionary a thaumaturge or new saint (Willems, 1940). Folk Catholicism stresses the belief in mystical experiences, in possessions and in charismatic leadership, and thus facilitates the transition to Pentecostalism. As pointed out before, a rich historical tradition of messianic movements, especially in Brazil, established numerous precedents for the second coming of Christ taught by many sects. Finally, the cult of the Holy Spirit is to be considered one of the more widespread and elaborate aspects of Latin American folk religion. In many regions of Brazil, the celebrations in honor of the *Divino Espirito Santo* actually constitute the pinnacle of the annual round of religious fiestas (Willems, 1949). The rural migrant who joins a Pentecostal sect thus finds himself on familiar grounds. Here, a lost element of his own religious background is brought back to him in a new and most exciting form.

20
The Functions of Pentecostalism

❖ The question of why the Pentecostal creed appeals so strongly to the unsophisticated masses of Chile and Brazil may be answered in a very general way by stating that it is almost ideally adapted to the aspirations and needs of the lower classes. There is of course nothing new in the statement that Pentecostalism is a class religion. It has been recognized as such in the United States and elsewhere (Clark: 1937), but outside Brazil and Chile it cannot be said to assume the proportions of a mass movement. In the United States, the Pentecostal bodies are typically small sects, while in Chile or Brazil the major Pentecostal sects have a larger constituency than all the historical Protestant churches together.

This difference is not surprising in view of the fact that in the United States the middle classes predominate, while in Brazil and Chile the lower classes constitute the bulk of the population. Without denying the existence of universal traits in Pentecostalism regardless of where it is found, we believe that there are certain affinities with the lower-class culture of Latin America which do not exist in the United States. One of these affinities has already been pointed out: Pentecostalism picked up the mystical tradition of Latin American folk Catholicism and converted it into a set of institutions that have a direct bearing on the sociocultural changes affecting the lower classes. Pentecostalism, along with Seventh Day Adventism and a few other sects, resumes an ancient tradition of messianism which, in Brazil at least, can be traced back to messianic Sebastianism of the sixteenth century.

True enough, the Pentecostal sects do not ordinarily announce the second coming of Christ at some future date. Their message contains the far more appealing prospect of an immediate coming of the deity. The repentant believer may expect the descent of the Holy Spirit *here and now* rather than in a distant future. And He comes to the individual person rather than dispersively to a group of people. Communion with or seizure by the Spirit is an everyday experience which may be observed whenever the members of a congregation gather for religious services. There is nearly *always* somebody who has visions, speaks in tongues or prophetizes. Various members of a large congregation of the Assembly of God in São Paulo affirmed that about 95 percent of their fellow members had at some time or other been "possessed" by the Spirit. In fact, we never encountered a practicing Pentecostal who had not been "baptized" by the Holy Spirit. It would seem that converts who fail to have such an experience withdraw from the congregation after a certain time.

Thaumaturgy or the working of miracles is another powerful tradition of folk Catholicism which the Pentecostal sects incorporated into their body of belief and ritual. There are two ways in which miracles are performed. The *tomada del Espiritu* is often accompanied by a miracle in the sense that the person who has been "seized" by the Spirit finds himself suddenly cured from some "incurable" ailment. Or another person, preferably the pastor, who has previously been seized by the Spirit, performs the miracle by touching the patient's head with his hands, or by uttering a prayer over him. Often collective prayers proffered by a group of brethren, all previously baptized by the Spirit, accomplish the miracle of *sanidad divina*.

Finally, an almost medieval belief in evil spirits, witches and demons of European, Indian or African extraction has been reduced, by the Pentecostals, to possession by the devil. In folk Catholicism there is a variety of ways in which evil spirits including Satan may intervene in human affairs, possession being only one of these. In their preachings and writings the Pentecostals admit that sometimes the devil seizes a member of the congregation and speaks and acts through his body. The faithful are constantly warned to be on guard against such manifestations which, according to Hoover (1948:33), already occurred in the temple of Valparaiso in 1909. Prayer rather than any specific exorcistic ritual seems to be the defense against such occurrences.

Certain powers or gifts of the Spirit are not directly related to existing religious traditions, but since they occur in combinations or clusters there is no feeling of discontinuity. Following the precedents of the Holy Scriptures, the Spirit illuminates and inspires the individual mind on which He descends. This power of *discernimento* (*alta percepción interior*) enables him to recognize and understand the truth, and the power of *persuasion* transforms him into a convincing preacher who finds himself under an almost irresistible compulsion to disseminate the Word of God.

The life history of a professional ballet dancer who at the age of 17 became a Pentecostal, presents some rather typcial aspects, particularly with regard to the acquisition of these two gifts. While still a member of the municipal ballet in São Paulo she "got completely disillusioned with life" and decided to kill herself. Before she could swallow the poison her little sister "found" her and thus "saved" her life. She began to pray and was converted during a casual conversation with an unknown woman in a street car. Shortly afterwards she was baptized by the Spirit and received the "gift of discerning the spirits," as she put it. She knows everything her brethren do including the sins they commit, and consequently she is able to offer advice. She also talks in tongues and interprets tongues, that is, "unknown languages." She spends all her free time with church work and preaching the Gospel in the streets. She of course left the battlet when she was converted and is now married to a dentist.

As a rule, the Pentecostals are proud of being uneducated and simple people, untrained for any intellectual task. Successful proselytism, especially the ability to hold the attention of a casual crowd and to make converts is invariably attributed to the presence of the Spirit in the preacher rather than to his intellectual skill.

Speaking in tongues and prophesying constitute perhaps the most respected and admired powers conferred by the Holy Spirit. To be sure, there is considerable confusion among the Pentecostal sects concerning the nature and intelligibility of the tongues spoken by a person who is being seized by the Spirit. Sometimes the "tongue" is believed to be a foreign language unknown to the speaker except during the *tomada*. More common, however, seems to be the belief that the "tongue" is no common language but a special idiom through which the Holy Spirit conveys messages to the congregation or certain of its members. Both versions of the belief seem to have gained ample currency. The following story, which was reported by one of our informants, appears to be a replica of the Biblical Pentecost.

A few *hermanos* had received a call (from the Spirit) to preach at the corner of San Diego and Alameda in Santiago. Now this was not one of our habitual meeting places because the noise of the traffic is almost deafening. When they reached the place they felt some kind of impediment weighing heavily upon them; for quite a while they remained without uttering a sound, but praying mentally. Suddenly one of the group began to preach in a very loud voice, but in a tongue which no other member of the group could understand. Many people stopped to listen, windows opened and before long the tenants of the nearby houses listened too. After the sermon had come to an end, a man, obviously a foreigner, asked the group where the preacher had learned to speak French for this was the language in which he had understood the sermon. And at a nearby window a lady showed surprise that the preacher could speak German because she had heard the sermon in the German language. Many people in the crowd were no less astonished for they had understood the sermon in Spanish.

"This is actually a universal language" the informant added. "The one who speaks it and while he speaks it, and those who understand it and while they understand it, are full of the Holy Spirit." Sometimes a person who speaks in tongues knows what he is saying, sometimes he does not. If he does, he communicates the content of the message in Spanish or Portuguese to the individual concerned or to the whole congregation. In one case we were able to observe a man who was praying in a loud voice who suddenly switched to an unintelligible "idiom," then back to Spanish. After a few moments another switch occurred, and after changing three times from Spanish to the unknown "tongue" he addressed the congregation as follows:

It is the will of the Lord that we work harder in His vineyard, that we obey Him in order to produce more fruit. I have seen the resplendence of His light in three distinct parts of this chapel while I was praying. The Lord is with us and wishes to remain here to lead us.

When the speaker of tongues proffers his measage in a trance-like state he may not remember his utterances or that he said anything at all. In this case a prophet who heard the message may translate its content to the congregation if it is believed to have some edifying value. The intimate association of the two powers—glossolalia and prophetizing—is also expressed by the fact that the prophet often uses tongues to communicate his inspirations which are believed to come directly from God. Indeed, the voice of the prophet or the person speaking in *tongues* is the voice of God.

The Chilean Pentecostals define the *tomada* as a kind of trance during which the recipient of the Spirit acts without being conscious of what he is doing. In Brazil, however, the trance has become associated with Spiritualism, another religious mass movement which is successfully competing with Pentecostalism. The tensions thus produced lead to emphatic distinctions between the two movements. Spiritualistic beliefs and practices including the mediumistic trance are branded as workings of the devil, and any trance-like characteristics of the *tomada* are emphatically denied by most Pentecostals. Our informants also assured us that the prophecies of the Pentecostals were "completely different" from the "divinations" of the Spiritualists. "The Holy Spirit cannot be called at will as the Spiritualists pretend." A woman, 60, housewife, was converted to the Assembly of God in

1938. Before her conversion she was a practicing Catholic and also a spiritualist medium. She "worked the table" and "gave prescriptions." When she wished to be baptized the pastor at first did not want her because he was not sure whether the "evil spirits" had actually left her. He told her to wait for the baptism of the Holy Spirit. She had to wait and pray a long time, but eventually she had a *tomada*. She is also a prophet. "The Lord has spoken many times through me to the brethren and to the Church." She claimed that prayer had cured her of a heart ailment and cancer.

There is no doubt that the *tomada*, charged as it is with highly pleasurable emotional experiences, provides a coveted change in the otherwise dreary and often hopeless life of the lower classes. It is valued for its own sake as a temporary relief from the miseries and frustration of a marginal existence, regardless of the social advantages that may accrue to the bearers of the mystical powers bestowed by the Spirit. Yet there is always a point where the religious symbolism of the *tomada* veers into social symbolism, where the powers of the Spirit turn into social powers with concomitant shifts in individual status and role, within groups of people who take great pride in their egalitarian constitution.

In the most general sense, the first *tomada*, which a Pentecostal seeks as anxiously as a Plains Indian seeks his vision, puts a seal of divine approval on the individual. Now he feels that he really "belongs." Many conversions begin with a *tomada* which may or may not be a recurrent event in the life of a Pentecostal. Many, however, are accepted and baptized in a sect without having had any such experience at all. It may take months or perhaps a year until their first *tomada* occurs, and during such a waiting period they cannot be elected or appointed to any office by the congregation. On the other hand, they may receive more than an ordinary share of powers from the Spirit, and if they do, a kind of professional career with the organizational framework of the sect is open to them. But, as said before, the supernatural sanction of the *tomada* must be validated by energetic and successful evangelization. Internally, the sect recognizes no source of social differentiation other than the powers of the Spirit. A man who has demonstrated his powers as a prophet is referred to as *el hermano profeta* or *interprete;* people listen to him in awe and follow his advice. In some sects, the voice of a prophet may even carry more weight than that of the pastor, as the following communication of a prominent Pentecostal leader in Chile indicates:

Anybody may become a prophet, just any member of a Pentecostal congregation, who receives the Spirit. The prophet stands up in the temple and corrects the pastor who deviates from the doctrine. And the pastor listens to him and submits to his inspirations. If he rejects the prophet, the Spirit leaves the church, and there will be no more prophets. The prophet also approaches the sinner and speaks into his ear; he tells him his sins and asks him to repent. Of course he does not know the sinner, nor does the sinner know him. The knowledge which the prophet has is given to him by the Holy Spirit. The sinner cannot resist the message of the prophet and confesses. Afterwards the prophet does not remember the content of the confession, nor the person he talked to.

The same person may become a prophet several times or just once. There is no way of knowing how long this phase will last, or who will be a prophet next. There are congregations which have never had prophets. This is so because the Spirit has been repelled by pastors jealous of their authority, or by members who refuse to believe in the Spirit.

The social implications of prophetizing are rather obvious. Vested in religious symbolism, it constitutes a mode of social control which may be exercised by *any* member of a congregation over anybody else, including the pastor. It minimizes the social distance between the common members and the pastor, between laity and clergy. It is an institutionalized way of keeping authority within the group in a state of continuous flux. In sects that have adopted the hierarchical and authoritarian tendencies of an episcopal structure, prophets cannot be tolerated. As a matter of fact the Iglesia Metodista Pentecostal of Chile does not recognize this kind of spontaneous prophetizing because of its subversive nature. "Whether in error or not, the pastor is the voice of God," remarked a minister of this sect. "In our churches people do not pay any attention to the prophets because they lead to errors and divide the congregation. *The one who does not respect the authority of the pastor is not called by the Lord.*"

To receive the powers of the Spirit constitutes the only recognized way in which human authority can be legitimatized in most Pentecostal sects. Their members are aware and sometimes proud of their lower-class extraction and do not recognize such criteria as wealth, family background, education, or occupation as ranking principles of social organization. Since as a class they are not allowed by the "world" to attain distinction in any of these aspects, they deny their validity altogether. Social egalitarianism thus becomes a dogma, and aspirations to distinction and leadership must be validated by divine sanction manifest in the powers of the Spirit. In a sense, this is subversion of the traditional social order in the language of religious symbolism. Goldschmidt's observations (1944:354) fully apply to the Pentecostal sects of Chile and Brazil:

The appeal of the emotional religion and the asceticism for the disfranchised is this: It denies the existence of this world with its woes. *It denies the values in terms in which they are the underprivileged and sets up in their stead a putative society* in the kingdom of God, where, because of their special endowments (which we call emotionalism) they are the elite. It is the society of the saved. Millenarianism is of the essence, for it is thus that the putative society is created; asceticism is the denial of the world in which they have been denied; and emotional participation is public acclamation of their personal acceptance into this world of super-reality. [Italics added]

However, the Pentecostals were after all enculturated in the way of life whose scale of values they attempt to subvert. Among other things, they absorbed the social preconceptions attached to class status. No matter how hard they try to make a virtue out of their humble background, their simplicity and poverty, they still have to overcome a feeling of inadequacy, of inferiority perhaps, which a highly class-conscious society attaches to their social origins. Evidence of such feelings is to be seen in the eagerness with which the convert adopts the status symbols of the middle class, the dark suit, white collar and tie, sobriety, a respectable family life, and regular working habits. Thus the supernatural sanction inherent in the *tomada* and the powers bestowed by the Holy Spirit are not just enjoyable "emotionalism," a temporary escape from the miseries and frustrations of reality. They perform the function of compensating the convert for his feelings of a class-conditioned inadequacy. And at the level of Pentecostal leadership *the powers of the Spirit serve the more specific function of shifting responsibilities for decisions affecting the future of the sect to supernatural authority.*

Proud as the Pentecostal leaders may be of their lack of formal theological learning, they still live in a society wherein formal recognition of professional skill is highly valued and only the stamp of approval issued by a learned institution secures professional status. It is not surprising therefore that continuous supernatural assistance is sought to justify, before one's own self and before a critical congregation, the next steps to be taken in the development of missionary work, the construction of temples, the organization of charity, and so forth. All ultimate responsibility thus lies with the Spirit rather than with man, for it is the Spirit who really makes the decisions and even the most exalted leader is nothing but an instrument attempting to fulfill His will. By formally deferring to the will of the Spirit, the Pentecostal leader legitimates his decisions and validates his status within the sect.

It is not easy to present clear-cut evidence for a contention of this sort, yet a structural comparison of different sects yielded results that show at least a correlation between the extent to which the assistance of the Spirit is formally requested before decisions are made and the status of the clergy within the sect. In the Chilean Iglesia Metodista Pentecostal certain traits of the parent institution (the Methodist Episcopal Church) have been preserved. The highest authority is a bishop who is, together with his immediate assistants, irremovable. Although these functionaries have no formal theological training, they command a degree of authority without parallel in other Pentecostal sects. The right of tenure is not extended to the pastors, but these too are expected to exact obedience, and usually they impose their decisions in a fashion criticized by other sects as "authoritarian" and "undemocratic." Prophets and dissenters are not tolerated, and recidivists are excluded from membership. One hears little about formal invocations of the Spirit, except on important occasions. The voice of the bishop or pastor is *implicitly* the voice of God. The leader apparently feels secure in his role, and the assistance of the Spirit is taken for granted by the congregation. Only on the lower levels, among the guides and *pastores probandos* who have not yet been anointed or ordained, the need persists to legitimatize their calling and to consolidate their position in an incipient and relatively unstructured congregation by leaning heavily on their relationship with the Holy Spirit.

Most other Pentecostal sects, particularly the Iglesia Pentecostal de Chile, resemble the congregational rather than the episcopal type of organization. The social distance between laity and clergy is considerably reduced, no functionary is irremovable, and dissent and competition from prophets are recognized as genuine manifestations of the Spirit. Here the greater need for deference to supernatural decisions and responsibilities is reflected in frequent invocations of the Spirit.

The extreme opposite to the Iglesia Metodista Pentecostal is represented by the Congregação Cristã do Brasil (Christian Congregation of Brazil). This sect, which in many respects occupies a position *sui generis* within the Pentecostal movement, has reduced the distinction between laity and clergy almost to the point of obliteration. There are neither bishops nor pastors. The "spiritual" leadership of the sect is entrusted to a self-perpetuating Board of Elders, "revested with the gifts of the Spirit," meaning that they must have been baptized by the Holy Spirit.

Three requisites are to be fulfilled before a novice may accede to the Board. First of all, the choice made by the Board must be confirmed by the Holy Spirit. The novice is presented to the assembly of Elders who seek illumination by the Spirit in silent prayers. If the choice is confirmed the novice is "ordained" by the oldest member of the Board. Finally, there must be unanimous agreement of the congregation to which the new member belongs. Neither the elders nor their assistants, the deacons and co-operators, receive salaries or any form of remuneration. They must even defray the cost of travels which they may be called to make in the interest of the sect.

"*Os profissionais da religião estragam tudo*" (the professionals of religion ruin everything), we were told when we asked an Elder why there were no salaried pastors. When we remarked that the work of the Elders was a full-time job and, consequently, they ought to be remunerated to free them from the obligation of earning a living, our informants recoiled in horror, as if we had committed a sacrilege. All Elders appeared to have some regular occupation. One was a plumber, another owned a small printing establishment, still others were bricklayers, porters, and railway employees. There was also the co-owner of a large industrial plant who, at the request of his family, seemed to devote most of his time to the sect.

All business affairs of the sect are transacted by a separate Board of Administrators, but decisions on any level require approval of the elders, deacons, and co-operators. But first of all, the matters to be decided upon "must be presented to the Lord in prayer." In fact, it turned out that no matter how trifling a decision might appear to an outsider, it is only made after a formal invocation of the Holy Spirit. Even the choice of a Biblical passage to be read and commented upon in church, is made only after the presiding elder has prayed for inspiration. And no elder would assume pastoral functions during a service without first seeking confirmation by the Spirit.

In an interview with a prominent elder of the *Congregação*, Léonard (1953:102) was told:

I have not read the whole Bible, but only the passages which the Spirit has indicated to me.—But when do you prepare your sermons?—I do not prepare them. We have been instructed not to worry about what we have to say. By the way, how should I be able to prepare them when I do not know whether or not I have to give testimony. Tonight, Wednesday, together with another elder I shall preside over our meeting in the Braz (industrial district of São Paulo City where the central temple is located). I do not know whether I will be allowed to speak. Some time ago I arrived at a meeting convinced that I would not have to speak. Now it happened that the other elder had not received anything either (from the Spirit). We both knelt down and I prayed: Lord, is it Thy will that these people leave empty-handed? I heard a voice which said to me: "You speak.— Well, Lord, but about what?—Psalm 10.—I stood up and said to my brethren: I did not believe that I would have to speak to you. But He ordered me to do it, and on Psalm 10. I do not know it. Let us take our Bibles and read it.

Unlike all other sects we had opportunity to investigate, the Christian Congregation repudiates the idea of a pastoral mandate instituted by ordination and based on the assumption of implicit legitimacy. The functionaries of the sect, regardless of rank and merit, must seek divine validation for each individual act they are called upon to perform. In fact, only the Holy Spirit has the power to make decisions, and the sect's functionaries are mere executors of His revealed will.

The course of development which the Christian Congregation has taken in Brazil clearly constitutes a regional adaptation of sectarian principles as they are interpreted, for example, in the United States. In this country, the small Christian Congregation prefers salaried pastors, trained in seminaries. An American visitor, a pious member of the sect, showed surprise and enthusiasm about the humility of his Brazilian brethren. "Over there, in the U.S.," he remarked, "we have seminaries, and there is a lot of vanity. You see? Here they let the Spirit work, and this is the reason why the Church goes on."

Oscillating between thaumaturgical leadership and a literal conception of the priesthood of the laity the Pentecostal movement presents the extremes as well as every conceivable combination of both. But whenever laymen who have no worldly credentials to lean upon assume a leading role, the Pentecostal creed makes it possible to validate their acts by transferring decision making with its inherent responsibilities to the intervening deity.

This function of the *tomada* which has been confirmed, to some extent at least, by a cursory comparison of different Pentecostal sects bears some relationship with the function of spirit possession in general which Raymond Firth (1955:4) stated in a somewhat different context.

In many social situations an intermediary may be not actual but putative— he may be provided not by an external person but by an extrapolation, or extrajection on a part of the actor's personality. *This putative agent is assigned the responsibility of decision and frequently has an authority unlikely to be exercised by the person himself.* An obvious example of this is the use made by many primitive and other peoples of the organizing function of pronouncements made by spirit mediums in a dissociated state. I would indeed suggest that externalization of responsibility is an important function of spirit possession. [Italics added.]

21

Cohesion and Security

✤ The functions analyzed so far are social in the sense that they exercise notable influences on the status of the individual as perceived by himself and by the members of his congregation. If he was a "nobody" before his conversion, he is "somebody" now—a person who has become a recipient of special supernatural powers, who belongs to a "chosen people." But the functions of Pentecostalism are social too in a somewhat different sense.

The Pentecostal sect is, as all sects, a tightly woven group, almost a community which provides a new cultural focus in a largely unfocused and disorganized society. It is indeed, as already pointed out, a personal community that provides a high measure of security, both psychological and material. This of course applies, although in varying degrees, to all Protestant churches. But the extent to which the Pentecostal sect absorbs the interests and energies of the individual member seems to exceed the norms of participation observed in the historical churches. The difference lies, above all, in the emphasis placed upon proselytism and the way in which it is pursued.

In the historical churches missionary work is assigned to specialists, trained colporters, and evangelists. There may be some missionary effort on the part of zealous members who on occasion attempt to convert neighbors, friends, or relatives, but such efforts are neither organized nor continuous, and many congregations prefer to "consolidate" their position rather than to add new converts to their ranks. In the Pentecostal sects proselytism is pursued as a concerted action of the whole congregation. Every militant member is a missionary who is willing not only to devote his spare time to the diffusion of his faith, but also to conjugate his personal efforts with those of his companions. At least one major facet of the associational efficacy of the Pentecostal sects is seen in certain devices developed for the purpose of expansion. The blueprints for these organizational devices were not introduced by foreign missionaries but emerged gradually from accumulated experiences with evangelizing under particularly adverse circumstances.

The usual course of action follows a set pattern. Initially, prayer meetings are held by a local congregation to seek inspiration as to where God wishes the new church to be located. Once the site has been determined, the congregation develops intensive preaching activities in the chosen sector which ordinarily covers part of a *población* or *barrio*. Three or four times a week a group of faithful go to a previously selected area covering from six to eight city blocks. The group is then divided into as many subgroups as there are blocks. At one of the corners of each block at least one member of every subgroup preaches a sermon attempting to attract the attention of the neighborhood.

When this is done, the subgroups walk in procession toward a central point. Following the model of Catholic street processions, the members sing hymns to the accompaniment of guitars and, if available, violins or accordians. The style of Pentecostal music keeps always close to that of Chilean or Brazilian folk music, but there seems to be a curious difference between the ways in which such music is executed in the two countries. The somewhat diffuse lyricism of Chilean folk music underwent a reinterpretation by the Pentecostalists who apparently felt some need for more rousing rhythms. They adopted a faster beat, often a marching rhythm which never fails to stir the congregation and most certainly contributes to the state of emotional excitement that characterizes the Pentecostal cult.

Brazilian folk music, however, contains an African component which already provides the rhythmic exaltation required by Pentecostalism. Thus the hymns are sung in the unadulterated rhythm of the *samba* or some other folk dance. In either country, Pentecostal music is directly adapted to the aesthetic patterns with which the people are thoroughly familiar and which stand in sharp contrast to the ritualistic solemnity of the usual Protestant hymn.

The point of convergence for all groups is usually a public square, where a service is held with prayers and hymn singing. The whole procedure is repeated in different sectors of the chosen area until the congregation has accumulated enough funds to buy a piece of land where the temple is to be located. This may require a year or two of strenuous efforts. The building process itself is, as everything else, a collective undertaking in which all militant members participate in one way or another. Large congregations are usually able to raise enough contributions in labor and building materials that cash expenditures can be kept to a minimum.

It should be noted however that other Protestant churches build meeting places in a similar fashion, although contributions in labor vary according to the occupational composition of the congregation. There is of course a heavier concentration of menial workers in the Pentecostal groups, and consequently a large number of members are given opportunity to participate directly in the building process. The erection of the church thus becomes a shared experience of the whole congregation. Those who lack the skills of bricklayers, carpenters, roofers, plumbers, or electricians assist in many other ways. Women often cook food and take it to the construction site to feed the workers. In Temuco, 57 out of 93 interviewed Protestants declared that they had donated their labor to the construction of a temple.

When the temple is finally completed, the sponsoring congregation attends the dedication ceremony *in corpore*. On this occasion the *guia de classe* who directed the entire missionary endeavor is consecrated *obrero* or *pastor probando* of the new congregation.

In some sects the tutelage of the sponsoring body may continue for a certain period of time to secure the stability of the new congregation. It is, for example, a common policy to send the *escuela espiritual*, or a "class" of volunteers who are in charge of such missionary tasks, to attend all services in the new church. The local residents are impressed by the large number and the fervor of the participants. *Tomadas* and miracles begin to happen almost immediately, and the local residents are drawn in increasing numbers by rumors of "divine cures" and other blessings received by those who "obeyed." Only when the success of the new congregation can no longer be doubted, the *escuela espiritual* of the sponsoring body withdraws to commence similar tasks elsewhere.

The foregoing account by no means exhausts the action program of a Pentecostal congregation. There are of course the age groups found in all churches, but instead of engaging in recreational activities, they all devote their leisure time to visiting hospitals, prisons, and the homes of brethren who are afflicted with sickness or some other calamity. But many congregations carry their proselytic zeal beyond the boundaries of the local community. Many Chilean congregations have organized *clases rodantes, los ciclistas,* or members who own bicycles and are willing to spend their weekends on trips to neighboring villages and towns, sometimes even to faraway and isolated localities. The objective of such trips is to prepare the way for the foundation of new congregations. The bicyclers constitute, in a very real sense, the frontiersmen of Chilean Pentecostalism. During the annual conferences, which the Chilean Pentecostal sects inherited from the Methodist church, 500 or more *ciclistas* have been observed. (At least two Chilean Pentecostal sects have formed branches in Argentina and Uruguay.)

The *clases rodantes* are autonomous. They set up their own programs and carry them out independently, without interference from local pastors and boards of elders. From time to time they present progress reports and turn over recently initiated missions to their boards which then take further steps in order to consolidate the new conquest.

Ordinarily, charity is practiced in an informal and strictly personal fashion. Institutional charity in the form of orphanages, hospitals, and homes for old people seems to be incompatible with the Pentecostal conception of Christian brotherhood. On the basis of considerable comparative data, we reached the conclusion that of all the Pentecostal sects, the Congregação Cristã do Brasil has probably taken the most uncompromising attitude so far as the practice of charity is concerned. The word *caridade* (charity) does not seem to exist in the vocabulary of the sect. *Obra de piedade* (work of piety) is used instead, and all of it is carried out by the *ministério da piedade* (ministry of piety), a sort of department which is operated mostly by women.

The *obra* is centralized in São Paulo City, and all business is transacted in one of the several dependencies of the main temple. The weekly meetings are attended by approximately one hundred women who perform duties comparable to those of social workers. Many of them present cases requiring some sort of assistance. All applicants must be members of the sect in good standing; the ultimate decision of whether an applicant is worthy of help is left to the Spirit. The presiding deacons seek inspiration in silent prayers, and consult each other before a case is decided upon. In this manner, some applicants are turned down, and the others are attended after a careful scrutiny of personal circumstances.

Sometimes the needy members receive food, clothes, fuel, or household items; sometimes small sums of money to help them over periods of unemployment or sickness. In particular cases the board may find it advisable to assist a member financially to establish him in some sort of modest business. Sick members without family receive prompt personal attention. We were informed that besides food, clothes and personal care, approximately 50,000 cruzeiros ($250 in 1960) in cash were distributed every week among the poor. All expenditures for charitable purposes are covered by special gifts the donors of which are kept anonymous.

The recipients of charity are never allowed to learn the names of their benefactors, because "all glory belongs to God." In fact, the sect adheres to the principle that "human vanity should not be permitted to interfere with the *obra de piedade*," and consequently the names of donators are never revealed to the congregation. Likewise, anything that would publicize the activities of the sect is avoided as much as possible.

These are the words of a prominent leader of the Congregação (Léonard, 1953:100):

We do not have religious journals, we do not correspond with those who publish them, and we do not collaborate with them. In the Word of God we have everything that is necessary; we thus march in the doctrine of God, with the guidance of the Holy Spirit. We do not want other lights. Times change, but the Word of God is unchangeable. Men change, but the Lord is the same, and eternally loyal.

Equally noteworthy is the fact that other mass media such as radio and television are strictly avoided in the missionary activities of this sect.

Although the Congregação generously, but anonymously, contributes to existing institutions such as the Evangelical Hospital, the Bible Society and others, it does not maintain hospitals, orphanages or homes for old people. Old and invalid members of the sect are cared for on an individual basis. Many of the volunteers in the *obra de piedade* have accepted old people in their homes where they are cared for as if they were members of the family. The *obra* maintains a "placement service" and pays subsidies if a family is unable to defray the expenses caused by such household additions.

The point we are trying to make here is that the Pentecostal sects found means and ways to mobilize their vast human resources to the last man. No matter how humble, unskilled or uneducated, the individual convert immediately feels that he is needed and relied upon; he is respectfully addressed as "brother," his services are requested by people who speak his own language, share his tastes, worries, and interests, who work with him at the same tasks and share with him the certainty of belonging to the "people of God" as the Pentecostals often call themselves.

Writing on life in a *favela* of Rio de Janeiro, Andrew Pearse (1961:200) refers to "anxiety and disapproval" his informants expressed about associating with other *favela* dwellers. An exception to the general tendency to keep to oneself, however, was found among the

Protestants whose little congregations were free associations whose members entered into a pseudo-kin relationship (brothers-in-Christ, etc.) and who were prepared to take something at least of the responsibility for one another that they would take for genuine kin.

The cohesion of the Pentecostal groups is of course constantly reinforced by collective acts of worship such as the following, related by a sympathetic eyewitness (Davis, 1943:82–83):

I was invited to attend the Sunday evening service in the Pentecostal tabernacle of a southern Brazilian city. The church has two thousand members, but on account of a heavy storm less than half were present. The great hall seated 1,400 people. The choir loft seated one hundred. An orchestra of thirty two pieces—string, wind, and percussion instruments—filled the rostrum. The congregation was very largely of people of the lowest economic and social status; one fifth were Negroes. Fully one half were young people. Some women carried their babies and led little children. The pastor, a trained musician, turned around in his pulpit to conduct the choir and orchestra. His skilled leading drew forth from orchestra and choir a fine expression and the best that they had to offer. I was thrilled by the music. Each performer seemed to pour out his soul upon his instrument. The orchestra vitalized the congregation and lifted it to an unusual fervor in singing. There was prayer, Bible reading, hymn singing, and special musical numbers by orchestra and choir which were rendered with flourish and zest. There followed a period of impassioned prayer led by pastor and members from the congregation. The whole company prayed together, groaning, ejaculating, and repeating the sentences of the leader. There was the sound of innumerable voices but all was orderly and controlled, and after a few minutes the praying ceased. The pastor called upon a Negro deacon to speak. The man came to the pulpit and gave an intelligent, inspirational witness to Christ's power in his own life which received the closest attention of the congregation. These hundreds of underprivileged people found a release from the drabness of their lives in the various channels of emotional expression provided by the service. Through music the pastor has won the devoted following of one hundred of his young people—they meet for practice four nights a week—and through instruments and song they not only express themselves in service to the Lord but provide an atmosphere and an artistic program through which a great company of the city's poor are lifted up and inspired.

It is not an accident that those church demonstrations in Brazil which are growing the fastest are these which are recognizing the emotional inheritance of the people and are giving it full opportunity for expression.

The events thus described do not refer to either one of the two largest Pentecostal bodies in Brazil, but most passages of the description apply, almost verbatim, to the services which the Christian Congregation of São Paulo holds every Wednesday in Braz, one of the working class districts of the city. The temple itself is a remarkable structure. Built of reinforced concrete, its moderately modern lines reveal an esthetic conception that contrasts favorably to the barn-like structures most Protestant congregations seem to prefer. The temple is large enough to seat five thousand; it is equipped with a powerful electric organ and indirect light. On Wednesdays no other temple in the city has scheduled services in order that all members of the Christian Congregation may find opportunity to worship *in corpore*. These Wednesday rituals are apparently designed to preserve and reinforce a sense of corporate strength and unity. The actual attendance doubtless bespoke the success of this rather ambitious design, especially in view of the particularistic congregationalism of most Protestant sects. When we entered the temple, all seats had already been taken, and together with hundreds of other people we had to stand in the aisles. After a full working day, more than five thousand had found time and energy to defy the distance and the unspeakable transportation system of a congested metropolis to attend an act of collective worship.

The seating arrangement is such that the men occupied the right section of the temple while the women kept to the left. This and the veil with which the women covered their heads may conceivably be carry-overs from the rural version of Italian Catholicism. An orchestra of approximately sixty musicians, mostly composed of string and woodwind instruments, accompanied the hymns and played solos in a pronouncedly operatic style of Italian provenience. The prayers which everybody proferred in a kneeling position revealed the usual individualism, but the general tone was rather subdued compared with the unbridled spontaneity of other Pentecostal services, including those of local congregations of the same sect. Some men in our immediate vicinity were heard to pray in tongues. The sermon offered by one of the elders was, as always, an improvised comment on a Biblical passage. A woman and two men rose from the audience to give testimony of miraculous cures which seemed to hold the closest attention of the crowd.

The Christian Congregation established certain rules that make it possible for presiding elders to screen the members of the congregation who wish to present testimony. Thus it is not permissible to vent sentiments of hostility against any "brother." Furthermore, special care should be taken lest a testimony become a manifestation of self-conceit. And no testimony should ever mention "the exploits and deeds of the enemy" (meaning the devil).

Following the service, there was a brief social gathering in the vestibule of the temple. Numerous brethren were seen to greet each other with the *ósculo santo*, the "sacred kiss" which the sect instituted as a symbol of harmony and brotherly love according to the Biblical model. The *ósculo santo* however is not permissible between men and women, nor is a woman allowed to be alone in a room with a man who is neither her husband nor a relative of hers. Again, these restrictions may be carry-overs from rural Italy. Such gatherings are merely chats among friends who otherwise do not have much opportunity to see each other. They were found to reinforce the pattern of reciprocal social acceptance or egalitarianism which plays such an important role in all Protestant churches. In fact, these gatherings appeared to play an important role regardless of denominational differences.

If one sums up the social functions performed by the Pentecostal sects and weighs them against the "pleasures of the world" which the faithful must renounce, one may find that the "advantages" outweigh the "disadvantages," or at any rate, a change in current value orientations "makes sense" in terms of lower-class culture. Pentecostals are forbidden to indulge in illicit sex, to drink, gamble, smoke, dance, attend movies or theatrical performances, join athletic associations, use cosmetics or expose the body on public beaches. Most of these prohibitions the Pentecostal sects share with other Protestant groups, although a few of the historical churches have in recent years relaxed the stringency of their discipline, at least in their urban congregations

The Pentecostal sects have remained adamant, but there is a notable difference in this respect between the Christian Congregation and all other Pentecostal groups. Much of what is strictly forbidden and coercively enforced elsewhere is merely "advised against" in the Christian Congregation. The consumption of alcoholic beverages, the epitome of sinful behavior to the more puritanical churches, contra dicts the standards of the Christian Congregation only if it is done immoderately. In fact, the communicants take fermented wine, in contrast to the grape juice preferred by the more puritanical groups. This may be interpreted as a concession to the Old World heritage of the sect, but at the same time it fits a pattern of behavior that seems to be unique within the universe of puritanical Protestantism.

To the members of the Christian Congregation, compliance with external rules is meaningful only if it springs from internal motivation, from a real desire to act as one is expected to act. "One must obey the Commandments only if one feels the internal desire to do so." Therefore, the categorical and constant refusal regarding everything reminiscent of legalism. Tithing, observed by many zealous Protestants, is banished as a "commandment." The faithful are free to exceed it in their donations, something that happens quite often. Observance of Sunday, to which all Evangelical denominations of Anglo-Saxon origin lend such an importance, is regarded as a servitude contrary to the Spirit—and this peculiarity of the Congregation constitutes the supreme heresy to many Protestants, and, at the same time, a very great opportunity for expansion of the "Glorias," a popular designation for the Christian Congregation which thus does not create for its members, the majority of whom are wage-earners, conflicts of conscience difficult to solve in modern life, particularly in the cities (Léonard, 1953:97–98).

22

Protestantization as a Selective Process

We attempted to show in the preceding chapters that the introduction of Protestantism in two Latin American countries has been a selective process. The different Protestant creeds and their ecclesiastic organization do not have the same appeal to different strata of the population. Generally speaking, and without regard to denominational distinctions, Protestantism is better adapted to the aspirations and needs of the lower and lower middle classes than to those of the upper classes. The lower strata began to respond to the proselytic efforts of the various churches and sects in increasing proportions as they were drawn into the vortex of sociocultural change. The needs and aspirations which the acceptance of Protestantism seems to satisfy stem primarily from the disintegration of the traditional society and the chances thus afforded to conquer a more respectable social position. This relationship between Protestantization and class structure will be further explored in a subsequent chapter.

The varying success met by different Protestant denominations since the date of their introduction suggests selective responses still in quite a different sense. Protestantism in Latin America is indeed what it originally intended to be—a protest movement, not just in the narrow theological sense, but a movement against the religious monopoly of the Catholic Church and its traditional ally, the ruling class. Protestantism is, in one word, a symbolic protest against the traditional social structure whose shortcomings are perceived in the mirror of recent revolutionary social changes. *If this interpretation is correct, one may expect that the farther removed the ideology and structure of a particular Protestant denomination from those of the traditional society, the greater the appeal it holds for the common people. Inversely, those denominations which in some sense and to some extent resemble structural and ideological elements of the repudiated society are likely to be less successful in their proselytic endeavor.* In fact, this hypothesis is borne out by the quantitative development of the three principal historical churches: the Methodists, the Presbyterians, and the Baptists. According to the most recent available data the membership figures are as follows (Read, 1965:217):

All Methodists	53,000
All Presbyterians	167,000
All Baptists	235,000

The situation differs in Chile insofar as, after a promising beginning by the turn of the century, Presbyterianism has made little progress; its total membership is now less than 2,000, but the differential rates at which Methodism and the Baptists have grown are comparable to those in Brazil.

Of the three denominations, the Baptist Church seems to be most consistent with the aspirations of the common people. Freedom of conscience, and from ecclesiastical authority, complete autonomy of the local congregation and the right of all communicants to decide on church matters in a totally egalitarian way represents ideological and organizational principles which the major institutions of the larger society deny to the lower strata. No matter how humble and unsophisticated, the voice of a Baptist carries as much weight within his congregation as that of anybody else. The pastor is elected by the congregation, and there are no high church dignitaries to impose decisions and to command obedience. It seems more than mere coincidence that of the three denominations, the Baptists hold the strongest appeal to the lower classes, and they are more militantly anti-Catholic than are either Presbyterians or Methodists.

In contrast to the Baptist church, Methodism has retained some ideological and structural principles clearly reminiscent of traditional Latin American society. "The Methodist Episcopal Church," writes Léonard (1952:145–146),

evinces here as elsewhere in the world a compromise in which Episcopalism prevails over Methodism and where the European Wesleyans would not encounter their traditions at all. If one reads the reports in the activities of its central organs in the *Expositor Cristão*, one feels the presence of a great administration in which the regulations and the hierarchy occupy an important place. So far as respect of the hierarchy is concerned, it suffices to read the apologies—so regrettably ridiculous—presented by a *provisionado* (nonordained minister) when he deals, in the official organ, with issues which only first-class ministers with a degree in theology are allowed to discuss. Incidentally, the pastor of a large community clearly expresses how little the individual, be he pastor or layman, counts vis-à-vis the hierarchy representing the Church, when he rejoices in the supplementary powers bestowed upon the bishops by the last *Concílio Geral* with regard to the utilization of "their" ministers: "The *senhores bispos* will have much more liberty to move their men. . . . We are beginning to see and to understand that man is a mere accident in the general economy of the Church; it is the cause of Christ that is permanent." "To move their men": This becomes a game of chess. The bishops alone, it seems, have the right to speak as individuals in the first person, and they use it in a tone which undoubtedly would surprise the true bishops. We find 'cabinets' everywhere, and the smallest parishes are directed by a "pastoral cabinet." So far as the simple laymen are concerned, their importance is not very great in the development of the Church to judge by the last *Concílio Geral* where there were only 24 among 48 pastors.

Faced with a choice between a hierarchically structured denomination which seems to pay relatively little attention to the individual, and an egalitarian denomination in which the individual, particularly the layman, is in full control of church affairs, the common man tends to prefer the institution which makes his conversion most meaningful in terms of a symbolic protest against the traditional social order.

Although the Presbyterian Church of Brazil is closely organized, it has neither bishops nor a hierarchy. It is avowedly a "federation of local churches" (Manual, 1960:8) and within the local congregation each communicant member participates fully in decisions regarding the election of ministers and church officials. The existence of regional and national representatives with delegated powers does not curtail individual participation, nor does it diminish the functional role of the layman in favor of awe-inspiring hierarchical dignitaries.

One may object to the assertion that the denominational structure and its inherent ideological norms are to be considered the sole determinants of preferences expressed by the people of Brazil and Chile. Surely, there may be other variables involved in the choice of a denomination. The intensity of proselytic endeavor and the geographical distribution of missions within a given territory constitute possible examples of such variables. It seems reasonable to assume that the number of missionaries kept in the field by different denominations at any particular time, and the use of different approaches to evangelization on the part of these missionaries may conceivably account, to some degree at least, for the denominational preferences shown by the converts.

It was not unusual for "competing" denominations to divide a given territory among themselves and thus to avoid duplication of missionary establishments in the same area. In Chile as well as in Brazil such agreements existed at one time or another, a condition which obviously removed the choice from the people to the mission boards. Without denying the possible effects of these variables on membership figures it would seem that, by and large, the proselytic efforts of the three main church bodies are comparable with one another. All three have been supported by large and powerful mother churches in the United States. Enough time has elapsed since the beginning of their missionary activities to test the receptivity of the Brazilians and Chileans to each particular creed. Dates and figures reveal that the Methodist Episcopal Church instituted missions in Brazil before the Presbyterians and Baptists did but that in terms of membership figures the Methodists have been the least successful of the three. This seems to support our hypothesis.

Of course, the selective nature of Protestantization becomes even more obvious if the historical churches are compared with the Pentecostal sects. In order to account for major selective differentials we attempted to analyze the functions of Pentecostalism in contrast to those of the historical churches. Our contention that Pentecostalism is more congenial with lower-class culture in Brazil and Chile will probably be resented or refuted by most leaders of the historical churches in both countries. Asked to express their opinion about the success of Pentecostalism, most interviewees pointed out that the masses were attracted by any display of uninhibited "emotionalism" (or "sensationalism" as one Baptist minister put it) and that the Pentecostal sects "made it easy for anyone to join."

This means that the Pentecostals fail to employ the screening procedures of the historical churches and do not bother about indoctrinating their prospective members before admitting them to the status of communicants. In other words, selection is reciprocal in the historical church but unilateral in the Pentecostal sects. The frequent assertion that the Pentecostals make it easy for anyone to join, however, refers only to admission procedures. In our previous anlysis it was found that the sort of participation expected from the active members of Pentecostal sects places responsibilities upon the individual which are at least equal to if not heavier than those of the historical Protestants.

Preferences are not only expressed in the exercise of choice between different denominations; they make themselves felt in schismatic movements such as the one that gave origin to the Iglesia Metodista Pentecostal in Chile. Uncounted minor movements which at one time or another split up local congregations of the historical churches, expressed preference for inward exaltation as opposed to conventional ritualism. One of these occurrences which signalized the advent of Brazilian Pentecostalism was described as follows (Mesquita, 1940:136–137):

In April of 1911 there arrived in Belém two Swedish gentlemen, Gunnar Vingren and Daniel Berg, who declared to be Baptists. . . . The basement of the temple was offered to them and there they stayed to learn the language and to assist Nelson (the pastor) in his missionary work. When this good missionary made one of his many trips to Piauí he left these men in the church in the sweet hope that they, even without knowing the language, would be of some help. It happened that shortly afterwards, during the meetings (of the congregation), these Baptists began to shake and to shout, and at this point they were already imitated by some Brazilians. What is this? What kind of new religion is this? These were the questions everybody asked. They answered that this was the *baptism of the Holy Spirit*. Tongues and false messages transformed the cult into horror. . . . The entire church was being contaminated, for many already talked in tongues, except the deacons who did not make this kind of "progress." What was there to do? The evangelist, assisted by Feli de Barros Rocha, organist of the Church, called an extraordinary meeting, declared the Pentecostals who already constituted the majority, out of order, and, with the help of the minority, he excluded those who had deviated from the doctrine.

Many such movements never really break out into open conflict, but smolder on in revivals and more or less articulate reform ideologies expressing preference for religion as an emotional experience rather than, according to one Methodist leader, "as a sanction of the status quo." All historical churches in Brazil and Chile have their "Pentecostal wing" whose position is perhaps most clearly formulated in the writings of a Brazilian Baptist leader (Tognini, 1960:21–22):

There is, not only among the unsophisticated members of our denomination, but also among the ministers and some of our most eminent scholars a dangerous fear regarding the doctrine of the Holy Spirit, especially insofar as some of its major aspects are concerned. When for example the baptism of the Holy Spirit is mentioned, many brethren of ours become deeply concerned only because the Pentecostals constantly refer to this aspects of Biblical doctrine. However we should not fear anything that is found in the Bible. . . . To surrender to the Pentecostals, out of plain fear, a Biblical issue as important as the baptism of the Holy Spirit, strikes me as incongruous and very harmful.

As everybody knows, I am a Baptist, and, as the saying goes, one with a capital "B." And because I am a Baptist I am free. I am consistent. I am sincere, I practice the rules of hermeneutics. I try to interpret the Bible scientifically. I have no fear of any scriptural text. I accept the Bible thoroughly. But I cannot agree with many of my fellow ministers who try to obscure the baptism of the Holy Spirit as it is presented in the Bible.

The pamphlet from which this topic was translated has had two editions already. Its preface was written by a Baptist teacher who "after being converted did not feel happy with her life *without power*." She prayed until the Spirit came and "inundated her soul with a glory and *gozo* that were almost unbearable." (Tognini, 1960: 109.) Power and *gozo*, the gifts of the Spirit, symbolize indeed the aspirations of an underprivileged class which historical churches and sects alike are confronted with, and will be for a long time to come.

PART V

Protestantism as a Factor of Culture Change

23

Inherent Changes and Contingent Changes

❧ In analytical approaches to the process of culture transfer oc-
curring between discrete societies some attention is usually paid to
the different phases of that process. Ralph Linton (1940:470 ff.),
for example, refers to "initial acceptance" of some novelty "by innovators," or in our case, by members of the recipient society who are
the first to embrace the new faith. What follows is a phase of "dissemination" whereby the new element is gradually transmitted to a
widening circle of people. In our case, the second phase is concomitant with the constitution of new Protestant congregations. The third
phase is one of "modification by which (the novelty) is finally adjusted to the preexisting culture matrix." Some Protestant schisms
and emancipation movements have undoubtedly been carried out to
counteract and belie accusations of foreign domination or of representing an unassimilable un-Brazilian or un-Chilean "ideology." Thus
the adoption of nationalistic values and attitudes may be interpreted
as an adjustment to a "pre-existing culture matrix" by which at least
one source of conflict with non-Protestants was gradually eliminated,
and final integration of Protestant institutions became viable.

Adaptive modifications of course occurred also in the non-Protestant sectors of the society insofar as their attitudes of antagonism and
hostility gave way to acceptance, tolerance, and even respect. In
virtually all those Brazilian and Chilean communities where Protestant churches were established many years ago, their presence is
now accepted as a matter of course. In other words, institutional
integration has been accomplished.

At this point one could raise the question whether the foregoing
remarks bear any relationship to the hypothesis to be examined in this
part of our inquiry—that Protestantism may cause culture changes.
Does the transfer of Protestant denominationalism comprise or imply
all previously hypothesized changes?

Religious conversion is often seen as a "rebirth" of the individual.
This presumably means a rather sudden emotional experience of high
intensity whereby a person is endowed (by the "grace of God") with

a new way of coping with the supernatural and with a new outlook on life. Insofar as this happens to a number of individuals belonging to the same community, the culture of that community has indeed begun to change. As soon as the converts form a cohesive group or congregation the ethical corollaries of the conversion presumably begin to affect the relationships among the converts and, to some degree at least, those between the converts and the non-Protestant members of the community. To the extent that the structure of the new group can be identified as a Protestant congregation in contrast to non-Protestant associations, a culture change has indeed been accomplished. The statement that such a change has been "caused" by Protestantism is of course a tautology.

Actually, the ethical system of Protestantism is expected to transcend the religious conversion proper and to affect a convert's relationships with his family, neighbors, employers, employees, customers, and government agencies. Seen as emerging patterns of behavior, such changes may be expected to bring about discernible differences in marriage and family life, in the education of children, in economic transactions, or in the acquisition and use of material possessions, to mention only a few possibilities. Yet ordinarily these changes, if they occur at all, are time-consuming, certainly more time-consuming than the conversion itself or the constitution of a religious congregation. Furthermore, the ways in which denominational leaders interpret or seek to apply the Protestant ethic are far from being invariant. Whereas withdrawal from worldly matters appears to be imperative to some, active participation in community affairs is rather vehemently insisted upon by others.

Active participation is not, however, just a matter of interpretation and leadership. In underdeveloped regions, the Protestant virtues of thrift, sobriety, and hard work are rarely rewarded with more than an extremely modest measure of success. Or the chances to moralize the political process by voting for "honest," preferably Protestant, legislators or executive officers may be severely limited or totally absent because the political structure of the country makes such participation unpromising or impossible.

On the other hand, economic development and democratization of the power structure may lead to new situations in which the Protestant ethic is given a better chance to succeed. In other words, the possibilities of Protestantism becoming an agent of change are conditioned by the general cultural process or, more particularly, by its variations in time and space. It will be shown, for example, that some Protestant churches have played a pioneer role in the diffusion of modern agricultural technology. Nevertheless, there are in both countries rural communities with sizable Protestant congregations where agriculture has not advanced at all.

These observations suggest the need to distinguish between changes *inherent* in the introduction of Protestantism in a community or region, and those changes that appear to be *contingent* on the direction and momentum of the cultural process. Both are directly related to Protestant initiative, but while proselytic Protestantism seems unthinkable without the former, its diffusion and continuity are not dependent upon the latter. Returning to the problem of transfer it would seem that both inherent and contingent changes tend to proceed along the lines proposed by Linton.

24
Changes in the Community Structure

❖ There is no need to repeat here what was said about the inherent changes brought about by the emergence of Protestantism. But internal changes within the Protestant groups should not be confused with the impact the continuous presence of Protestant congregations has on the traditional community structure. In pre-Protestant Brazil and Chile, the union of church and state, the constitutional exclusivity of the Catholic Church, and the recognition of religious unity as a symbol of national unity characterize the kind of monolithic structure which is manifest at the local level in the *parish system* "by which a whole community was embraced within the church and subjected to its discipline." (Hudson 1961:27–28.)

Actually, of course, the parish system has always been an extremely precarious institution in either country. The scarcity of priests, their inadequate training and supervision, combined with a population thinly distributed over huge areas, prevented the Church from establishing the kind of discipline typical of European Catholicism. But no matter how lax and unorthodox religious participation might be, there was a distinct tendency to identify oneself with the Church as a *cultural symbol*. Thus the appearance of resolute and iconoclastic groups of Protestants acted as a disintegrating force splitting the community and creating a situation that varied from antagonism and tension to open, sometimes violent, conflict.

The second phase could be described as one of accommodation in which the dissenting factions reached some kind of *modus vivendi*. Eventually integration was achieved on the basis of mutual toleration and respect, encouraged or otherwise santioned by economic or political groups whose members acted unter the influence of Protestant purchasing and voting power. Some communities passed through this process half a century ago while in others, as in the previously described town of Sertão Novo, it took place in recent years. Yet whatever the particular circumstances, the change involves a breakdown of the monolithic parish system and the gradual emergence of religious pluralism with a wide range of possible repercussions on the community structure. The extensiveness of religious pluralism in Brazil is reflected by the fact that in 1960, 1,643 or 57.5 percent of a total of 2,855 *municipios* reported one or more Protestant congregations. So far as Chile is concerned, no breakdown by *municipios* is available, but the census of 1952 verified the existence of Protestant congregations in all 25 provinces.

As a rule, a Protestant congregation endeavors to involve its members in a number of activities large enough to leave little time for association with non-Protestants, except of course those deriving from occupational obligations. This means that the Protestants cease to share interests and activities that were once shared by most members of the community. In rural localities and smaller towns very few people are prepared, for example, to pursue their daily round of activities without continuous appeal to the supernatural. *Promessas* to the saints accompany all important steps in life. Participation in numerous religious festivals, in novenas, processions, pilgrimages, and certain choreographic and musical performances mainly derive from compacts with particular saints.

From this universe of saintly helpers, in which the people move with considerable familiarity and little awe, the Protestant convert finds himself completely severed. He learns that the cult of the saints is to be abhorred as idolatry. The compact as well as any of its multiple manifestations is expected to disappear from the life of a true *crente*. The sacred symbols of the community, the status of the patron saints, the banners of the religious brotherhoods, the little chapels and crosses on the wayside—mementos of piacular acts or miracles—the crown worn by the Emperor of the Divine Holy Spirit, the dances and chants performed in honor of Saint Benedict, all these objects as well as the ancient traditions and beliefs which support them and serve as a mainspring of communal solidarity, are meaningless to the Protestant. Nonparticipation in the ritual life of the community does not even bring relief from a financial burden as it does in Guatemala, for example (Nash, 1960:50), for any religious office involving major expenditures in cash or services either falls to well-to-do farmers or becomes a source of income to its holders (Willems, 1949:407).

Withdrawal from community affairs further extends to such secular institutions as the festive working party among neighbors. Protestants refrain from taking part in such co-operative enterprises because they object to the kind of entertainment that follows work and comprises dancing and the consumption of large quantities of alcoholic beverages.

To evaluate the disruptive effects which nonparticipation exerts on neighborhood organization one ought to consider the fact that the working party requires the co-operation of large groups of people and covers practically all kinds of work, such as weeding, harvesting, road and bridge repairs, and house construction. If the Protestants constitute a minority, as they usually do, nonparticipation affects them rather than the community; if they form compact neighborhoods they may rely on their own mutual aid organizations, but in either case the cleavage between Protestants and non-Protestants splits the rural community right down to its very foundations.

In urban centers where integration with the outgroup occurs predominantly on a secondary level requiring less intimate forms of association, withdrawal from activities classified as *mundanismo* is unlikely to disrupt the community. The anonymity of the individual makes it easier to adhere to a value system of his own choosing and to spend his free time in close association with those who share it. But rural and urban congregations alike must have something to "offer" to their members, not only to justify the things they are expected to "give up," but something to fill their leisure time, to "keep them busy" in activities that instill a sense of accomplishment, of worthwhileness. Thus prayer meetings, Sunday school, and choir or orchestra practices alternate with weekly meetings of six or more different associations encompassing men and women, as well as the different age grades. In addition to these continuing activities there is an annual round of specific observances.

All those occasions, needless to say, provide ample opportunities for secular entertainment, both formal and informal, frequently to an extent unparalleled by comparable non-Protestant institutions. The pattern of sociability as found in the Protestant congregations of Latin America, is alien to the native society. It was introduced and is being reinforced by American missionaries who take it for granted and tend to consider it an integral part of church life. It is particularly attractive to the women who formerly found little if any opportunity to get away from the monotony of domestic chores, to be socially accepted by a group of sympathetic people and to engage in a variety of activities without ever incurring the risk of losing respectability. The Catholic parish is no match for this kind of sociability. The vastness and anonymity of its membership, the scarcity of priests and the heavy workload they are bound to carry, prevent the kind of social intimacy that characterizes the Protestant congregation. Furthermore, the Catholic priest has no wife to assist him and to provide the sort of auxiliary leadership the pastor's wife is expected to provide.

The social function of the Protestant congregation in Chile and Brazil is both compensatory and substitutive. Severing his ties of primary association with people who shared with him the "pleasures of the world," the *crente* retreats to the group of fellow believers that offers him not only something *to live for*, but something *to live in*, a kind of miniature community rather than the usual church congregation, limited to scheduled performances of rather peripheral interest to the individual member.

This brief description may have conveyed the impression that once religious pluralism has been established no further changes occur.

This is far from being the case. If withdrawal from the world and relative isolation of the Protestant group once was the predominant attitude, there is now a growing emphasis on participation in community affairs, if only within the historical churches. Since these recent reorientations seem to lie in the realm of contingent rather than inherent changes, they will be dealt with in subsequent chapters. There is obviously a significant difference between a community with a few isolated Protestant groups and one in which Protestant participation in municipal politics, administration, public education, and welfare is to be reckoned with.

25
The Protestant Family

✠ Any attempt to analyze the structural changes inherent in the emergence of Protestant denominationalism would be incomplete without considering the family. Latin American familism, or the institutionalized predominance of family and kinship over all other sectors of the society, is of course at variance with a strong and self-determining congregation. Not only does this imply a change in the institutional rank order of the traditional value system but also changes of those aspects of the family usually defined as "patriarchalism."

There is little need to insist upon the incompatibility of the double standard of sex morals with the model of the Protestant family. The double standard is a survival of agrarian patriarchalism, obviously out of step with the emerging industrial society. The fact that the Protestant congregations have been relatively successful in eradicating among their membership the customary male privilege of committing adultery with impunity should be weighed against the changing role of the women in the economic structure. Widespread and growing female competition in the labor market suggests that at least the economic determinant of female submissiveness is losing its former power.

But even in traditional settings untouched by industrialism and modernization, virtually all Protestant denominations assume an attitude of moral intransigence toward traditional sex privileges of the male. *This appears to be one of the major reasons Protestantism has grown slowly in the more tradition-bound areas of Brazil and Chile.*

Our data indicate that membership in a Protestant church indeed reinforces the position of the married woman vis-à-vis a husband relapsing into customary sex behavior. "The woman whose husband is a *crente*," writes Saunders (1955:160–161),

is able to protest effectively against his sexual irregularities, and very often does so by bringing the situation to the attention of group leaders who then take the necessary corrective steps, in the form of a committee that first admonishes the member against his behavior, then asks for a resignation, and finally, if necessary, engineers the formal expulsion of the individual from the group. Because of loss of face, severance of group relationships, possible fear of supernaturally inspired consequences, and the fact that it is nearly impossible to keep secret extra-marital sexual relations over a long period of time, this has proved to be an effective means of social control.

Unwillingness on the part of Protestant women passively to accept the age-old pattern of marital infidelity, and the willingness of the sinning husband to submit the accusation of the spouse to the decision of ecclesiastical authority indicates a second major change in the relative position of the family within the general social structure. Neither the protest of an offended wife, nor the husband's acceptance of supra-family authority adjudicating such intimate matters as sexual misbehavior, would have been conceivable in the old social order. Traditionally, the husband was expected to be the supreme arbiter of his own sexual behavior. To surrender that authority to "outsiders" would have meant to jeopardize not only his status within the family but the status of the family within the community as well. As a highly self-centered unit, it was expected to settle its internal disputes without external interference, and during centuries it jealously defended that privilege against communal, judicial and ecclesiastical encroachments (Pinto, 1949:186 ff.).

Our data show that in Protestant families the wives can and do resort to church authorities in the case of troubled relationships with husband or children, and that the members of the family including the husband generally accept the role of pastors and/or elders as arbiters and peacemakers. Thus the family implicity recognizes its subordinate position vis-à-vis the congregation, as well as certain changes in its internal structure.

In Concepción and Temuco, eighty-eight informants answered our question whether they would accept their pastor's advice in the case of serious family troubles. Sixty-six said they would without restrictions, nineteen somewhat qualified their willingness, and only three signified that they would neither seek nor accept pastoral advice. Asked whether they would accept advice of the elders of their congregations in similar situations of family trouble, sixty-two gave their unqualified assent, and sixteen showed qualified willingness. Four informants failed to answer the question.

Some informants emphasized their acceptance of the minister as arbiter with remarks such as these: "The pastor cannot be wrong because God ordained him," or "the pastor is the only one to be trusted with family problems," or "he is the instrument of the Lord." There were no significant differences between the different denominations. Sect members showed as much willingness as members of the historical churches.

While adultery is severely punished by suspension or expulsion from the church, it seems much more difficult to enforce premarital chastity of the male.

Although premarital sexual relations are also frowned upon, breaches of this norm on the part of girls are practically unknown (because of its consistency with the outgroup norm it is not a problem), and when it occurs on the part of boys . . . and if it were known for a fact, [the culprit] would probably not incur the maximum penalty of exclusion from the group, but merely group censure and disapproval. Although this behavior is then to some degree tolerated . . . the individual is nevertheless made to feel the group's displeasure. When this norm is internalized and a break of it occurs, this situation may result in a conflict within the individual between his desires and the behavior expected of him, while not altering his religious convictions. Such was the case with one member who, although born in a Protestant home, felt his sexual activities to be incompatible with his church membership. He therefore dissociated himself from the group until after marriage when he was able to achieve harmony between actual and expected or ideal behavior in this matter. It should be stressed that this is a problem faced only by the male, who, as already indicated, is encouraged by the cultural environment to indulge in sexual relations at will before marriage. This is made all the easier by widespread prostitution. [Saunders, 1955:158–159.]

The changes in the internal structure of the family and its relative position in the community should not be interpreted in terms of "losses"—loss of male prerogatives and loss of autonomy—but rather in terms of far-reaching rearrangement and redefinition of roles. Particularly in Brazil, the active Protestant family has assumed the new role of a cult group. This could be achieved only by incorporating male *and* female members of the family into a worshipping unit—no minor accomplishment in a society that tends to leave the practice of religion to its women.

In a number of cases we witnessed the unusual phenomenon of family gatherings during which passages from the Bible were read, prayers recited and hymns sung in unison. Particularly in rural communities, such gatherings are preceded by the evening meal which congregates all family members around a large table. Needless to say, all meals begin and end with a common prayer. Such commensal behavior stands in the sharpest possible contrast to the eating habits of the lower class of rural Brazil, where the family members, especially the men, seek to isolate themselves and swallow their food without uttering a word.

Where schools are unavailable or distant, fathers are sometimes seen teaching their own children the rudiments of reading and writing, a rare sight indeed in a society that knows only the choice between government-provided schools and illiteracy. The father-teacher apparently assumes a responsibility above and beyond what non-Protestant fathers would be willing to recognize as their personal responsibility. It may be considered a sample of what our numerous informants had in mind when they referred to the "greater sense of responsibility" inherent in the role of the Protestant parent.

Curtailment of male prerogatives, assumption of mutual responsibilities, and assignment of new functions, such as the *culto doméstico* (family worship), involve reduction of the traditional social distance and therefore greater intimacy between husband and wife, parent and child. When thirty-six Presbyterian ministers were requested to define the influence which, according to their own experience, conversion to Protestantism has on family life, they used such expressions as "more gentleness," "forgiveness," "better humor," "more understanding," "respect," "sincerity," "more attachment," loyalty," and "affectivity" to define the changes that had affected the relationship among the members of the Protestant family. As said before, the industrial revolution in Brazil and Chile inevitably leads to a more egalitarian family structure. Protestantism seems to perform the function of channeling and validating these changes with its own brand of ethical and supernatural sanctions.

26
Economic Changes

Prescribed and Proscribed Behavior

✦ Planned diffusion of the ethical components of American Protestantism acted simultaneously in two directions. It sought to implant certain attitudes and to eradicate others. Industriousness, thrift, and sobriety were taught on the assumption that the "inherent dignity of a Christian life" is incompatible with the abject poverty predominant in the lower classes. On the other hand, habits or attitudes held to be sinful were the favorite target of puritanical evangelism, and their eradication, coupled with the emotional experience of conversion, was equivalent to the spiritual renewal or "rebirth" of the individual. Both changes were bound to affect the level of living of the converted, particularly if economic development tended to reward the effort of those who were sufficiently motivated to improve the material conditions of life. The adoption of ascetic attitudes did not necessarily imply renouncement of all hedonistic values; the objective to be attained was not freedom from wants but the substitution of permissible gratifications for "illicit" pleasures. The shift occurred from what the missionaries regarded as irresponsible, improvident economic behavior toward a sustained productive effort and judicious consumption.

Some Protestant churches are quite explicit in their attempts to change traditional economic behavior. According to the precepts of the Brazilian Methodist Church, for example, one must avoid "damaging the state by purchasing or selling property without paying the taxes due, or by carrying out any public or private transaction using subterfuges to circumvent the law." (Cânones, 1950:II.) The obligation to comply with the law which is, according to the testimony of numerous local officials, rather strictly adhered to by Protestants, constitutes one of the sharpest possible contrasts to non-Protestant business ethics. Brazilian public opinion takes it for granted that the people are continuously defrauded by thievish officials and politicians. Such alleged dishonesty is seized upon to justify any kind of tax evasion or deceit resorted to in order to "get even with the government."

Another major change in economic behavior is reflected by the Protestant norm that a specified part of one's income should be given to the church. The "pledge" and, to a lesser extent, tithing have actually been accepted by nearly all Protestant churches and sects, but it is virtually unheard of among Catholics. Catholics deposit, perhaps as often as not, a small coin on the collection plate which circulates during Mass, and if the coin the giver happens to carry in his pocket is not small enough, he takes some change from the plate. Of course, generosity, or lack thereof, varies from parish to parish, yet it is safe to say that hardly any parish priest could possibly live and maintain church services on the spontaneous contributions of the faithful; thus fees for all special services such as baptism, marriages, and funerals are normally charged by all priests.

We were unable to discover a Protestant congregation in which tithing was practiced by all members. Out of a random sample of 42 heads of families belonging to a variety of denominations in Temuco and Concepción in Chile, 27 or 64.3 percent declared themselves tithepayers. In southern Brazil, 48 pastors of Presbyterian, Methodist, and Baptist congregations stated that a varying percentage of their parishioners paid tithes. The distribution was as follows:

TITHING IN 48 PROTESTANT CONGREGATIONS
(Southern Brazil)

Percentage of Tithepayers	Number of Congregations
1–10 percent	12
11–20 percent	14
21–30 percent	11
31–40 percent	2
41–50 percent	3
51–60 percent	2
61–70 percent	2
71–80 percent	2

Although no figures were available, the pledging of a fixed amount seems to be far more common than tithing. It is probably safe to state that, including the tithepayers, at least 50 percent of the active members of the Protestant churches in Brazil and Chile donate a fixed percentage of their income to the church. The response to requests for extraordinary funds, particularly for the construction of churches, schools, and playgrounds, may be judged by the fact that even numerous smaller congregations have found it possible to build rather impressive churches from such voluntary contributions without outside assistance. It must be said, however, that many such contributions are made in labor rather than in money or kind. For example, among 58 Protestants in Temuco and Concepción, 44 (75.8 percent) had contributed labor to various construction projects. As indicated before, labor contributions are relatively more important in the Pentecostal sects, many of whose members are not in a position to contribute anything but their manual skills and part of their time.

In contrast to the Catholic concept of *esmola* (alms) which one is supposed to give to the church, the Protestant concept of the pledge comes actually close to that of a voluntary tax, although most *crentes* would probably refuse the term as too secular to interpret the meaning which their contributions seem to convey. The "blessings" derived from generous giving may be inferred from the testimony of one *crente* (Moura, 1938:7):

I am surprised, I am really very surprised. And it is of myself that I am surprised. Listen, my brethren, to what I am going to tell you about it, for I am surprised with the blessings of God, and I became so astonished that I wish to tell you about it: After I decided to give to the Church a part of my earnings according to the determination of the Word of God, I can testify that I am surprised with the quantity of money that I always have for the Kingdom of God, with the progress of my spiritual well being, with the facility with which I meet all my expenses and pay my bills, with the ease with which I administer all that God grants me and with how there is enough of everything and nothing is ever lacking. Finally I am surprised at myself, wondering why I did not adopt this divine plan of tithing during my first days as a *crente*. How was it that I spent what I should not have spent, and which was not mine, but which belonged to the kingdom of my Lord? I am surprised at the calm and peace that I now feel in my conscience.

There are three different indices of economic change causally related to Protestantism: preference given to Protestants by non-Protestants in economic matters; awareness of economic change subjectively expressed by Protestant converts; actual changes objectively observed, described and, if possible, measured. In the following pages some data concerning all three indices will be presented.

Preference Given to Protestants by Non-Protestants in Economic Affairs

In the preceding part, the social ascent of the Protestant churches was described, to some extent, as a consequence of the realization by the non-Protestant sector of the community, that the Protestants had adopted patterns of behavior that not only explained the relative successfulness of their economic pursuits but of which non-Protestants could profitably avail themselves as well. In other words, Protestants gradually acquired a reputation of being dependable, industrious, and efficient employees; fair employers; honest merchants; and proficient professionals with high ethical standards. None of our numerous informants thought or implied that such virtues could not be found among non-Protestants, but there was obviously a general expectation that Protestants did in fact live up to standards far from being collectively adhered to by non-Protestants. An American Catholic missionary, John J. Considine (1958:253), observed that "the best carpenters in Temuco are *canutos*. They have worked hard to learn their trade, they give an honest day's labor, they are never off the job on account of drunkenness, because they do not drink."

According to various informants, some years ago industrial and commercial companies in Santiago often advertised for Protestant employees in daily newspapers. The fact that no such advertisements could be found in 1959 was generally attributed to a slump in the labor market and to widespread unemployment. A former executive of Chile's largest papermill formulated his experiences with Protestant laborers as follows:

For twenty years I was *jefe del personal* and thus able to make a lot of observations about the attitudes of the workers who had embraced the Gospel. I don't know how they do it, and how they come to change their customs, but when they adopt those practices they certainly give up drinking, they become responsible, obedient, cooperative, loyal to their *jefes*, and very *positivos*. I know many of them on the agricultural estates of the company in Lota and Coronel. More than once I attended their meetings. I didn't understand their practices which seemed *extremistas* to me. These activities took place at night. During the day they behaved as indicated; I never had any problem with them, nor did they have any problem with other workers.

The present *jefe del personal* (personnel manager) expressed his views in similar terms:

The Evangelical element is scarce but those [who are employed by the coi pany] distinguish themselves by their good attitudes towards work. They are appreciated by the group. One of them distinguished himself as union leader. We called him *el canuto Henríquez*. A positive, conciliatory man; an efficient mediator between *jefes* and workers. Loyal to the Company. They did not attach themselves to political elements. I wish we had more pure Evangelical laborers.

"I wish we had a hundred Protestants in our factory" an executive of another large industrial plant told us, "the few we have do not give us any cause for concern; they are dutiful, responsible people."

Chilean Pentecostals, at least those in the cities, seem to avoid wage-earning jobs with schedules that interfere with their missionary endeavors. Out of 294 gainfully employed Protestants of Población Los Nogales near Santiago, 90, or 30.6 percent, turned out to be self-employed. Most of them are street or market vendors, carpenters, cobblers, painters, mechanics, and the like. The majority of the remaining 204 hold jobs with somewhat flexible working hours. Many are laundresses or domestic servants who can change jobs easily and often.

To test the reputation of Protestant employers in Brazil, 30 Presbyterian pastors of widely different parts of São Paulo and neighboring states were asked whether and how often they had been approached by non-Protestants with the request to recommend members of their congregations for employment. Of these, 31 or 58.3 per cent answered affirmatively. During his twenty-three years of pastoral activities, one minister had been approached about twenty times by persons looking for domestic help. One pastor had been requested forty times in a period of only two years to recommend *crentes* for white-collar positions, industrial, agricultural, and domestic jobs. One had been asked twice to recommend Protestant lawyers, another one had received a request for an insurance inspector. The reasons given for such preference were invariably two: honesty and efficiency. Stating that their choice was determined by previous experiences, these employers felt they could entrust their houses, merchandise, and cash to *crentes* without having to worry about theft or embezzlement.

Further inquiries made in São Paulo City revealed a significant difference between the behavior attributed to the members of Pentecostal sects and the one which was expected of other Protestants. Most informants whose experiences with Protestants was limited to sect members emphasized the docility of the *crentes* who refuse to become involved in labor disputes and whose peaceableness contrasted strongly to the contentiousness of non-Protestant workers. Although reputed to be honest, the Pentecostals were found to be lacking ambition and efficiency. The non-Protestant manager of a metallurgic plant in São Paulo informed us that there were thirty crentes among his 250 employees. According to his experience, these Protestant workers (all members of Pentecostal sects) were unexcelled so far as assiduity, honesty, loyalty, and obedience were concerned, but they lacked efficiency. "This is so," he added, "because they seem too preoccupied with the other world to care seriously about material things." He also commented on the behavior of one of his Protestant section chiefs.

He is not very efficient, but he is the best of all when it comes to loyalty, veracity and obedience. He can be relied upon as long as his work is of the routine kind. He is easy to get along with, and he does everything in an orderly fashion. However, whenever confronted with something unusual he would not act without receiving explicit orders. Even when ordered to do something of that sort he still isn't sure whether he is committing a sin or not.

With regard to his Protestant workers in general the manager emphasized that whenever I am faced with some service requiring great responsibility, things that demand competence, vision, and initiative, I would not choose a *crente*. I would perhaps ask somebody who is not as constant and well-behaved as the *crentes*. But when it comes to routine jobs requiring honesty, patience and assiduity I entrust them to *crentes*.

His twenty most dependable workers were *crentes*, but among the twenty most competent workers, only two or three were *crentes*. The manager of another plant informed us that two of his twelve section chiefs were Protestants, and these ranked among the six most efficient ones. Both belonged to historical churches. Equally highly ranked were the three Protestants of a crew of forty-eight workers. All three were classified among the "ten most efficient, assiduous and well behaved workers." And one Protestant ranked highest among the five best workers of the plant.

The owner of a banana plantation in São Paulo informed us that all the planters of his district agreed on the desirable qualities of their Protestant workers. He added that he had no complaints about his own, very carefully selected workers.

But the *crentes* among them [he pointed out] have something which the others do not have. When I set up a schedule for some sort of work, the *crente* is always on time. And when he cannot be there at the established time he sends somebody over a day before to inform me that he cannot come for some reason or other. The others almost never do this kind of thing.

Actual Economic Achievements

Los Nogales.

To compare economic achievements of Protestants with non-Protestants in the urban setting we chose Población Los Nogales, one of the many shantytowns in the vicinity of Santiago. Los Nogales is quite homogeneous in class composition. Only people who definitely belong to the lower class can be forced to accept the living conditions of a *callampa*. Furthermore, Los Nogales had been in existence for a period of at least thirty years; it is thus old enough to show whatever economic differences may have emerged among its approximately 20,000 inhabitants. The department for Adult Education of the Chilean Ministry of Education had carried out a census in Los Nogales, in which data on church affiliation and housing conditions had been included. Since almost everybody builds his own "house" in these shantytowns and attempts to improve it whenever he can afford it, housing conditions may be considered as one index of economic achievement. To classify the dwellings into "bad," "average," and "good," a number of criteria had been taken into account, such as building material, number of rooms, floor space per capita, existence or nonexistence of plumbing facilities and wooden floors; number and quality of windows (glass panes or wooden shutters), and others of minor importance. It was found that 563 residents of Los Nogales were Protestants and with a few exceptions members of different Pentecostal sects. To compare the housing conditions of the Protestants with those of non-Protestants we selected at random 563 non-Protestants from Los Nogales. The result is shown in the following table:

HOUSING CONDITIONS IN LOS NOGALES

Housing	Protestants		Non-Protestants	
Bad	93	16.5 percent	193	34.3 percent
Average	362	64.3 percent	298	52.9 percent
Good	108	19.2 percent	72	12.8 percent
Total	563	100 percent	563	100 percent

Thus the number of non-Protestants living in "bad" houses is more than twice as high as the number of Protestants whose housing conditions were found to be bad, and the percentage of Protestants living in "good" houses is significantly higher than that of non-Protestants living in houses of that category. Calculation of the chi square with one degree of freedom indicates that the present distribution would occur by chance less than one time in a thousand ($p > .001$); consequently it is safe to state that there is indeed a very significant difference between Protestants and non-Protestants insofar as "good" and "bad" housing conditions in Los Nogales are concerned.

Volta Grande, Cume, and Pádua Salles.

In order to analyze economic achievements following the introduction of Protestantism in rural areas, our choice fell upon three communities in notoriously underdeveloped regions of the state of São Paulo: Volta Grande, Cume, and Pádua Salles. These three villages differ from one another as much as they differ from any of the more developed agricultural communities of the state. All three are quite representative of "older" culture areas where some economic development occurred in the past but where a number of unfavorable circumstances led to stagnation or deterioration of economic conditions. These cases will be described here in some detail merely to show what *may* happen if people are sufficiently motivated to utilize existing human and natural resources and to entertain a concerted effort to raise the prevailing level of living. The evidence presented here is not of the kind to justify generalizations. It is not meant to imply that wherever Protestantism is accepted, economic conditions change as they did in these three villages.

Volta Grande with its fifty-eight inhabitants lies on the bank of the Ribeira River, in the southern part of São Paulo. The Ribeira Valley and the adjacent plains were once a rather prosperous rice-producing area. The port of Iguape with its numerous empty and decaying town houses and the ruins of several rice-processing plants are mute testimonies to past prosperity. The construction of more modern port facilities elsewhere and the opening of other agricultural areas nearer to urban markets are responsible for the general neglect of the Ribeira Valley by the State government which failed to build roads and railways and let the port of Iguape fall into disrepair.

A few kilometers from Volta Grande is another village of almost identical size, Jipovura, which remained untouched by Protestant missionary endeavor. Quite obviously, these two communities do not differ from each other in topography, soil conditions, ethnic composition, cultural background, and social composition. Neither place can be reached by road, rail, or telephone, but only by river boat or canoe. According to the prevailing stereotype, the local inhabitants resemble the *praianos*, the mestizo fishermen and farmers of the coast. They are supposed to be easy-going, indolent, undernourished and suffering from hookworm, malaria, and alcoholism.

When we first visited Jipovura in 1941 it was a largely progressive settlement of Japanese immigrants. There were several general stores, a rice-processing plant, a sawmill, postoffice and several other business establishments, but when the Japanese moved to more promising areas, Jipovura reverted to the lethargic way of life that characterizes most localities in the Ribeira Valley. Except for the two remaining Japanese families which own motor boats, the local residents do not even have canoes, but depend on the little river boat that stops in

Jipovura every other day. A few people engaged in agriculture are tenant farmers who plant some rice, manioc, and beans in a rather desultory fashion. One would look in vain for the small vegetable gardens so typical of Brazilian farms in other areas. Occasionally the men do some fishing, but there is not a single head of cattle in Jipovura. Most family heads work for the cannery in Volta Grande.

The local diet consists, as among most river *caboclos,* of beans, rice and manioc flour. Meat is seldom available, and milk, butter, eggs, vegetables, and fruits (except bananas) are almost never consumed. All water comes from the river and nobody bothers to boil or filter it. Most houses are wattle and daub structures in a poor state of repair and almost devoid of furniture and ornaments. People sleep on *esteiras* (straw mats) and use tiny oil or kerosene lamps that make it barely possible to discern the outlines of people and objects in the room. Only the Japanese and two Brazilian families live in relatively comfortable houses; at least they sleep in beds and use chairs, tables, and cupboards.

About twenty years ago the Japanese of Jipovura built a school house and donated it to the community. After the Japanese left, the building gradually deteriorated, for the people showed no interest whatever in preserving it. Actually, they helped destroy it by breaking window panes and carrying off windows and doors. In 1960 it could no longer be used, and the twenty-five school children were taught in a small room made available by one of the two Japanese families. Most parents are illiterate, but they want their children to attend school. Since neither reading material nor incentives to read are available in Jipovura, the children will probably forget the little knowledge they may pick up in two or three years of grammar school. By 1:00 p.m. the children appear in class unwashed, unkempt, barefoot, and most of the time without having had either breakfast or lunch. Parents and children alike are unwilling to co-operate with the teacher in maintaining minimum standards of cleanliness and hygiene. The only family that sends its children to high school in the nearby town of Iguape is of Japanese extraction.

There is a little building called "the Club" erected and owned by the Japanese who encourage their youngsters to meet there for ping-pong and other games. The Brazilians use *O Clube* only for occasional dancing parties. Other forms of organized recreation are nonexistent.

The men spend a considerable part of their ample leisure time playing cards and drinking sugar cane brandy (*cachaça*). Drinking bouts on weekends and holidays are quite common and the teacher reported occasional drunkenness among children attending school. The Catholic church in Jipovura is an ample and well-built structure, but like the school it has been so utterly neglected that it can no longer be used for religious services. Once in a while Jipovura is visited by a priest, but except for occasional participation in major Catholic festivals in Iguape, the people of Jipovura do not engage in any kind of organized worship.

Volta Grande, on the opposite bank of the Ribeira, presents a strikingly different aspect. Its simple brick or clapboard houses are well kept and some of them are, by regional standards, unusually well appointed. All families use water filters and three produce their own electricity. With two exceptions, all families own at least a canoe, but there are also three motor launches that are constantly used for business transactions in Iguape. Almost all the people of Volta Grande are small farmers who cultivate manioc, beans, rice, corn, bananas, and near their houses such vegetables as collard greens, tomatoes, lettuce, and peppers. Three families cultivate rice on a commercial scale, and two produce bananas for export. Furthermore, two families own small herds of dairy cattle, and considerable quantities of milk, cheese, and butter are consumed locally. The main source of income for the people of Volta Grande and surroundings, however, is a fish cannery which from October to March, when the river teems with *manjuba* (a fish of the anchovy family) employs an average of 120 workers. The plant is well appointed with modern machinery and produces its own electric power. The proprietor of the cannery also owns a grocery store in Iguape and a truck to ship the products of his cannery to the city of São Paulo. According to our informants, the net profit of the cannery amounts to an average of $3,000 per year.

The people of Volta Grande have taken up most of the food habits characteristic of urban civilization. All families consume coffee, milk, bread, butter, eggs, pork, vegetables, and fruits, besides such regional staple items as manioc flour, corn, beans, and rice. Almost all families raise chickens and hogs for home consumption, and from time to time the proprietor of the cannery slaughters a cow and sells the meat to his neighbors.

The children of Volta Grande formerly went to school in Jipovura, but when the school building fell in disrepair the people of Volta Grande did something almost unheard of in this type of community. They pooled their meager resources and built their own schoolhouse which was then donated to the state government with the stipulation that a teacher be provided and remunerated by the State Department of Education. The building is modest but quite adequate for local needs. According to the regional school supervisor, Volta Grande now has the best school in the entire area. The children attend class well dressed, clean, and adequately fed.

The people of Volta Grande are well informed about political events, both domestic and international. In most houses newspapers, magazines, and a variety of religious literature are read. Three families own small collections of books, and of course all read the Bible. There is no illiteracy in Volta Grande. All aspire to their version of betterment, and most of them have already purchased some land to build a house and plant subsistence crops. Grammar school education seems no longer sufficient to some people. In fact, the children of two families already attend high school in Iguape.

About twenty years ago, Salvador R. moved from Iguape to Volta Grande to exploit the seasonal occurrence of the *manjuba* for industrial purposes. Salvador was a member of the Brazilian Presbyterian Church and before long Volta Grande became a *ponto de pregação* (preaching point). Eventually all the local people were converted and became active Protestants who took to the puritanical rules preached by the missionaries and the local pastor in Iguape to whose congregation they belong. Drinking, gambling, and "other vices", even smoking, had to be given up, and steady working habits began to be regarded as a virtue. In the midst of a population where regular work is seasonal and never exceeds six months in any single year, the people of Volta Grande, like the Japanese settlers of the area, have found it rewarding enough to work steadily all year round. Since the pastor from Iguape comes only once a month, a local church member directs Sunday School and the religious services held three times a week in the little church of Volta Grande. The "family-worship"— widespread among Brazilian Protestants—assembles each individual family after dinner for Bible reading, praying and singing. Six hours a week was found to be the average time a person spends in the performance of his religious obligations.

It is probably true that Volta Grande owes its development to the initiative and entrepreneurship of Salvador R. But Salvador was born and raised in the same region, and his family background hardly differs from that of most subsistence farmers of the Ribeira Valley. His education, personal habits, and aspirations he owes to the fact of having been raised by Protestant parents. Numerous culture elements whose presence was noted in Volta Grande can be traced directly to the introduction of Protestantism. Modern hygiene, the consumption of vegetables, fruits, and dairy products are among the traits introduced by Presbyterian missionaries who, incidentally, were all Brazilians. Discouraging the use of the traditional sleeping mat (*esteira*), one missionary taught his parishioners how to make beds and mattresses. In Volta Grande the sleeping mat has virtually disappeared.

Exposure to cultural diffusion through Protestantism in Volta Grande seems comparable, in some respects at least, to the exposure of Jipovura to the way of life of the Japanese settlers, which constitutes the most effective single factor of cultural development in the Ribeira Valley. The people of Jipovura, without being persuaded to do so, could have at least copied some of the Japanese culture elements that would quite obviously have resulted in immediate profits and practical improvements of some sorts. The fact that they do not suggests that mere exposure to manifestly advantageous culture elements is not always sufficient to produce actual changes. On the other hand, the profound changes proposed by the missionaries were deemed palatable by the people of Volta Grande in spite of the price they were asked to pay in terms of cherished personal habits now branded as vices. Apparently, the Protestant missionaries succeeded in transforming the value system of Volta Grande—something that mere contact with the bearers of an alien culture failed to accomplish. Whatever motivated the inhabitants of Volta Grande and failed to motivate the people of Jipovura seems to lie in contextual differences between the two contact situations.

The Japanese never showed the slightest interest in changing the culture of the "natives," whom they despised. The people of Jipovura in turn assumed an ambivalent attitude towards the Japanese; they envied their skills but hated their alien way of life. Nevertheless, the exodus of the Japanese apparently demoralized the community, whose members failed to maintain such institutions as church and school. Their low morale is reflected in the fact that they proceeded to wreck the school building that the Japanese had erected at considerable cost. The effects of the implantation of the Protestant "culture" on the morale of Volta Grande were diametrically opposed to those which contact with Japanese culture had on the morale of Jipovura.

The Cume community is part of Cunha, a municipio of São Paulo, whose Protestant congregations were already dealt with in a previous chapter. Relatively prosperous as a way station on an old road linking the port of Paratí with the mining districts of Minas Gerais, Cunha fell into isolation and economic stagnation when in the second half of the past century Paratí succumbed to competition with other sea ports and to new railway lines that led to widespread ecological reorganization in some areas of Southern Brazil. To the peasants of Cume it meant return to a kind of subsistence economy that differed from the one of the Ribeira Valley only insofar as the people of Cume were more vigorous producers who lived up to their reputation of sturdy and hard-working farmers. Although the ethnic composition of Cume is similar to that of the Ribeira people—the people are of mixed Portuguese, African, and Indian descent—they live in a mountainous region between the coast and the Paraiba Valley of northeastern São Paulo. The average altitude being close to three thousand feet, neither coffee nor tropical crops can be grown in the area. The farmers depend largely on the cultivation of corn and black beans and the raising of hogs. There are about 70 Methodist families in Cume, but the community is not homogeneously Protestant as is Volta Grande, nor does it possess the characteristics of a village. Cume is merely the name of a bairro, a district with a number of rather isolated farms. With very few exceptions, the Protestants of Cume are small landowners (sitiantes), while most farm workers prefer to prac tice their own version of folk-Catholicism.

There is a noticeable difference between the Protestant and the non-Protestant sitiantes of the region. The latter adhere to the routine swidden agriculture and show little desire for technical improvements. The Protestants, on the contrary, are prone to experimen with new tools and techniques and some of their religious magazine provide them with practical advice on agriculture and animal husbandry. On the whole, the Protestant farmers are economically better off than their non-Protestant neighbors. They are better dressed, have better houses, and try to give their children a better education. In fact, they built their own little schoolhouse which is also used as a church. As has been indicated, this in itself constitutes an unusual achievement for a Brazilian peasant community which ordinarily waits for the government to provide such facilities.

The only electric generator in Cume was found in the house of a Protestant farmer who also operates his own sugar mill and manioc press, the only ones in the entire region. This farmer is one of the few whom the local people call *curiosos*, i.e., individuals who invent and build simple machines and are always experimenting with more effective technical devices. He actually invented a grater, a pulverizer and peeler for the processing of the manioc tubers. The farmer's brother, head of another large Protestant family, is the only person in the community who owns land-surveying equipment and knows how to use it. This again is to be considered an outstanding achievement in a region where exceedingly few holdings have been surveyed, and where hardly anybody knows how many acres he actually owns.

Although the Methodists of Cume are very meticulous in fulfilling their religious obligations, they are not proselytically inclined. As in Volta Grande, there are no self-styled evangelists.

Pádua Salles is, like Cume, an agricultural community composed of one hundred families. A district of Conchal *municipio*, it is located in an old farming area of central São Paulo which has seen better days. The land is not very valuable, and many people from other municipios thus found it possible to purchase *sitios* in Pádua Salles. Subsistence farming and commercial production of manioc constitute the economic basis of the independent *sitiantes*. The State government purchased 1.865 alqueires or 11.060 acres in Pádua Salles for reforestation purposes. A team of 87 laborers under the supervision of an administrator have already raised and transplanted more than two million pine trees on *Fazenda Campininha* as the state property is called. The payroll of the fazenda represents the largest single source of cash income for the community. The first of the present residents came to Pádua Salles in 1890, but the majority moved in since 1930, and very few of the adults were born in the community.

All local Protestants are members of the Assembly of God, and the administrator of *Fazenda Campininha* is its pastor. An evangelist of this sect began to preach the Gospel in 1947. His first convert was a tubercular woman on whom he performed a cure that was generally believed to be a miracle (no such cures were reported from either Volta Grande or Cume). Very soon, people began to be "baptized with the Holy Spirit." The present pastor was at that time a laborer on *Fazenda Campininha*. According to his own testimony he had been a "bad husband and father" who constantly quarreled with his wife and neglected his children.

I was so irresponsible that my sister-in-law had to take care of my wife and children. I smoked, drank and gambled, and often enough I got involved in fights with people in the village. Whenever there was a *cateretê* [secular folk dance] or a *dança de São Gonçalo* [semireligious folk dance] I used to play the *violão* [guitar].

Eventually he was converted and received the "baptism of the Holy Spirit." Most of his *companheiros de farra* (companions of drinking bouts) are now members of the Assembly. The conversion changed his whole life, as it changed that of all the other crentes in Pádua Salles.

After several years of successful evangelizing he became an ordained pastor in 1959. As the congregation grew, the village developed from a *lugar largado* (neglected place)—as one of the older non-Protestant residents put it—into *lugar bonito* (pretty place). The Assembly of God, numbering 170 members, succeeded in building, without assistance from the outside, a church that accomodates about three hundred. By checking and cross-checking interviewees, we discovered that the pastor performs his role as administrator of Fazenda Campininha to the satisfaction of the employees.

When he was appointed to this job he discovered that the productivity of the workers was rather low. He introduced a wage system according to which the laborers were paid for the amount of work done rather than for the time they spent on the job. The production has risen considerably since. The owner of one of the three general stores in Pádua Salles joined the Assembly at the age of forty nine and immediately ceased to sell alcoholic beverages, tobacco, cigarettes, and cosmetics. Approximately 90 percent of his customers are Protestants. Since he opened the store, thirty non-Protestants but only four

Protestants have left Pádua Salles without paying their debts. The proprietor of one of the two other stores informed us that approximately 5 percent of his customers failed to pay up their debts regularly, but there has never been a Protestant customer among these. To compare the economic achievements of the Protestants with those of the non-Protestants, ownership of brick houses was selected as a criterion. On a socioeconomic level where wattle-and-daub structures constitute the predominant pattern, the brick house must indeed be considered a significant achievement. Both Protestants and non-Protestants were thoroughly familiar with both types of construction. We found that 43.7 percent of all Protestant families and 37.3 percent of all non-Protestant families owned brick houses. This difference may not seem significant, but only so long as the time element is left out. Actually, 64.1 percent of the Protestants as against 32.8 percent of the non-Protestants settled in Pádua Salles after 1940. Thus, considering the fact that on the whole the non-Protestants had more time than the Protestants to attain the present level of economic achievement, the aforementioned difference is more significant than the figures on house ownership suggest.

It has not occurred to the Pentecostals of Pádua Salles that they could conceivably use the church as a schoolhouse and part of their revenues (about $600.00 per year) to pay a part-time teacher. They prefer to wait for the government which apparently promised the villagers a consolidated school (*grupo escolar*) instead of the present *escola rural*, or one-classroom school.

Different as these three communities are from one another, they share one characteristic which can hardly be overestimated. *The hacienda system is conspicuously absent from all three, and the local farmers are typically small landholders.*

Protestant Churches as Agents of Planned Technological and Economic Changes

While the Pentecostal sects have not concerned themselves with deliberate and planned attempts to raise the level of living of their members by introducing or disseminating new skills, the historical churches very early began to co-ordinate their missionary effort with a broad range of educational endeavors. Léonard (1951:180) writes,

The practical faith of the North American churches led to a conspicuous development of "para-ecclesiastic" institutions which offered the advantage of permitting indirect propaganda by contributing to the creation of a "Christian civilization," if not to the realization of the Reign of God on earth, more or less consciously identified with the economic system of the United States.

The present chapter is solely concerned with the planned introduction of technical skills designed to raise directly the level of living of the masses. The creation of general educational facilities will be dealt with in a separate chapter.

Of course, churches are not equipped to cope with problems of underdevelopment on a large scale. They have neither the trained personnel nor the financial resources necessary to solve problems of this kind. Their endeavor to teach new agricultural techniques or mechanical skills needed in a society which is making strenuous efforts towards industrialization, tends to remain subsidiary to their ethical and religious objectives. Nevertheless, some Protestant churches contributed, in their own limited way, to the diffusion of scientific knowledge and its practical applications to a variety of development problems, at a time when such initiatives were rare or nonexistent.

In Chile, the Anglican Mission and The Methodist Church have played an active role in the acculturation of the Mapuche Indians. Beginning in 1895, British missionaries sent by the South American Missionary Society attracted the first Indian converts by providing schools and medical service.

In the schools the boys are taught carpentry, agriculture, fruit-culture, and gardening. The girls . . . learn to weave, cook, sew and mend, keep house and exercise a controlling influence over their younger sisters. . . .

The results of the faithful instruction given and received are seen today in the improved conditions prevailing in the parts of the country where the ex-pupils of the school live. Modern machinery is being used on the farm, up-to-date methods are employed in agriculture generally, and plantations of fruit trees abound. Many of the Indians live in nice frame buildings with zinc or shingle roofs, and often a delightful flower garden or fruit orchard is planted along-side their houses, and in the homes themselves, presided over by the girls who have had the advantages of education, there is a marked increase in the way of neatness and cleanliness, and contain many objects of furniture which their husbands have made by their own efforts. (George, 1931:42–43) "Many of them," the same observer remarked, "are now on the same level with their Chilean neighbors, especially the boys who have passed through our agricultural school in Pelal." (George, 1931:71.)

In order to reach the poorest and most unacculturated Indians of Cautín province, the Methodist Church established a Granja Agrícola in Nueva Imperial. This agricultural boarding school is fed by a number of rural grade schools where Methodist lay teachers instruct the Indian children in the three Rs. Approximately three hundred out of a local Mapuche population of three thousand are members of the Methodist Church. The brightest children are sent to the *Granja Agrícola* where they learn the rudiments of modern agriculture and animal husbandry in a practical way by working in the fields and stables with their own hands. The Granja Agrícola helps feed students into a larger agricultural establishment of the Methodist Church in El Vergel which has played a historical role in the modernization of Chilean agriculture. In 1919 the Foreign Mission Board of the Methodist church purchased a 3,800-acre hacienda near Angol in Malleco province.

During the many years of El Vergel's experience, countless agricultural practices have been tried and proved successful or found wanting. Much experimental work has been done, for example, in finding the best combination of grasses, grazing, and fertilization for good pastures in the hill land of the farm. Likewise, numerous species of trees have been used for reforestation work, and their responses to different soil and climatic situations have been carefully noted. New varieties of fruits and ornamental plants have been developed in the nursery. Much valuable experience has been gained in "top-grafting" different apple stocks with other varieties to obtain heavy-bearing, disease-resistant trees. In connection with the livestock enterprises, attention has been given to the production of low-cost, balanced rations. There is a veritable 'gold mine' of agricultural information available at El Vergel. (Maddox, 1956:88–89.)

At a time when Chilean agriculture and husbandry was almost entirely dependent upon the initiative of the individual hacienda owner, El Vergel became a major focus for the diffusion of new farming and breeding techniques. All the major crops of the country, except grapes, underwent improvements in quality and quantity. Since the Methodist church has been consistently opposed to drinking, vineyards are conspicuously absent from El Vergel. In recent years, large-scale experiments in reforestation and the introduction of new grasses for pastures have been combined with new techniques designed to combat soil erosion, one of the most menacing problems of Chilean agriculture. The fact that El Vergel has been, from the very beginning, a highly profitable enterprise has made it possible to reinvest regularly large amounts of capital in the hacienda and its agricultural school. In 1959, eighty students were enrolled in this coeducational institution with a curriculum now equivalent to that of an agricultural college. Since 1928, forty-two Mapuche Indians have been graduated from El Vergel. Among these, twenty are now either farmers, teachers in agricultural schools, or employees of agricultural enterprises. A sample of eighty-one non-Indian students representing about 25 percent of all students who received instruction from the school, shows the following occupational distribution: eighteen or 22 percent are farmers, thirteen or 16 percent are technical employees of haciendas, eight or 9.9 percent are employees of the Institute of Inter-American Affairs, four or 4.9 percent are employees of various ministries of the Chilean Government, and eight or 9.9 percent have served as agricultural instructors in El Vergel, twelve or 14.8 percent are teachers in public schools and the remaining eighteen or 22.2 percent took up activities totally unrelated to agriculture. El Vergel does not provide agricultural extension service; the school has been the principal instrument of cultural diffusion.

The hacienda system is more amenable to technical innovations than to the development of human resources. On many farms, the use of modern agricultural techniques contrasts strangely to the lack of skill and productivity of the labor force. The American missionaries of El Vergel recognized this lag and attempted to develop the human resources connected with the farm. When El Vergel was purchased the work habits of its *inquilinos* or resident laborers were indistinguishable from those of other laborers of the surrounding haciendas.

As elsewhere in Chile, *San Lunes,* or the custom to skip work on Mondays, had virtually become a social institution. Traditionally, Mondays were used to recover from the effects of heavy drinking over the weekend. Not only were wine and chicha outlawed on El Vergel, but an additional incentive was provided by the commitment to pay wages corresponding to a seven-day week if the *inquilino* worked on Mondays. Otherwise, Sunday as well as Monday were discounted from his weekly wages. Interestingly enough, El Vergel anticipated Chilean social legislation which later adopted an identical clause for all labor contracts.

In addition to increasing labor productivity, the administration induced the *inquilinos* to send their children to school. Two primary schools were established on El Vergel, and the national law of compulsory school attendance was strictly enforced. About 150 families supply labor to the hacienda but only sixty-five actually are *inquilinos*, and almost all of these belong to the Methodist church. "They have a community organization that conducts a recreational program in a large hall and gymnasium located on the farm. Included in the activities are an athletic program, movies, first-aid courses, a blood bank, concerts, and an annual farm fair." (Maddox, 1956: 87.) At the present time, thirty-seven children of farm laborers employed by El Vergel go to public high school in nearby Angol against only five children from the seven haciendas adjacent to El Vergel, which, taken together, have a population several times that of El Vergel.

The Brazilian counterpart of El Vergel is the College of Agriculture in Lavras, Minas Gerais. Founded in 1908 by the Board of World Missions of the Presbyterian Church in the United States, it has played a pioneer role in the modernization of Brazilian agriculture and animal husbandry. Like El Vergel, it was many years ahead of similar initiatives by state and federal government, but in contrast to the Chilean institution it has never engaged in large-scale experimental work. According to Maddox, the Lavras school is to be credited with making decisive contributions toward three major changes. Following the model of the American land-grant college, it combined a practical system of instruction with the academic standards of a university.

The importance of this innovation can be fully understood only if one takes into account the deep-rooted Latin American prejudice against manual labor. Traditionally, a person of middle- or upper-class background does not defile himself by working with his hands. If he must acquire applied knowledge about soils, crops, animal nutrition, veterinary medicine, and the like, he prefers to listen to lectures dealing with such subjects or to watch practical demonstrations performed by farm employees.

The Lavras school was probably the first institution in Latin America to disregard the social stigma attached to menial work and to gain recognition for its pioneer intrepidity. This break with a powerful tradition was accomplished by lifting agricultural instruction to the university level. Thus

by giving scientific agriculture the status of a professional career, it attracted the sons of wealthy farmers. They no longer had to become lawyers, physicians, or politicians to maintain social status; agriculture no longer put a man in the class of a farm foreman or an estate manager. (Maddox, 1956:98.)

Finally, the Lavras school provided agricultural extension services. It became a center of systematic diffusion of new agricultural skills to the farmers of the surrounding area.

In recent decades, however, the potential benefits that Brazilian agriculture might have reaped from the Lavras school have been neutralized, to a considerable extent, by new employment opportunities which a rapidly expanding federal and state bureaucracy offered to the graduates of agricultural colleges. The gradual realization that *o Brazil é um pais essencialmente agrícola* (Brazil is essentially an agricultural country) reversed the traditional neglect of agricultural progress but created, along with new agricultural schools, a vast governmental bureaucracy which began to gobble up the graduates of agricultural colleges almost as fast as they were being produced. Thus much of the best agricultural talent returned from the laboratory and experiment station to office work in some government agency where they had little opportunity to use their knowledge except on paper.

At the present time, such institutions as El Vergel or the Lavras school no longer stand alone in their effort to introduce and disseminate a new technology. State-supported schools of agriculture with similar objectives and curricula have been established in Brazil and Chile. Many of their graduates go to the United States for postgraduate training, and the United Nations has played an increasingly important role in the process of changing obsolete technological patterns. As Maddox has pointed out, the agricultural colleges established by mission boards or churches no longer fill a vacuum, and the costs of operating such institutions effectively is growing rapidly (Maddox, 1956:107).

The problem of whether the Protestant churches are in a position to carry on indefinitely the increasingly complex and costly task of diffusing technical knowledge and skills need not concern us here. But in a complex society split by class cleavages such as those found in most Latin American countries, organized culture change must be generated on different levels if it is to reach more than a privileged sector of the society. If a higher level of living is indeed the desirable objective of deliberate change, certain technical innovations directly brought to the small landholder, the tenant farmer, and sharecropper would seem to be one of the possible shortcuts to the attainment of that objective. Some of the Protestant churches actually recognized the need of reaching the peasantry directly by setting up such centers as the aforementioned Granja Agrícola in Angol or the Instituto Rural Evangélico in Itapina, Brazil. Under the sponsorship of the Methodist church, the latter comprises a boarding school for about fifty boys and girls who "come from extremely poor farm families, and few of whom have received any schooling before they arrive at the institute. It is common to see teenage youngsters in the first of the five grades. Most of the students are Protestants referred to the institute by Brazilian pastors of rural Methodist and Presbyterian churches.

The courses in agriculture and home economics are extremely practical: boys work on the farm four hours per day, and girls spend an equal amount of time working in the kitchen and dormitories. Much of their classwork is directly related to the jobs that they perform daily. Buildings and facilities, all of which are crude but quite in keeping with the local style, have either been constructed by student labor from bricks and tile made at the school or been repaired by the students with local materials. Nearly all the food consumed by the students and staff, who eat together in one dining hall, is produced on the farm. The meals are substantial and, because of a large irrigated garden, usually well balanced. The daily menu is determined by what is available from the farm and garden. The traditional black beans and rice are the staple items, just as they are in millions of Brazilian homes because they can be grown and stored easily, but meat and green vegetables are added. (Maddox, 1956:60–61.)

In Angol and Itapina, planned change is carefully adjusted to skills that can be absorbed easily by the peasantry and do not go beyond a fuller and more rational utilization of existing resources. Similar objectives have been pursued by the Presbyterian mission in Ceará, a state that combines, as all the other states of northeastern

Brazil, a high population density with technical and economic under-development. Ceará is further plagued by droughts which period-ically decimate the population and force many thousands to seek refuge in the cities or to migrate to southern Brazil. In fact, the *flagelo da seca* (literally: the scourge of the drought) constitutes one of the most devastating social calamities of contemporary Latin America. Over the last thirty or forty years the Brazilian federal government has constructed a number of *açudes* (artificial lakes) in the northeast which brought some relief to a few thousand people' but failed to solve the irrigation problem proper.

Of the seven haciendas operated by the Presbyterian mission, two are designed to develop modern irrigation techniques by means of deep wells and windmills which can be installed at relatively small cost to the farmer. When a drought strikes, one of the haciendas takes up to 1,000 refugees who are given housing and temporary construction jobs. The other haciendas are more or less specialized in such pursuits as the production of high-quality cotton seeds, fruits, and the breeding of a new strain of beef cattle. It takes only fourteen months for cattle of the Santa Gertrudis variety to attain its maximum weight, in contrast to the three or four years required by the ordinary cattle of the region.

The Presbyterian mission in Ceará, which is headed by an American, operates on different social and technological levels. On the one hand, it co-operates on a regional level with other Brazilian, American, and international development agencies; on the other hand, it reaches the local peasants directly by such "low-level" projects as the intro-duction of the ox as a draft animal. In most regions of Brazil ox and oxcart are symbols of a traditional technology, not to say of back-wardness and poverty, but in Ceará they are virtually unknown. The head of the mission proceeds on the assumption that the local peas-antry is not yet, ready, either economically or technically, to adopt devices that would be more in accord with the machine age. Since *immediate* relief from intolerable economic conditions is judged more important than complex and time-consuming changes affecting the entire economic structure of the region, the introduction of the ox and ox-drawn plows and carts, seems to be a desirable and feasible improvement that fits the cultural context of the region.

The American missionary and Brazilian members of his staff perform a pioneering role in still another field. A few years ago when the local government planned to build a new road to one of the most unaccessible and backward regions of the state the American missionary was entrusted with the administration of the entire construction project. Assisted by Balbino, a former *cangaceiro* (bandit) who had become a faithful member of the church, he hired three thousand laborers, supervised the construction work and made all payments connected with the project. Again in 1959 when the northeast was devastated by floods, the same missionary participated in the administration of funds and supplies that had been made available to the stricken population. In both cases, the services of the missionary were enlisted to prevent public funds from being misused by dishonest officials and corrupt politicians. These instances indicate that "Protestant behavior" is in line with a widely felt need for greater honesty in public administration.

27
Excursus On Protestantism and Social Class

Self-Image and Community Expectations

As Niebuhr (1929: 28) points out,

One phase of the history of denominationalism reveals itself as the story of the religiously neglected poor, who fashion a new type of Christianity which corresponds to their distinctive needs, who rise in the economic scale under the influence of religious discipline, and who, in the midst of a freshly acquired cultural respectability, neglect the new poor succeeding them on the lower plane. This pattern recurs with remarked regularity in the history of Christianity. Anabaptists, Quakers, Methodists, Salvation Army, and more recent sects of like type illustrate this rise and progress of the churches of the disinherited.

The rise of proselytic Protestantism in Latin America, particularly in the two countries under scrutiny, has been interpreted in the preceding chapters as a vindication of the "neglected poor" or "disinherited" against the traditional social order and one of its main symbols, the Catholic church perceived as a class-bound institution. Initially, Protestant denominationalism reflected scarcely more than a multiplicity of contact situations and the opportunities it afforded to encourage a movement of social transformation and ethical renewal. It has been shown here that differentiation among the historical churches and the emergence of sects with definite class ties are concomitant with and functionally related to the process of sociocultural change.

It would, of course, be sheer nonsense to argue that Protestant ethics created the Brazilian and Chilean bourgeosie. Along with far more powerful secular forces, Protestantism may be considered merely as a contributing factor toward the reorganization of the traditional society. Technological and economic change, combined with the opening of agricultural frontiers, afforded unprecedented opportunities to the lower classes, whose members began to perceive for the first time the promise of economic and social rewards for such "Protestant" virtues as hard work, thrift, honesty, sobriety, and economic initiative.

In this context, the acceptance of Protestantism as a way of life makes social sense. In addition to eternal salvation and the acquisition of a social identity, it furthers the chances for economic betterment as demonstrated by those who had already embraced the new creed. There is a folklore of economic success attached to Protestantism. Regardless of denominational affiliations, the Protestant congregations built up a self-image in which economic success is perceived as an outstanding trait.

"Protestantism," remarked a Presbyterian pastor in São Paulo, "is a religion of character discipline which inspires work and a simple life without immoderate luxury. It fights against gambling and vices in general and converts the Evangelical Christian into a citizen whose economic life certainly becomes prosperous." "A Protestant," another minister of the same faith observed, "does not cheat the government. He pays his taxes religiously and he never becomes an adventurer in his business operations."

A Baptist minister in São Paulo pointed out that "Protestantism makes powerful contributions to the economy because a Protestant is sober, free from vices and a hard worker." One Presbyterian minister apparently knew his Max Weber when he told us that "the Protestant peoples do not suffer from malnutrition and financial difficulties. This is where capitalism comes from: By influencing people's behavior it [Protestantism] makes them prosperous and efficient in their ways of controlling capital."

"What God puts in our hands," another Presbyterian pastor remarked, "should be well administered and can only impart beneficial effects to the economy." These as well as a score of similar statements gathered from our interviews with Protestant leaders, reflect the firm belief that obedience to doctrinal precepts leads to economic prosperity. There is undoubtedly a high degree of awareness of economic rewards which the faithful are allowed to reap.

On the other hand, this self-image is constantly reinforced by the expectations which the community attaches to Protestant economic behavior. From initial hostility, intolerance, and contempt the attitudes of the non-Protestant public changed to tolerance and respect. "Instead of being a liability it is now almost an asset to belong to a Protestant church," remarked a middle-class Presbyterian of a small town in São Paulo. "People like to do business with you because you pay your debts. They know they can trust you." Similar observations were made by Donald Pierson and Emile Léonard (Pierson, 1951: 180; Léonard, 1953:97).

The reputation of *honestidade* (honesty) and *seriedade* (seriousness) that the community attributes to Protestants is to be understood in the light of prevailing business patterns. In both countries (as elsewhere in Latin America), local business practices facilitate accumulation of debts, the perpetration of frauds, and arbitrary price manipulations. Everything, particularly food items, are bought on charge account, and customers are supposed to pay their bills monthly. Actually, however, a considerable proportion of patrons fails to do so. Most merchants would rather sustain heavy losses than resort to legal action.

On the other hand, profit rates are such that "normal" losses are covered rather generously. In addition to these practices, a number of store owners, especially in rural areas, manipulate prices in such a way that illiterate and slow payers are heavily overcharged. This system works because buying is noncompetitive to the extent that one prefers easy credit, general accessibility, and a group of friendly neighbors (who habitually gather in the store) to lower prices. Although relationships between merchants and patrons are characterized by considerable reciprocal tolerance, sharp distinctions are drawn between honorable and dishonorable business practices. To say that a man is *serio* means that he does not indulge in such practices.

There seems to be a reciprocal reinforcement of actual behavior of the Protestants as a group and the expectations which the community holds towards the group's behavior, but one should be aware that much of the effectiveness of this control mechanism derives from the status of the Protestants as a minority group. As are all minority groups, it is overexposed to criticism and consequently highly sensitive to the reactions of the community. This and its tightly woven structure strengthen the self-regulatory capacities of the Protestant minority to a degree that must be considered unusual in the easygoing and self-indulgent way of life of most Latin American communities.

Writing on a Methodist congregation in Rio de Janeiro, Saunders (1955:166–167) noticed that

one of the most marked features of the *crente's* viewpoint are his concern and preoccupation with the activities of his fellow *crentes* in so far as they are likely to cast an unfavorable light on the group. The *crente* feels, and not without some justification, that censurable actions by a single member will be interpreted by the out-group as reflecting unfavorably on every member of the group. It cannot be denied that generalizations of this type by members of conflicting groups are common, especially so perhaps when the censured group is a minority. The *crente* is aware of this danger. As a result of his strong sense of identification with the group, he tries to avoid the development of any situation or action by a group member which might expose the group to censure. Thus every *crente* is a self-appointed guardian of the group's ethics and behavior, constantly on watch for omissions and transgressions.

Thus investment in terms of "Protestant" virtues is not an act of lone individuals, but it flows from identification with the group, is sanctioned by it, and the rewards are to be interpreted primarily as group rewards. In this social atmosphere of group sanctions and community expectations, it is of course up to the individual to get his share of economic success and bourgeois respectability.

The Social Composition of the Denominations

The introduction to the present volume alluded to the fact that the early Protestant missionaries in Brazil and Chile approached their work very much in the revivalistic spirit with which the American West had been evangelized. Their message was featured to reach the "common man," and because of peculiarities of the existing social structure it happened that the "common man" was essentially uncommitted to the value system of the upper strata and consequently "available."

Although the "common man" was, roughly speaking, synonymous with the "lower classes," some qualifications are necessary. By the time the first Methodist and Presbyterian missionaries set foot on South American soil, there was a class of people who by occupation, education, and level of living differed from the vast rural proletariat. These were the small landowners (*sitiantes, chacreros*) and tenant farmers, the owners of tiny *vendas* or *almacenes*, a sort of general stores which could be set up with very little capital, the artisans and low-level employees of business establishments, banks, railroads, and factories, and finally the lower echelons of the government bureaucracy. It seems a matter of semantics whether these categories are to be considered "upper-lower" or "lower-middle" class. Either classification could be justified, but in order not to suggest parallels with the American class structure, we prefer to call this rather heterogeneous conglomerate the "transitional class."

The transitional class was of course quite different from the middle class of business men, professional people, civil servants, including teachers, and owners of medium-sized *fazendas* or *fundos,* but its upper reaches tended to fuse with the lower ranks of the middle class. In fact, considerable fluidity may be expected from a class structure dependent on the vicissitudes of a boom-and-bust economy, but on the whole Brazil has proved more resilient than Chile, and economic setbacks that affected the entire society in Chile often had only regional effects in Brazil.

The chronic instability of the transitional and the middle class made it virtually impossible to erect boundary-maintaining mechanisms at these levels, a condition that has probably added to the chances of Protestantism as a factor of social mobility. At any rate, it seems that the transitional class contributed about as many converts to the first Protestant nuclei as the lower class.

The number of faithful was of course small, and if local congregations were to survive at least some of its members would have to be in a position to make contributions to the construction and maintenance of a church (Arms, 1923: 30, 40, 46–47). One may assume that the first missionaries made a deliberate effort to establish a foothold in the transitional class. Commenting on the fact "that the membership of most of the Protestant churches has come from the upper brackets of the lower classes," one observer (Nida, 1958:101) describes the strategic role of that class as follows:

The leadership within the churches has seemed to come primarily from the families of independent tradesmen and merchants, e.g., carpenters, shoemakers, blacksmiths and shopkeepers. It would appear as though the gospel had an attraction for just those groups which had much to gain, e.g., education for their children, a sense of importance (as co-laborers with God in the Kingdom of Heaven), and recompense for having been so largely excluded from the upper brackets of Latin American society. Conversely, these same people had very little to lose by becoming Protestants, for they were not so likely to lose their jobs, were not dependent upon some one person for their social and economic security (as in the case of the day laborer or peon), and had never been cultivated to any great extent by the Roman church, which has concentrated most of its attention upon the elite class.

This is what in a preceding chapter was called "interstitial penetration" of the traditional social structure by individual converts who were in a position to defy the prevailing value orientations and their sanctions. The transitional as well as the middle class proved to be more accessible in Brazil than in Chile, and toward the end of the nineteenth century, Protestantism had already established a solid bridgehead in the Brazilian bourgeosie.

By 1895, a Baptist missionary (Crabtree, 1927:116) noted that

the prestige of the Evangelical merchants was remarkable. Coffee, pharmaceutical and other products sold by Protestants got a tremendous acceptance in the market. A Baptist plumber in Amargosa, although constantly denounced as a dangerous heretic by the priest, was unable to carry out all the orders of his customers who appreciated the honesty of his work. A seamstress crente of the same town was denounced by the priest accompanied by a crowd of his followers, and henceforward her orders began to increase more and more. Everywhere the people showed confidence in the word of a Protestant and believed in the honesty of his services. Taking advantage of this popular sentiment, a criminal declared to be a Protestant was acquitted by the Jury.

Protestantism thus fed on revolt against the Catholic Church; it attracted members of the incipient and struggling middle class, and conversion against the odds of a powerful opposition paid off in the form of increasing prosperity and status advancement.

Unlike the Chilean "aristocracy," the upper class of Brazil was not entirely unreceptive to the preachings of the early missionaries. In 1878, for reasons unknown "seven ladies of the highest Brazilian aristocracy," to use the words of the historian (Ferreira, I, 1959:1965–1966) joined the Presbyterian Church of São Paulo.

These families were not a sterile acquisition for the Protestantism of São Paulo. Dona Rosa Edite de Souza Ferreira married Professor Remigio de Cerqueira Leite, he himself a scion of an ancient lineage of the land. A granddaughter of Dona Antonia da Silva Ramos, Dona Ernestina Rudge, joined the faith four years after her grandmother, on September the seventeenth, 1882; on the twenty-first she married a young man of the same social level, son of a high military officer, Cesario Pereira de Araujo who had joined the church four years before; this marriage was a remarkable event for the society of that city. However, it was another family of the same city which became, for the number of converts to the reformed faith and for its religious zeal, the center of the Presbyterian Church of São Paulo: the Souza Barros whom the genealogists relate, through the kings of Portugal, to the emperors of Leon and Charlemagne, without forgetting the Indian chiefs Piquerobí and Tibiriçá to whom the ancient houses of São Paulo proudly trace their descent.

Léonard (1952:450–451) mentions other members of the landed aristocracy who became Protestants:

The names of Macieis in Minas Gerais and Nogueira Paranaguá in Piauí are particularly meaningful. It is significant that the pastor and professor Ernesto Luis de Oliveira was, for some time, Secretary of the Department of Agriculture in Paraná, and the Baptist Luiz Alexandre de Oliveira, member of the federal legislature for Mato Grosso; that the reverend Antonio Teixeira Gueiros, pastor of the Presbyterian Church in Belém, was vice-governor of Pará. There is certainly no indiscretion in the statement that the pastor of the Presbyterian Church of Fortaleza, the Reverend Natanael Cortes, is one of the great *fazendeiros* of the region, proprietor of sugar mills and a bank.

Emile Léonard (1952:451), the historian of Brazilian Protestantism, found that

the professions and commerce are abundantly represented in contemporary Brazilian Protestantism. . . . Regarding lawyers, doctors, and businessmen it suffices to open the last pages of the Protestant newspapers to inform the reader that there is no want of coreligionists to take (medical) care of him, defend him (in court), or represent his interests. Business, both wholesale and retail, affords handsome success to merchants and businessmen who commend themselves mainly for the kind of honesty which is generally recognized among Protestants. Business circles often show pride in the rapid economic and social ascent of many of their members.

The question we wish to raise at this juncture is this: What effects did the social ascent of the historical churches have upon their structure? Have they absorbed middle-class culture to the point of losing contact with the lower classes? In other words, have they become churches of the rising middle class? To answer these questions, the social composition of a number of congregations was examined. Since we had to rely on informants and interviewers, no attempt was made to go beyond the conventional tripartite division, lower-middle-upper, with which all our co-workers appeared to be familiar. "Lower class" denotes, within the cultural context of either country, mostly unskilled or semiskilled menial work, complete dependence on wages, poor housing and a high illiteracy rate. The "upper class," according to current local definitions, is composed of the liberal professions, owners of haciendas, well-to-do merchants, industrialists, real estate owners, and individuals in high managerial or civil service positions. The "middle class" is defined as a residual category composed of interdependent artisans, small merchants and entrepreneurs, small landowners, white-collar workers and civil servants in subordinate positions. Due to its heterogeneous composition and somewhat amorphous characteristics, we prefer, as already indicated, the designation "transitional class."

The concept of the upper class is somewhat ambiguous. By small-town criteria, the individuals identified as members of the upper class actually belong to the highest stratum of the *local* community. By metropolitan and national standards, however, they would undoubtedly be considered middle class. Since none of the Protestant congregations under scrutiny appeared to have any members belonging to the *national* upper class, the term was dropped altogether and the designation "middle class" was chosen instead.

In a random sample of sixty-seven Protestant families belonging to

various denominations in two Chilean cities (Concepción and Temuco), the three social classes were distributed as follows:

Lower	53 percent
Transitional	9.1 percent
Middle	37.9 percent

Information about class composition was obtained from ministers
and informed members of different congregations. Classification was
based on the criteria of occupation, education, and material possessions. Since none of the more refined measuring techniques could be
used, the following tables should be considered mere approximations.
The obvious shortcomings of this rather crude approach were, at least
in part, counter-balanced by the fact that we were dealing with
relatively small groups, the members of which knew each other well
enough to supply a wealth of information bearing on class status.

In a Chilean Methodist parish (Santiago) 60 percent of the members belonged to the lower classes, 30 percent to the transitional and
10 percent to the middle class. Out of 104 families affiliated with the
Seventh Day Adventist Church of a Chilean city (Concepción), 47.5
percent belonged to the lower class, 37 percent to the transitional and
15.5 percent to the middle class.

The analysis of the membership of thirty-four Presbyterian congregations in São Paulo and neighboring states yielded the following
class distribution:

Lower	59.4 percent
Transitional	34 percent
Middle	6.6 percent

These congregations, however, appeared to be so heteregeneous that
a more detailed scrutiny seemed to be in order.

Table XVIII shows that in 22 out of 34 parishes people of lower-class
extraction represent more than half of the total membership, and only
one congregation declared to have no lower-class members at all.

In order to obtain a sample of class distribution in a metropolitan
area, three congregations from widely differing residential districts
of Rio de Janerio were selected (Table XIX). Methodist I is located
in a predominantly proleterian suburb; Methodist II lies in a district
where transitional- and middle-class people are predominant, and the

Presbyterian Cathedral, as it proudly calls itself, is located in a *bairro chique,* (fancy neighborhood) a predominantly middle- and upper-class residential district.

The class extraction of the clergy constitutes another criterion to measure the extent to which the historical churches have maintained contact with the lower classes. Table XX shows the class origin of three distinct groups: 36 Presbyterian pastors, 74 students of a Presbyterian seminary, and 43 students of a Methodist seminary in Southern Brazil.

At least two conclusions may be drawn from these tables:

The social ascent of the historical Protestant churches since their inception is a fact. The mean percentage of the transitional and middle class membership in a total of forty congregations amounts to 43.7 percent.

The historical Protestant churches did not lose contact with the lower classes. Much on the contrary, the mean percentage of the lower-class membership in these congregations represents 56.3 percent of the total.

The Brazilian Presbyterian Church is of course over-represented in our sample, and there are no figures at all on class distribution in the Baptist churches. Virtually all our informants, however, agreed that of the three main historical churches the Baptists appeal more strongly to the lower class than either the Methodist or Presbyterian church. Thus, if Baptist congregations were included in our sample, the figure referring to lower-class membership would probably be higher.

Furthermore, all Brazilian informants agreed that the Presbyterian Church had been more successful in attracting members of the middle class than the Methodists and the Baptists. (The Presbyterian Church in Chile has been so notoriously unsuccessful that the Brazilian Presbyterian Church is planning to send missionaries to Chile.)

So far as we are able to find out, the Protestant laity and clergy are well aware of the potential threat which internal stratification holds for the cohesion or esprit de corps of the individual congregation. Practically everybody whom we interviewed pointedly insisted on what he perceived as egalitarian behavior within the group. The pastor of the Presbyterian cathedral in Rio de Janeiro, for example, emphasized that the members of his congregation were "not class conscious at all. They all sit together during the services. A doctor sits next to a laborer." Reflecting the class composition of his parishioners, most deacons and presbyters are educated people, but some of them belong to the lower class. These were elected because they are *muito simpáticos* (pleasant), and get along very well with everybody.

A pastor of the Evangelical Congregationalist Church of Brazil emphasized the absence of class problems in his rather heterogeneous congregation. "People are not class conscious and everybody gets along fine with everybody else. It is quite common to see laborers sitting next to their boss during our services." Nevertheless, the social composition of this parish has changed from a "church of the elite" to a "church of the people." The lower-class members show more interest in church activities than the "elite" which has become rather *comodista* (lax). To counteract this tendency the pastor assigns some leading functions to members of the "elite."

In spite of the cultural origin of Latin American Protestantism, no traces of racial prejudice and discrimination could be discovered. *In fact, this appears to be one of the major adaptations American Protestantism underwent in Brazil.* There is no doubt at all that any attempt to establish separate "Negro Churches" would have been regarded as a public calamity in Brazil, and considering the virulence with which public opinion responds to violations of the doctrine of racial equality it could well have meant complete failure of Protestant missionary endeavor. The number of colored members of course varies enormously according to region and class composition of the individual congregation.

In the Methodist parish of a predominantly lower-class suburb of Rio de Janeiro, Saunders (1955:18) found that of a total of 142 members 47.9 percent were white, 29.6 percent mulattoes and 22.5 percent black. According to our own observations this is probably a typical distribution for communities of similar race and class composition. Even in predominantly middle-class congregations a sizable percentage of the members is colored. For example, among the 125 attendants of an evening service in a middle-class Baptist church in São Paulo City we counted a total of 31 colored individuals. In two Methodist congregations with a similar constituency, the percentages of colored members were 21 percent and 25 percent. The churches seem willing to go any length to prevent racial stratification within their congregations, as the following observation by Saunders (1955:150–151) shows.

Another interesting aspect of the group's informal organization is racial discrimination, in the sense of *distinguishing*, or discriminating *among*, not *against*. This also indicates a degree of racial self-awareness, and an attempt to classify every member in either one category or the other, although the attempt has not been very successful. There is, however, a degree of racial self-consciousness among the "definitely white" and the "definitely black." It is necessary when organizing a *festa* or special church program such as Sunday School Day, to take care to include an equal number of white and black persons on the program, lest one of the groups feels offended and discriminated against. Similarly, the Sunday School superintendent, who is a Negro, states that he tries always to be impartial in this respect, in the choice of Sunday School teachers and other Sunday School officials, attempting to include equal proportions of Negro and White, lest he be accused of favoritism toward the black group members. It is interesting to note that the choir is tacitly assumed to be the special province of *gente de côr* or "people of color," and this element does in fact predominate it. It has been my experience that this also holds true for several other congregations in the Federal District.

Status Achievements and Social Aspirations of the Clergy

The social rise of an institution implies upward mobility of its individual members. This is mainly achieved by a conjunction of economic advancement and the full utilization of educational facilities. More will be said in forthcoming chapters about these aspects of culture change. Within the context of the present chapter, however, our attention will be focused upon the institutional exponent of historical Protestantism, the native clergy, its achievements and aspirations in terms of social mobility.

To assess the status achievements of the Protestant clergy, especially in Brazil, it ought to be pointed out that the individual career does not often proceed solely within the channels of a theological institution and a church. Of course, nowadays most pastors of the historical churches are graduates of a seminary, but frequently they exercise a second profession, or, if they do not practice it, they have at least a qualifying degree for such practice. Thus whatever class position they may have achieved in a community, it cannot adequately be evaluated solely in terms of the pastorate. "There are numerous examples" wrote Léonard (1952:459), such as Pereira, Trajano, Erasmus Braga, Ernesto de Oliveira, Henrique Vogel, Otoniel Mota e Jeronimo Gueiros, who exercised the teaching profession and achieved fame in it. There never was a want of pastor-physicians and much less of lawyers and business men. The most surprising example of this multiplicity of aptitudes and functions was the Reverend Bento Ferraz, assistant of Eduardo Carlos Pereira and founder of the Conservative Presbyterian Church. Pastor in São Paulo, he also was professor of the state college in Campinas, lawyer in Minas Gerais, businessman, owner of sugar mills and banks in São Paulo and Rio.

This astonishing versatility appears to be deeply rooted in Latin American culture. The traditional concept of the *homen culto*, the Latin American intellectual, requires encyclopedic learning and a broad range of interests. Entrepreneurship or commercial ability are often associated with the image of the *homen culto* as a concession to a "new civilization" and its opportunities for economic advancement. It would be easy to quote scores of non-Protestant Brazilian intellectuals of national repute who also amassed fortunes as industrial entrepreneurs or businessmen.

Sometimes, however, a congregation is too poor adequately to support a minister and his family, and in these cases the exercise of a second profession becomes a must. The churches discourage this trend, but they have never really been able to halt it. In 1950 the magazine *Puritano* reported a case of this sort which is not as unusual as one is inclined to believe (Léonard, 1952:460):

The pastor exercised the teaching profession. He was professor in three *colegios*; his average teaching load was thirteen hours per day; this activity would be sufficient to exhaust any human organism. Even so, this minister attended all meetings of the departments and associations of the church; he preached three or four times every week; he supervised his field which was quite large with a good number of congregations; he did all the work requested by his presbytery; nor did he neglect work in the city and cooperation with other denominations. When invited to think of the impossibility of continuing in this rhythm he resigned his teaching jobs which of course involved a great material sacrifice.

A sample of twenty-three Protestant pastors taken in São Paulo City, shows that the trend to achieve competence in various professions, practiced or not, has by no means altered. Thirteen out of these twenty-three clergymen obtained professional degrees or practiced some profession in addition to the pastorate.

Professional Achievements of Protestant Ministers—São Paulo
Denomination

Presbyterian: Degree in theology. Degree in medicine. Practicing physician.

Presbyterian: Degree in theology. Two years of social sciences in university. Professor of psychology, education, history of education, and philosophy.

Presbyterian: Degree in theology. Attended law school but was not graduated.

Presbyterian: B.A. in theology and D.D. Teaches in *Colegio.*

Presbyterian: Degrees in theology and B.A. in philosophy. Teaches philosophy and is practicing professional journalist.

Baptist: Degree in theology. Teaches in Colegio.

Baptist: Degree in theology and law. Teaches in Colegio.

Baptist: Degree in theology. Attended law school but was not graduated.

Baptist: Degree in theology. Professor of Portuguese.

Baptist: Attended seminary but has not yet been graduated. Has degree in law and accounting. Attended school of medicine for two years.

Baptist: Degree in theology (M.A.). Doctor of medicine.

Adventist: Degrees in theology and accounting.

Adventist: Degrees in theology and law. Practices law.

The trend to achieve professional competence in some field other than the pastorate is further illustrated by the educational background of 118 Methodist and Presbyterian candidates to the ministry. Out of 43 Methodist students 15, or 34.9 percent had some amount of other professional training. Among the 75 Presbyterian students 20, or 26.7 percent had acquired some other professional skills.

The ministry has been a channel of upward mobility. According to Table XX, 30.6 percent of a group of 36 Presbyterian pastors came from a lower-class background. In a sample of 75 Presbyterian seminarians, the lower-class contingent (29 or 39.2 percent) appears to be greater than either one of the two upper strata. And of a group of 43 Methodist seminarians more than one third (16 or 37.2 percent) came from lower-class families. Some understanding of the ways and means by which social ascent has actually been achieved may be provided by the following brief excerpts from a number of interviews with Protestant pastors in São Paulo City.

A. C., METHODIST PASTOR of a congregation with 245 members, was owner of a small store before his conversion to Protestantism. He was graduated from the Methodist Divinity School and became successively minister in eight different towns until he was placed in a parish in the state capital.

A. S., PRESBYTERIAN MINISTER of a congregation with 200 members. Was grammar school teacher in a neighboring state. After his conversion to Protestantism he was graduated from a Presbyterian seminary and became successively minister in eleven communities, mostly small towns in different parts of the interior. In 1935 he received his present parish in the state capital.

E. M., BAPTIST MINISTER of a congregation with 610 members. Before taking up his studies for the ministry he worked on a farm and later as a salesman in a small store. He attended law school for several years, but lack of time prevented his completing the requirements for a degree in law.

R. A., BAPTIST MINISTER of a congregation with 105 members. He worked on a small farm, and at the age of 15 he became a clerk in a country store. After being graduated from the seminary he exercised the ministry in two towns in São Paulo. In 1956 he was elected pastor of his present congregation.

S. P., METHODIST PASTOR of a congregation with 122 members. Before taking up his theological studies he was assistant mechanic of a telephone company.

E. T., BAPTIST MINISTER of a congregation with 122 members. Illiterate, he learned to read and write by himself. He was, successively, a farm laborer, fisherman, railway worker, sailor, policeman and taxi driver. In 1926 he became a Protestant and shortly afterward he prepared himself for the ministry.

D. A., BAPTIST MINISTER of a congregation numbering 435. Before his conversion he was a truck driver and completely illiterate. Invited to attend the preaching of a missionary, he accepted the Protestant faith and began to attend night school. He completed his education in the seminary, and in 1945 he was elected pastor by his present congregation.

E. C., BAPTIST MINISTER of a congregation with 285 members. Came from a Protestant family. Before he took up his studies for the ministry he was a tailor. After his ordination he did two years of mission work in the Amazon region. Later he was successively minister in eight different towns of the interior. In 1958 he was elected pastor by his present congregation.

T. M., BAPTIST MINISTER of a congregation numbering 900. Before his conversion to the Protestant faith he was a farm laborer and commercial employee in northern Brazil. He has degrees in theology and medicine. During nine years he was pastor in two cities of the north. In 1929 he was elected pastor by his present congregation.

Within the traditional scale of values, urban parishes carry more prestige than small town or rural parishes. Consequently, the somewhat tortuous moves of some pastors from obscure localities to larger towns and finally to the state capital ought to be interpreted as upward steps on the social ladder.

In the traditional rank order of Latin American town society, the priest belongs, together with the mayor, the doctor, the judge, and other "dignitaries" to the local upper class. The class status of the Protestant minister, however, is still somewhat equivocal. In the past, the Protestant congregations including the ministers responded to prejudice and antagonism by cutting themselves off from the main stream of "worldly" events. More recently, increasing participation in community affairs has changed the position of the individual Protestant, particularly the minister, who now tends to define his position in the class structure and to assume a leadership role which transcends the boundaries of his own congregation. The school where he acquired his professional training has been upgraded, at least by his church, to the rank of a *faculdade de teologia* (school of theology), the graduates of which should be able and willing to assume a position comparable with that of other college graduates.

Is the individual candidate to the ministry aware of this "struggle" for higher status in which, *nolens volens*, he has become involved? How does he conceive of his position as a community leader and exactly what are his social aspirations? To answer these questions, the students of the aforementioned divinity schools were asked to express their opinions on whether the Protestant minister should be on an equal footing with the other community leaders such as priest, judge, doctor, and whether the minister should be invited to attend official community affairs, such as patriotic commemorations, civic campaigns, and dedication of public works. Out of 43 students of the Methodist divinity school, 39 or 90.7 percent felt that the rank of the minister should be equal to that of the other local leaders, and 38 or 88.2 percent thought that the minister should be invited to participate in outstanding community events which, by their nature, offer opportunity to reaffirm class status. One candidate was unsure of "these things" and the remaining three failed to answer the question.

Among the 75 students of the Presbyterian institution 57 or 76 percent responded positively to both questions, 9 or 12 percent were unsure, and the rest failed to answer.

To further clarify the nature of participation in community matters in which the students felt they ought to engage, a list of five typical associations or institutions were presented to them with the request that they point out those of which they would seek to become members.

STUDENTS' PARTICIPATION PREFERENCES

Associations or Institutions	Methodist	Presbyterians
	Number/Percent	Number/Percent
Local directorate of political parties	4 or 9.3 percent	23 or 30.7 percent
Clubs	13 or 30.2 percent	21 or 28 percent
Masonic lodges	13 or 30.2 percent	12 or 16 percent
Municipal government (mayor or councilor)	6 or 13.9 percent	12 or 16.0 percent
Civic associations of a non-political nature	36 or 83.7 percent	59 or 78.7 percent
No participation at all	0	2 or 2.7 percent
No answers	7 or 16.3 percent	7 or 9.3 percent

An overwhelming majority in both groups wished to be recognized as members of the local upper class, but when it came to choosing possible alternatives of participation in community institutions, the groups revealed differences that seemed to reflect two distinct denominational traditions. The Presbyterian group showed considerably more willingness or desire to participate in political affairs than did the Methodist group. Political participation in leading positions is perceived to constitute more of a threat to the moral integrity and the religious ideals of the individual than any other of the aforementioned forms of participation. Of all forms of participation the exercise of political leadership was rated the most worldly. Thus, to the extent that our subjects are willing to assume positions of political leadership in the community, they are actually making a radical break with the "otherworldliness" of the past. That the Presbyterians showed so much more willingness to do so than the Methodists, seems understandable if one takes into account the worldly achievements of the Presbyterian "elite" of the past.

The question regarding the social position the pastor should hold in the local community raised some comments. One Methodist student for the ministry felt that the pastor should be in close contact with the "most influential people in town without neglecting the other classes." Another student of the same institution thought that "as a leader the pastor should concern himself with all the political, social, and religious problems of the community like the other leaders." "The pastor is a guide of the people of his town," declared a third student, "a guide in spiritual things as well as any other aspect of life."

A student at the Presbyterian institution felt that "the minister ought to be aware of the necessity of not being inferior to other community leaders." Another thought "the pastor should be a lawyer too; in fact he should be above everybody else." One student suggested that "the pastor be in touch with 'high society' in order to exercise his influence and to take advantage of any opportunity to spread the Gospel." "Participation is all right" declared another student, "but it should not be an obligation, and it should not be at the expense of one's pastoral obligations." Two students whose fathers were manual laborers felt the pastor "should not seek equality with the upper class." "If the town is very small," advanced another student, "the pastor should be equal to the leading citizens. He should participate in all phases of community life."

The Churches as Way-Stations of Social Mobility

The Protestant churches have served the function of furthering upward mobility by capitalizing on the virtues of Christian asceticism, but they have become victims of the process they have helped to develop. "Parents who have been blessed materially through the practice of self-discipline are eager to give their children the advantages which they themselves were denied." (Davis, 1943:123.) Equipped with the educational resources for further social advancement, these second generation Protestants may find it more advantageous to drift away from active church membership to nonparticipation. No longer do they want "to be associated with obscure groups of *crentes*," they are not motivated by the evangelical ardor of the parent generation, and Christian asceticism seems singularly unrewarding once professional and financial success is deemed obtainable merely by secular effort.

Writing in 1943, Davis (1943:119) already reported a considerable loss of younger church members. In fact, many congregations were losing from 20 to 70 percent of their youth to the hedonistic values of a highly secularized society.

Not a few of the pastors admitted that in the estimate of many young people the church stands as a negation of nearly everything they like to do. Dancing, smoking, card-playing, and theater and movie attendance are all in the same category of sins; games of any kind or picnics and walks on Sunday are ruled out.

Most churches had no program of recreation to substitute for forbidden pleasures. Thus the old cultural conflict which the parent generation seemed to have overcome crops up anew among the second-generation Protestants. Meanwhile, many urban congregations have at least relaxed their puritanical strictness, often to the scandal of their rural brethren. Many urban congregations do have a recreational program, and Protestant student associations seek to maintain some measure of control over Protestant youth away from home.

Loss of younger members was also reported by Chilean pastors. Pious Protestant parents often make great efforts to provide a college education for their children. The families living in the provinces have to send their sons to Santiago where they tend to become estranged from the church. A Baptist churchman in Southern Chile estimated that there were approximately 30,000 persons in Chile who at one time or another had been baptized in the church, while the official membership of the Chilean Baptist Convention (for 1957) was only 7,957. By the end of 1958, the number was down to 7,205, mostly because of exclusions and resignations (*La Voz Bautista*, 1959:12).

In Brazil, all Protestant churches and sects reported 66,335 exclusions in 1956 and 84,814 in 1957 (*Estatística do Culto Protestante*, 1951:1; 1960:1). There is of course no evidence that all or even the majority of these exclusions involved individuals "on their way up." As indicated in a previous chapter, there is considerable drifting from one denomination or sect to another, and a large proportion of the people listed as exclusions by one group appear as new members in some other group.

The Pentecostal Sects and the Class Structure

The social stratification within the historical churches in Brazil and Chile rules out the hypothesis that the acquisition of "new cultural respectability," to use Niebuhr's terms, has led to the neglect of the "new poor." Nevertheless, the overwhelming appeal that the Pentecostal sects hold for the lower class requires some explanation in view of the fact that the historical churches have by no means lost their lower-class constituency. A much larger proportion of new members joined the sects rather than the churches, but the sects did not simply succeed the churches by taking over their lower-class members; they rather began to compete with them for such membership, and their relative success appears understandable in the light of certain ecological and structural peculiarities of the sects.

The relationship between a particular church or sect and the class structure is reflected, to some extent at least, by its location in a given area. In any sizable settlement residential segregation by social class occurs, and the geographical distribution of institutional facilities must be geared to the pattern of segregation. The location of Protestant temples in Santiago, for example, presents the following ecological pattern.

A total of 111 Protestant temples could be located in the metropolitan area. Thirty-nine, or 35.1 percent of these belong to the historical churches; the others represent thirty-five different sects, mostly of the Pentecostal variety. Except for a German Lutheran Church, no Protestant church was found in the residential area of the upper-middle and upper class. (Barrio de Providencia). The center of the city, circumscribed by Mapoche Ricer, Alameda O'Higgins and Quinta Normal contains five historical churches and, on its periphery, one "Baptist Pentecostal" temple. This area contains the civic center, top business establishments, recreational facilities, office buildings and numerous middle-class apartment houses. No Protestant church lies in the immediate vicinity of the center, but as one moves towards the southern, western or northern districts of the city Protestant temples become increasingly frequent.

To judge by the buildings, the transitional and lower classes predominate in these sectors. Interspersed among the Pentecostal temples, one finds a varying number of historical churches. North of the Mapoche River there are two Methodist and two Baptist churches against nineteen sectarian temples. West of the main railway track, two Methodist, one Presbyterian, and two Baptist churches are located among nine Pentecostal temples. The southern sector, the most industrialized of all, has four Presbyterian, three Baptist and two Methodist churches, but twenty-two Pentecostal temples. In the southeastern districts, next to Providencia, fifteen Pentecostal temples, but only two small Baptist churches could be located. The remaining churches lie in the suburbs, *poblaciones callampas* (shanty towns) and lower-class housing developments.

Within the city districts under scrutiny, the number of Pentecostal temples increases as one moves away from the center toward the periphery, while the proportion of historical churches remains either constant or diminishes. In Temuco, São Paulo, and Rio de Janeiro we were able to discover a similar pattern of distribution.

Many of the historical churches, especially in Santiago, have small constituencies, while Pentecostal temples in their immediate vicinity may be attended by one thousand or more people. This discrepancy tends to increase as one moves towards the *poblaciones* which form an outer ring around Santiago. In Población Los Nogales, for example, 563 residents declared themselves Protestants. Among these, not more than forty-two, or 7.5 percent belonged to historical churches (thirty-one Methodists and eleven Baptists). The rest were Pentecostals, except ten, who were members of Jehovah's Witnesses.

In order to explain the competitive advantages of the sects we

need not repeat what has been said about the functional compatibility between Pentecostalism and lower-class culture. Our own findings confirm what John L. Gillin wrote about these affinities in 1910:
"Sects originate generally in the lower classes which have been shut
out from any part in the socializing process." The lower classes, he
continues, "are not represented in the state as it exists, consequently
they organize themselves so as to be able to deal as classes with the
upper classes." (Gillin, 1910:239.)

The Pentecostal sects of Chile and Brazil are class organizations,
the historical churches are not. Like most sects, the Pentecostalists
refuse to accept the traditional symbols because these are symbols
of the upper classes. The Pentecostal sects are protest movements
against the existing class structure, while the historical churches, to
the extent that they include members of the middle and upper classes,
clearly accept such traditional values as educational and occupational
achievements, wealth, political power positions, and the like. In fact,
they attempt to reconcile class tensions and antagonisms in their own
structures. Their accomodative attitude makes them less attractive
to those who seek redemption from the evils of a social order which
is felt to be unjust.

The aggressiveness of the sects if further reflected in their approach
to the organized diffusion of the Gospel. The sects thrive on proselytism; every active member is not just a churchgoer but a missionary
who does not recoil from the ridicule and contempt which the public
may heap upon him. In the cities of Chile the historical churches
have virtually withdrawn from street-corner evangelism which is held
to be incompatible with the dignity and respectability of their constituency. To preach in the public square implies to be confused with
the *canutos*, a designation which has become almost synonymous with
a social stigma.

The Brazilian churches are more aggressive, but in both countries
the boundless missionary zeal of earlier times has given way to a
more cautious attitude that in many local congregations has resulted
in almost complete abstention from any missionary effort whatso-
ever. In its stead, one hears nowadays much talk about "consolidation." "The leader of our church believes" one Chilean critic remarked, "that the mission field lies in Africa, Korea, India, or China
but not in Santiago or any other part of Chile. When I criticized the

lack of missionary zeal in our church, I was told that I was stepping out of line."

A further advantage of the Pentecostal missionaries is to be seen in their class origin associated with the lack of formal training. They are not given opportunity to develop status aspirations in an institution of higher learning. Their "low" level of living enables them to work anywhere and under any conditions. As Davis (1943:85) accurately stated, "such humble leaders can live upon an economic level which would be impossible for highly trained men."

It would be unrealistic, however, to describe the relationship between the Pentecostal sects and the class structure solely in negative terms of abstention and protest. The sects do not live in Utopia; their members cannot withdraw from the dynamics of sociocultural change, and more often than not they are engulfed by it. True enough, as a rule they do not cultivate the ideals of economic and professional advancement; their attitude toward educational achievements is that of indifference or antagonism. Mere literacy is deemed sufficient because a *crente* must be able to read the Bible, but even this modest level of aspiration is not incompatible with a measure of bourgeois respectability.

The practice of asceticism never fails to be of some help in attaining at least a modest degree of economic security. The rigidity of the class structure and the lack of economic opportunities in Chilean society make such changes very difficult. Consequently, the Chilean sects are socially much more homogeneous than their Brazilian counterparts. Especially in São Paulo, it is not unusual for white-collar workers and small businessmen to belong to the Christian Congregation or to the Assembly of God. In the most urbanized areas of São Paulo, perhaps one fifth of the Pentecostals belong to the transitional class and a few have been able to accumulate considerable wealth. Léonard (1953:72–73) has observed:

Incidentally, there too the Protestant communities are clearly and rapidly undergoing the general process of *embourgeoisement* because of their conditions of convinced and educated minorities rather than an alleged idiosyncracy between Reformation and capitalism; observers are impressed by the petit-bourgeois nature of the congregations, at least in the cities.

Assuming that further economic development and increased social

mobility will change the class composition of the Pentecostal movement, a change from "otherworldliness" to a "worldlier" value orientation, from protest to increasing conformity may be expected. At
least this seems to be a viable hypothesis for future studies of this sort.

28
Political Behavior

Historical Commitments and Protestant Withdrawal

✤ The political forces predominent in Brazil and Chile in the second
half of the nineteenth century were either openly hostile or indifferent
to the emerging Protestant churches. The union between the Catholic
church and the state imposed constitutional restrictions upon any
form of heterodoxy, particularly upon practices interfering with the
monopoly of the Catholic church. To the average Protestant, politics
mostly meant defense of the status quo, and thus participation in
party politics would have been equivalent to self-destruction. Furthermore, to identify oneself with a political party, no matter how
lofty its overt program, would have implied endorsement of the
covert "immoralities" which public opinion and the press incessantly
attributed to party politics. Thus political abstention was consistent
with the general withdrawal from "worldly" activities in which the
crente might become involved to the detriment of the ideal of living
up to the principles of his faith.

This attitude, however, has changed during the last three decades,
at least within the historical churches, while the position of the Pentecostal sects has been determined by a number of contradictory factors
that make generalizations difficult. These changes are roughly concomitant with the gradual democratization of the political process in
Brazil and Chile, especially with the development of opportunities
for minority groups to protect themselves more effectively against
discrimination. In view of the structural differences between the two
countries, it is not surprising that the political activation of the Protes-

tant bodies should have begun at different times, proceeded in different fashions and with widely varying intensity. Above all, one should be aware of the fact that Chile terminated its official association with the Catholic church only in 1925, or thirty-five years after Brazil had taken the same step by enacting its first republican constitution. The main differences between the Brazilian and Chilean party systems, as they developed during the first half of the twentieth century, may be defined in the following terms:

1. The Brazilian party system, according to the decentralized federative political structure of the nation, tends to be regional rather than national, while the highly centralized political structure of Chile created a nationwide party system with components tightly controlled by their headquarters in Santiago. This difference of course reflects differing constitutional arrangements providing for full-fledged elected state and municipal governments in Brazil, but confining local democracy in Chile to the election of inexpressive and almost powerless communal governments. (The Brazilian constitution of 1946 requires that all political parties be national rather than regional. Whether or to what extent this measure has contributed to an actual centralization of party politics is open to question.)

2. Brazilian political parties usually shun ideological commitments beyond the general recognition of democratic principles, but most Chilean parties are, by statute or tradition, committed to Catholicism, socialism, "Christianity," anti-clericalism, or laicism.

3. The Brazilian party system is relatively fluid or unstable, while the Chilean system has a hard core of stable parties surrounded by a fringe of somewhat fluid groups that tend to split or combine under different labels in periods preceding national elections.

The Growing Political Awareness of the Historical Churches

Considering everything, it would seem that the Brazilian situation offered chances for an earlier and more massive participation of Protestants than the political situation in Chile. Since ideological commitments were rarely involved, Brazilian Protestant voters felt free to pick candidates deemed personally irreproachable, while the regional character of most parties made nationwide commitments dispensable. Of course, the totalitarian interregnum between 1930 and 1946, except for three years, offered little opportunity for the exercise of political rights, but since 1946 the growing Protestant contingent in the general electorate reflects not only increasing participation but also a growing church membership. In most parts of Brazil, Protestants are now recognized as a political force to reckon with, and most candidates running for office carefully avoid commitments that could alienate the Protestant electorate.

The extent to which Protestants are now encouraged to participate in political activities is reflected by the attitudes of thirty-six pastors of the Presbyterian Church of Brazil. Asked whether Protestants should protect their civil rights, especially freedom of religion, through some kind of political action, twenty-seven answered affirmatively. In fact, all pastors except one declared that they had encouraged the members of their church to participate in political elections, but only six admitted having suggested a particular party. All others were unanimous in that their action should be limited to emphasizing the importance of fulfilling civic obligations within a democratic society. They found that Protestants should be allowed to choose freely from at least those parties that were not in any sense opposed to the restriction of civil rights anchored in the constitution.

There was a rather widespread belief that none of the existing parties actually expressed the goals of Protestantism and that therefore the Protestant voters should be influenced by individual qualifications of candidates rather than by party platforms. One respondent thought that all Protestants including pastors should be integrated in a national organization for political action. Another respondent suggested that in local and state elections Protestant candidates be introduced to the congregation, and the members be invited to vote for them.

Two pastors voiced support for the Brazilian Labor Party for being "easy to understand." Three pastors thought that Protestants should be represented in all positions of importance in the country. Another one declared that he always conveyed to his congregation any information he had about the qualities and shortcomings of individual candidates running for office. Two pastors expressed their preference for the National Democratic Union because they believed it to be the party more in favor of individual liberty than any other. It was also believed most strongly committed to fighting corruption and disrespect of the law. There was only one case of militant anti-communism. It was generally felt, mostly by implication, that democracy was the best political organization for Protestants because it protected their rights as a religious minority.

The same thirty-six ministers were asked whether they knew cases of Protestants having been elected to municipal or city councils. Since official records do not show the religious affiliation of the members of municipal and state legislatures, we attempted to gather as much information as possible on this point in personal interviews. If the results are far from complete, they at least convey an impression of how widespread active political participation of Protestants in Southern Brazil is. The replies cover five states, but as most ministers interviewed come from localities situated in the state of São Paulo, the latter is overrepresented. The replies reported a total of thirty-four legislative bodies with one or more Protestant members. Almost all pastors referred to localities in which they were residing then, or had resided at some time in the past.

Since these data were collected, the number of Protestants including Pentecostals elected to legislative bodies seems to have increased considerably, as the following information on Manoel de Melo, a well-known sect leader in São Paulo, indicates.

Within the past three years many of his Evangelical candidates have been elected. Just recently, a fellow Pentecostal preacher was elected, with the Missionary's support, to be a federal deputy from the state of São Paulo. Another Pentecostal preacher was elected in the same way as a state senator. In the state of São Paulo, he has seventy-two whom he has supported in their elections to local city councils and are called *vereadores municipais*. He believes that the Evangelicals must place their own candidates in office and begin the long-needed reforms from within through them. [Read, 1965: 155.]

Asked whether in their opinion the political record of the Protestant members of legislative bodies was in any sense different from that of non-Protestants, all pastors except one replied that there were indeed differences, which they proceeded to formulate. Thirty-five pastors virtually agreed that Protestant legislators

—did "not defend personal interests"

—were "not sectarian" in the exercise of their mandate

—defended "freedom of conscience"

—had "more respect for human rights"

—were willing to assume "more moral responsibility"
—worked for "honest administration"
—"worked more"
—were "more interested in solving social problems"
—showed "greater strength of conviction"
—had "more idealism"
—had "a moralizing influence upon municipal councils"
—showed "more responsibility in spending taxpayers' money"
—showed "more interest in public welfare"
—had "more moral courage"
—were "more progressive"
—were "more democratic."

In 1960, four members of the national Chamber of Deputies were Protestants representing four different political parties (Socialist party, Brazilian Labor party, Republican party and National Democratic Union). All four were members of a Committee for Education and Culture. According to one of our non-Protestant informants, a member of parliament himself, three of these Protestant congressmen, one Baptist and two Presbyterians, always act as a "monolithic block" whenever a proposal of interest comes up for discussion. "Of course," added our informant, "like all politicians they defend their personal interests and those of their party, but they never forget that they are Protestants."

In order to determine the attitudes towards political participation among future members of the Protestant clergy, the student bodies of two theological schools in the state of São Paulo were asked whether, in their opinion, they ought to participate in local party leadership and in municipal government as elected councilmen or mayors. Out of a total of forty-three students of a Methodist institution four (9.3 percent) felt they ought to be members of a local party board of directors and six (13.9 percent) declared to be willing to participate in local government. Among the seventy-five students of a Presbyterian institution, there were twenty-three (30.6 percent) who felt obligated to participate in local party leadership, but only twelve (16.0 percent) showed willingness to run for office in the municipal government of their future place of residence. Most students seemed to feel that they could not be simultaneously minister and councilman without neglecting the obligation of either office or both.

Since party leadership requires only occasional action, refusal to participate cannot be ascribed to conflicting demands on time. The contrast between Methodist and Presbyterian students suggests a relationship with their position in the class structure. The attitude of withdrawal from "worldly activities" tends to become irrelevant as the status of the group rises within the social structure. There is little sense in denying a "world" which seems to reward one's spiritual endeavor with a measure of economic success and social recognition. A gradual reversal of the former attitude of withdrawal is obviously under way, at least in the historical churches, but it is geared to the general process of upward mobility of the individual denominations.

The Presbyterian churches have gained more ground among the upper social strata than any other Protestant church in Brazil; they not only have a wider variety of human resources to draw upon for leadership, they also seem to feel more at ease than the members of any other church in using these resources for worldly purposes which offer opportunities, as they say, to inject their "uncompromising ethical precepts" into a society deemed to be in dire need of such injections.

In localities where the working class looms large, the Braziliar. Presbyterian Church has made some effort to "awaken the class con·sciousness" of its members. Especially prepared teams of workers try to recruit members for the labor unions. Defective and weak as these unions may be, Presbyterian leaders nevertheless regard them as the most effective instrument available to defend the interests of the working class.

The attitudes of the sects toward participation in politics vary from thorough involvement to aloofness and explicit opposition. Manoel de Melo, leader of *Brasil para Cristo,*

has taken a political position that other religious leaders have not dared to take, but are apparently glad to see taken by someone. Several times he has endorsed political candidates and engaged in vigorous political campaigns to get them elected, only to be disappointed after all the votes were counted and the results known. He discovered that whether they won or lost, political loyalties were only temporary expedients and only skin-deep. Several candidates he helped elect gave him hardly as much as a hearty thank you. Consequently, the missionary has decided to put only Evangelicals as candidates for political office. [Read, 1965:155.]

In contrast to the point of view of Manoel de Melo and a few other sect leaders, the charter of the Christian Congregation "does not admit political parties of any description in the congregations" but recognizes the legal obligation of its members to cast their votes in political elections. So far as the election to political office is concerned, the charter is quite explicit:

No brother who has been called to serve the Ministry of the Word of God, or holds any kind of office in the work of God, is allowed to accept political positions.

Even for other brethren who, without holding office (in the sect), wish to serve God with a tranquil conscience it is advisable not to accept political office.

While it is possible to distinguish a sense of moral proselytism in the way Brazilian Protestants participate in politics, the predominant motive inducing Chilean Protestants to play an active role in political elections seems to be the felt need to protect the late conquest of complete religious freedom against restrictive schemes attributed to certain ultramontane groups. In Brazil, there is a distinct feeling of urgency about the civic mission of Protestantism, at least in the historical churches. According to the opinion of one outstanding Brazilian Protestant member of one of the southern state legislatures, political emancipation of the Protestant churches has been far too slow to take full advantage of the events that are changing the structure of Brazilian society. He harshly criticized the form of leadership provided by the Protestant clergy, especially what he called the "failure to grasp the golden opportunities of civic leadership" in communities wherein such leadership was not provided by any other group.

No such sense of urgency could be discovered in Chile. The fact that most Chilean parties have strong ideological commitments tends to restrict the possibilities of Protestant participation. The traditional alliance between powerful rightist parties and the Catholic church puts the Protestant minority automatically in a position of defense. Furthermore, the rightist parties are identified with the upper class against which the lower and lower middle classes, including the Protestant citizenry, are struggling for economic survival. This leaves the left wing of the center and leftist parties (excluding the Communist party of course) among which Protestants may choose without imperiling their own ideological position.

Actually the Partido Radical appeared to attract most Protestant voters. It was a representative of this party who attended the religious service celebrating the fiftieth anniversary of the Iglesia Metodista Pentecostal de Chile and who adressed the audience as follows:

The Radical Party, which respects all religious ideas, expresses on this memorable opportunity its respects and its highest considerations for the Iglesia Metodista Pentecostal. We know that we owe much gratitude to the Evangelical brethren because their prayers and also the aid of their votes permitted the election of the candidates of the Partido Radical. And this obliges us, as respectable citizens, to lend you our support in order that the work you are carrying out be every day more effective, more magnificent and more ample.

Mr. Bishop, in the name of the Partido Radical I express my congratulations, and I wish to declare that all deputies of the Partido Radical are at the disposal of your church in order to co-operate in the task of making our country every day worthier and more beautiful.

A pastor of the same church in Temuco, informed us that the members of his congregation had indeed voted for Bossay, the candidate of the Partido Radical in 1958. He added that such open support of a political party had been a reversal of the formerly predominant attitude of aloofness. "Nobody has the right to criticize the political situation of the country," he emphasized, "without participating in the elections. In the future, I shall follow any political directions issued by church authorities in Santiago."

A random sample of ninety-three Protestants in Temuco and Concepción who were questioned about party membership and participation in recent political elections, revealed relatively strong preference for the Partido Radical. Out of these ninety-three individuals, eighteen (19.4 percent) declared to be members of the Partido Radical, 2 (2.1 percent) were Socialists and 73 (78.5 percent) were not affiliated with any party. In the presidential elections of 1958, thirty-one (33.3 percent) voted for Bossay; twenty-one (22.5 percent) for Alesandri who, without having committed himself to any party, was supported by a coalition of the right and the center; and four (4.4 percent) cast their ballots for Allende, the candidate of the leftist coalition. There was a widespread agreement among Protestant voters that the Radical Party was "more democratic than any other party; more liberal and favored freedom of religion; defended the interests of the poorer and middle classes."

In this, as in many other instances, in Chile as well as in Brazil, we found that membership in a minority group, combined with an incipient or already achieved rise in the class structure, causes Protestants to be genuine protagonists of democracy. They clearly perceive the protective value of constitutional rights in their unobtrusive striving for recognition as a minority and a rising segment of the lower strata.

Political awareness as well as participation in political activities seems to be lowest in urban areas with heavy concentration of Pentecostals. In Población Nogales, a sample of 563 Protestants contained only fifty-two, or 9.2 percent non-Pentecostals. Of this total only fourteen, or 2.5 percent declared themselves "active in politics." (They were registered voters and/or sympathizers of a political party.) In the control group of 563 non-Protestants, however, forty, or 7.1 percent indicated they were politically "active." This seems to confirm the rather general attitude of aloofness from "worldly" matters that persists among the Pentecostals. Many of our life histories, including those gathered in Brazil, strongly suggest that Pentecostals entertain the notion that "corruption" or "rottenness," believed to be inherent in political activity, "contaminates those who allow themselves to become involved in its devilish designs." There seem to be two conditions that sometimes cause Pentecostals to take part in political action. One is the felt need for defense against suspected or actual encroachments upon religious freedom; the other refers to orders or suggestions issued by sect leaders. These are widely respected because it is God who speaks to them through their leaders.

Concerted Political Action

In 1959, all Pentecostal groups of Temuco had joined an ecclesiastical council composed of the pastors of the different denominations. The council convened for weekly prayer meetings and once every month for "special purposes." Contrary to their usual aloofness, the Pentecostal groups had joined the council because, we were given to understand, it represented a reaction against the proposal of a member of the Chilean Senate who had attempted to reintroduce compulsory instruction in the Roman Catholic doctrine in the public schools of Chile.

The only attempt made in Chile to integrate all Protestant denominations in a civic association with precisely defined political objectives, *not* exclusively devised for protection, is the Unión Civica Evangelica which in 1959 was established in the metropolitan area of Concepción. The fact that this happened in the largest and most rapidly progressing industrial area of Chile, aside from Santiago, can hardly be interpreted as a coincidence. In addition to the city of Concepción, it comprises the port city of Talcahuano, the coal mining districts of Lota and Coronel, the district of Huitchipato with its modern steel plant, and the textile center of Tomé. Twenty-seven Protestant denominations were found in this area and all except three had joined the Union. Two of the outsiders were Pentecostal churches, one being the Iglesia Evangelica Pentecostal, the most rigidly secluded of all Pentecostal bodies, which refused to join as a matter of principle. The other, a small local sect, did not join because its pastor was a candidate of the Democratic Party running for municipal office. The third denomination could not be identified. Political commitments at the top level of some Pentecostal bodies seem to contradict the general attitude of withdrawal from political as well as other worldly interests, but as pointed out before, the very considerable power bestowed on most Pentecostal leaders, the often discretionary use they make of it, and the frequency of schisms arising from personal rivalries, suggests the presence of the "caudillo pattern" which seems to make complete political abstention rather difficult.

The Unión owes its existence to the "sudden realization" that 80 percent of all Protestants in the Concepción area were not even registered voters. For the first time, the leaders of the movement carried out a campaign in order to increase the roll of Protestant voters. The initial number of member churches in the Union was small, yet gradually all joined with the aforementioned exceptions. The eventual acceptance of the Union was determined by three facts that clearly reflect the sort of suspicion surrounding ecumenical endeavors: The organizers were persons of excellent repute in church and community, they did not belong to any political party, and assurance was given that membership in the Union did not in the least affect the independence of the member churches.

The first steps toward the founding of the Unión Civica were taken in meetings of the Unión de Juventudes Evangelicas, an Evangelical

Youth Association affiliated with the Unión de Juventudes Evangelicas de Chile, and, with the Latin American Evangelical Youth Association. A young lay leader of the local Methodist Church played an outstanding role in launching the Unión Civica which finally, after "eight or ten meetings" of local church leaders took its present form as an interdenominational association designed to provide guidance in political matters, particularly in electoral campaigns. A sense of moral proselytism is expressed by those aspects of the program that refer to the social and spiritual responsibilities involved in the ballot "and to the need for honorable men who make Christian ideals prevail in government."

In January of 1960 the Unión met to discuss the way in which the member churches should participate in the forthcoming municipal election. Most of the delegates seemed to think that, once mobilized and registered, the Protestant forces could easily elect one or more *regidores* (council members) in the Concepción area, but it was not clear whether the Union should nominate its own candidate or endorse the candidates of one of the political parties. The Unión eventually agreed upon Protestant candidates uncommitted to any party cause. In the city of Concepción, the four men who had had a leading role in organizing the Unión were also nominated to run for office. Two of them were Methodists, one a Baptist, and the fourth was the pastor of a small local sect. The Methodist lay leader whose initiative and effort had been the most decisive factors in the process of launching the Unión was a lawyer and undoubtedly of middle-class extraction.

There is little doubt that the Unión would never have been launched without the initiative of Protestants affiliated with the historical churches. The fact that the Unión represents the only case of concerted political action among Chilean Protestants seems to be related, in part at least, to the relative weakness of the historical churches. Nothing compares with the two Presbyterian churches of Brazil and their outstanding leadership in political endeavors. Furthermore, the absence of a meaningful municipal government in Chile discourages political action at the local level.

29
Protestantism and Education

Protestantism and Education

✤ The nature of the changes which the Protestant missionaries endeavored to introduce into the prevailing value orientation of the recipient societies inevitably led to a rather absorbing concern with formal education. The high rate of illiteracy found among the social classes from which most Protestant converts were recruited was intolerable to the missionaries. It was necessary that a Protestant be able at least to read the Bible and the religious tracts which the colporters, often at the risk of their life, distributed among the people. Thus, very early in the history of proselytic Protestantism in Chile and Brazil teaching became closely associated with preaching. Schools had to be provided at any cost, and the missionaries were willing to go to any length to inculcate the need for education upon their congregations. Besides, how could the level of living of the lower class be raised without providing the basic instrument of literacy?

In order to compare the literacy of Protestants with that of non-Protestants we examined information supplied by thirty-five Presbyterian parishes in São Paulo and neighboring states. Eight of these had no illiterate members at all, twenty reported an illiteracy rate varying between 1 and 5 percent. In three parishes it varied between 6 and 10 percent, and another three had from 11 to 20 percent illiterate members. Only one parish in Minas Gerais reported a very high illiteracy rate of 87 percent. The average rate for all thirty-five parishes amounted to 3.54 percent. No recent comparative data for Brazil are available, but in 1950 the average illiteracy rate in Brazil was 51.65 percent; and in São Paulo state, where most of the thirty-five parishes are located, it was 34.63 percent. Although these rates may have been somewhat reduced since, they certainly are still several times as high as the average figure reported for these thirty-five Presbyterian congregations (Anuário, 1959:353). Even in the cities where more schools are usually available, Protestant congregations are more literate than the population as a whole. In a Methodist parish of suburban Rio de Janeiro, composed predominantly of members of the lower class, Saunders found an illiteracy rate of 7.1 percent which compares favorably with the 19.6 percent of the Federal District, now the state of Guanabara (Saunders, 1955:60). All historical churches have been actively engaged in promoting primary education, not only by organizing, staffing and maintaining numerous schools, but also by instituting *cursos de alfabetização* (instruction in reading and writing) for adult members whenever the need arises. No figures are available on the role which the Pentecostal sects play in primary education. Although intellectual pursuits are usually discouraged, all our Pentecostal informants stressed the need to be literate, and numerous congregations actually make some concerted effort to reduce illiteracy among their members.

Chile has been more successful in its attempts to provide at least a primary education for its citizenry. In 1952, only 19.4 percent of all Chileans more than fifteen years of age were illiterate (Statistical Abstracts, 1957:8). Consequently, differences between Protestants and non-Protestants are apt to be less pronounced so far as illiteracy is concerned. To test this hypothesis, the shantytown of Los Nogales was chosen. It turned out that among its 563 Protestants only sixty-six, or 11.7 percent, were illiterate, while in our "control group" of non-Protestants this number amounted to seventy-seven individuals, or 13.7 percent of the total.

While a difference of 2 percent between Protestants and non-Protestants does not seem significant, the same two groups differ sharply insofar as the existence of reading habits is concerned. Among the 563 Protestants of Los Nogales, sixty, or 10.6 percent, are not in the habit of reading anything at all. Among the 563 non-Protestants (selected at random), however, this figure amounted to 201, or 35.6 percent of the total. Although the significance of this difference can scarcely be doubted, it seems difficult to determine just what it means. About half of all Protestant readers satisfy their intellectual curiosity with the Bible, religious pamphlets, and magazines. Of the remaining half, only a few seem to go beyond daily newspapers and popular magazines (most answers were too vague for an accurate classification of preferred reading materials). No information was given about the extent to which these materials were read nor the amount of time spent in reading them. The only conclusion that can conceivably be justified in that Protestantism, even in its openly anti-intellectual versions, has somehow contributed to render literacy more functional, for whatever a person reads it seems to satisfy some need or desire.

The Traditional Educational System and Protestant Innovations

Our attempt to interpret the data on Los Nogales points to some of the basic differences between Protestant education and traditional Latin American education. As most other innovations introduced by Protestant missionaries, the new education was at the same time Protestant *and* North American. This is to say that it was, at least in the beginning, as much concerned with Bible studies and the transmission of Protestant ethics as it was action-centered and pragmatic in its outlook. At any rate, it was almost diametrically opposed to the prevailing Latin American emphasis on the humanities, including dialectic and rhetoric. The fact that the middle and upper classes of the recipient societies very soon took to the Protestant *ginásios, colégios,* and *liceus* indicates that there was a felt need for a major change in a venerable tradition, the foundations of which had been laid by the teaching orders of the Catholic church, especially the Jesuit fathers.

The demand for change in the existent system of secondary education ought to be examined in the light of its eight most salient characteristics:

The traditional school including the university was authoritarian. The principle of the *magister dixit* prevailed. The student was not encouraged to scrutinize critically and discuss materials presented by the teacher.

Lessons were dictated and committed to memory by the students without giving much thought to the actual assimilation of knowledge.

Emphasis was placed on language, literature, history, and geography. To the extent that the sciences were taught at all, the student depended on the textbook, the dictated lesson, and the formulae written on the blackboard and subsequently memorized. There was little or no experimentation in the laboratory.

A great many subjects were taught simultaneously without much effort to explore any particular one in depth. This so-called *enciclopedismo* has often been criticized by Latin American educators, yet the actual *reformas do ensino* have done very little about it.

The teaching programs were designed to imitate European models rather than to cope with the realities of the students' own society and culture. The creators of the public school system in Chile, wrote Francisco Encina in 1911 (1955:99), "did not understand that the type of education existing in the European countries cannot be transplanted to a less developed country whose evolution occurs in substantially different conditions without causing extremely serious moral troubles."

Teachers with professional training were exceptions rather than the rule. Anybody with a high school or college diploma who needed some additional income was allowed to teach in secondary schools. And the university professor was typically a lawyer, engineer, or physician who was willing to devote a few hours of his busy professional life to teaching.

The sexes were rigidly separated in the secondary schools. Coeducation was incompatible with the traditions of Latin American societies.

Little or no attention was paid to physical education.

Thus was the system at the time the first Protestant secondary schools were established. Unhampered by legal strictures, the missionaries changed the relationship between teachers and students, mostly by encouraging intellectual curiosity and free classroom discussion. The sciences began to be taught on a more experimental and practical basis, a change that undermined the traditional reliance on rote-learning. By adopting coeducation, the Protestant schools attempted, with considerable success, to free the relationship between the sexes from the restrictions of an "obsolete code inspired by the assumption of mutual irresponsibility."

The most difficult problem the missionaries were up against was probably the introduction of a new ethical standard of "honesty." Cheating in examinations was, as one missionary put it, "a game in which the student sought to outwit the teacher and which he pursued like a parlor game without the slightest trace of guilt feelings."

It should be noted that during the first decades of the twentieth century, secondary and higher education in Brazil and Chile were still allowed to develop without much interference from legislators and governmental authorities. Administrators and teachers alike had sufficient autonomy to change curricula and teaching methods according to the needs of the students and emerging trends of modern education. Taking full advantage of this situation, the Protestant institutions soon enjoyed the reputation of offering the most progressive secular education available in Brazil and Chile (as in some other countries in Latin America).

Samples of the "Anglo-Saxon" educational system, the Protestant *colégios* attracted the patronage of numerous middle- and upper-class families, even if these showed little or no interest at all in the religious foundations upon which these institutions were erected. At any rate, a very large percentage, sometimes the majority of the students, enrolled in Protestant schools came and still come from non-Protestant families. To attract non-Protestants and to convert or at least to expose them to the influences of "Protestant culture" was one of the main objectives of the schools, but the question as to whether they actually performed that function was, in the beginning at least, a highly controversial issue within the Protestant churches. In fact, it contributed, as already pointed out, to the schism of the Presbyterian church in Brazil, and a good many Brazilian Baptists resisted their American brethren who felt that schools were necessary "to educate the children of Baptists and to facilitate the evangelization of the Brazilian fatherland." (Crabtree, 1937:126.)

In the previously quoted manifesto of the Brazilian Baptists the opposition was formulated as follows (Léonard, 1951:429):

Education follows evangelization, but evangelization does not follow education. Besides, experience teaches us that large funds deflected from evangelization and spent on the construction of large *colégios* damage the Cause and delay its progress. The Brazilian fatherland will never be evangelized by the *colégios*. These are excellent subsidiary aids to evangelization as long as they do not deviate from the simplicity and the power of the Gospel, but they are a veritable impediment to evangelization in the opposite case. Experience further teaches us that many such *colégios* grow and become wealthy as they deviate from the Gospel. Many famous universities in the United States constitute irrefutable evidence of what we have just stated. The conversions in our *colégios*, which have been given so much publicity, are mostly hypothetical cases, premature and problematic.

Most American missionaries put the issue of the Protestant schools in a broad cultural context. Crabtree (1937:127), the historian of the Baptist church in Brazil, apparently believed that a transfer of Protestantism was dependent upon a radical change in the traditional culture, and no such change could possibly be accomplished without Protestants' participating in the educational process:

Regardless of the miraculous power of the Gospel in the immediate transformation of the ideas of the individual, the superiority of Baptist doctrines will not be demonstrated to the Brazilian people exclusively in the field of evangelization. The people will be convinced by the fruits of the Gospel. It is precisely in the field of education that the Gospel produces its select and superior fruits, namely, men prepared to speak with power to the national conscience.

There seems to be an irreconcilable conflict between Catholic and Protestant culture which reaches far beyond the realm of pure religion. Crabtree (1937:127) continues,

The two systems conflict with each other as the Reformation abundantly demonstrated in the following propositions: the supremacy of the Bible over traditions; the supremacy of the faith over deeds; the supremacy of the people over the clergy. These principles are basic and have many ramifications. The Gospel encompasses the principles of democracy, individualism, equality of rights, intellectual and religious freedom. And freedom is necessarily accompanied by responsibility.

Catholicism is

by nature anti-democratic. Vis-à-vis the absolute authority of the Church and the passive obedience of the people, the individual is deprived of all responsibility except passively to submit to superior authority in matters of religion. He need not read or study.

Personal responsibility in the face of God forcibly implies individual liberty to read and study the revealed truth in the Word of God. There is no responsibility without freedom. The right of free scrutiny and of private interpretation of the Bible spontaneously springs from personal responsibility.

Political democracy cannot flourish among a people without instruction. The success of Evangelical individualism also depends upon popular education, particularly in an environment dominated by Catholicism. [Crabtree, 1937:128–129.]

True to the tradition of American Protestantism, religion, political democracy, individual freedom and responsibility are perceived as necessary parts of a whole which is saturated with an unflinching faith in education. Needless to say, the American point of view prevailed. The role which the historical churches, especially the Presbyterians, Baptists and Methodists performed in the area of general education is comparable with and intimately related to the pioneer role they played in the field of technological change. The Protestant schools of Brazil and Chile contributed decisively, along with a few secular "foreign" institutions, to a redefinition of educational principles, objectives, and methods. By providing free secondary education to hundreds of Protestant children, they changed, among other things, the prevailing notion that access to *colégios* was a privilege of the "elite." In principle and practice, the Protestant institutions thus deviated from the accepted social function of the traditional secondary school system which by its very nature lent countenance to the existing class structure.

Rather than reinforce the status quo, the Protestant school system accelerated upward social mobility by awakening an increasing number of people to the opportunities of a changing culture and by making it possible for them to fill the many specialized roles of an emerging industrial society. What Saunders (1955:18) found in a Methodist working class parish in suburban Rio de Janeiro could be generalized without incurring the risk of exaggeration.

An individual will become converted to Protestantism, and as a result of the acquisition of the group's value system will be motivated to learn to read, in turn stimulating his children to pursue their studies as far as possible. As a result of higher educational achievement, the children obtain better paying jobs. The grandchildren often are property owners and achieve middle-class status. In one case at least, that of the church member with the highest income ($500.00 per month), the ascent in the social scale was made in the second generation of Protestants. This person's grandfather was Catholic. His father was converted to Protestantism and earns his living as a night watchman, while the individual in question owns an automobile and over $10,000 worth of property.

The geographical distribution of the principal Protestant institutions is such that the educational needs of each major area with a large Evangelical population are, to some extent at least, taken care of. In Brazil, Recife, Rio de Janeiro, Belo Horizonte, São Paulo and Porto Alegre are seats of major institutions, including primary and secondary schools, often a business academy and a normal school for teachers and, in a few cases, one or more *faculdades* (colleges). In Chile, comparable schools are located in Temuco, Concepción, Santiago, and Iquique.

Furthermore, a few smaller towns in Brazil and Chile have become centers of Protestant educational institutions whose "output" exceeds local or even regional needs. The outstanding examples of such localities are Presidente Soares and Lavras in Minas Gerais (Brazil), Londrina in Paraná (Brazil), and Chillán in Chile. The Instituto Filadelfia in Londrina appears to be a particularly outstanding example of concerted Protestant action. Londrina, the regional capital of one of the richest agricultural areas of Brazil, developed within thirty years from a tiny frontier settlement to a modern city of 70,000. The Instituto was founded in 1945 as a sort of nonprofit corporation whose original shares were acquired by the local Presbyterian, Methodist, and Baptist churches. The president and the vice-presidents are members of the Brazilian Presbyterian church, the president being at the same time a member of the state legislature. The Instituto Filadelfia, which is coeducational, maintains a *grammar school*, *ginásio* (first "cycle" of a secondary school), a *colégio* (second "cycle" of a secondary school), a normal school for grammar school teachers, a business academy and a small *faculdade de filosofia* (liberal arts college). There is also a *escola noturna* (night school) for those who are working their way through college. In 1960, a total of 2,500 students were enrolled in the Instituto Filadelfia. Of these, 10 percent were Protestants, a proportion which directly corresponds to the percentage of Protestants in the total population of the town (7,000 out of 70,000). The majority of the teachers were Protestants. In 1960 the *Instituto* was in the midst of a vast expansion program including four dormitories, a swimming pool, a soccer field, tennis courts, and a large gymnasium.

Like so many other Protestant institutions, the Instituto Filadelfia is respected by the local population for its "liberal attitudes" in educational matters. *There is no religious proselytism*, but daily Bible classes are offered for the Protestant student body and for non-Protestants who wish to attend.

The Instituto Filadelfia is certainly a far cry from the ideal which such missionaries as Crabtree had in mind when they emphasized the need for Protestant schools to "evangelize the Brazilian fatherland." In Londrina, the concerted effort of the historical churches created an institution whose secular functions clearly prevail over its religious ones. It acts, as do all Protestant schools in Brazil and Chile, as a channel of upward social mobility, *not solely for a Protestant minority, but for the population at large irrespective of religious affiliation.*

In contrast to Londrina, Presidente Soares is located in a highly conservative region with neither the drive nor the resources of northern Paraná. Located in the southeastern part of Minas Gerais, the town became the center of an agricultural *municipio* with a population of approximately 9,800 (1959). Of these, 2,800 live in the town proper. The first settlers were of European Protestant stock. In 1896, an American Baptist missionary attempted to found a congregation, but apparently the settlers rejected the unfamiliar idea of baptism by immersion, and the following year the Baptist was replaced by an American Presbyterian missionary.

By 1902 there already was an organized Presbyterian congregation with 105 communicants. In 1907 an Evangelical school was added which in 1923 developed into a full-fledged high school, the Ginasio Evangélico do Alto Jequitibá, as the town was called at that time. The extraordinary success of this Presbyterian institution made it necessary to add, in 1944, the Brazilian version of the junior college, designed primarily to prepare candidates for the universities. The *colégio* became the main attraction and the economic mainstay of Presidente Soares, which possessed neither industry nor any other source of urban development other than a few rather modest business establishments. The school attracted numerous students from the surrounding area, and since 1940 many families have moved to Presidente Soares because of the school which in 1960 had an enrollment of 715 students taught by 31 teachers. A little more than 50 percent of the students are Protestants.

Presidente Soares is not a predominantly Protestant town. At the present time, only 25 percent of its 2,800 people belong to Presbyterian, Methodist, or Baptist churches. The over-all figure for the entire municipio is 16.5 percent. The "elite" of the town, however, is composed almost entirely of Protestant families, many of which still bear the names of early settlers. The best houses and all important business establishments are owned by Protestants. One local Protestant constructed private water works which supplies water to other residents.

Otherwise, there is little economic progress in the *municipio*. The farmers stick to their traditional agricultural techniques, the availability of jobs for the graduates of the Colegio is extremely limited and most graduates consequently leave the region to seek suitable jobs. In fact, Presidente Soares has been educating its Protestant youth for other communities. São Paulo City; Rio de Janeiro; the Rio Doce Valley in Minas Gerais with its recent industrial developments; North Paraná, which since 1930 has become one of the fastest developing areas of Brazil; and, since World War II, Volta Redonda, with the largest steel mill in South America, have absorbed most of the migrants from Presidente Soares. The number of migrants from Presidente Soares was large enough in some of these localities to create new Presbyterian congregations.

It is thus safe to say generally that the possibility of the Protestant minority becoming a *privileged group by force of its own educational system and inherent chances for social ascent, has been eliminated by making the institutions accessible to non-Protestants as well.* This function of the Protestant educational system is becoming gradually more effective as the secondary school system expands and reaches an increasingly larger percentage of people whose parents had only the advantages of grammar school education.

Half a century ago, when secondary schools were generally considered a privilege of the "elite," the Protestant institutions attracted, as pointed out before, numerous non-Protestant students of upper-class extraction. Many of these students remained life-long friends of "their" school and of Protestant education in general. Whenever the distinctive traits and acquired rights of these institutions were challenged by the foes of Protestantism, they found loyal and able defenders among their non-Protestant alumni who more often than not occupied positions of considerable power in the political structure. Naturally, the defenders invariably enhanced the usefulness of these schools as samples of progressive education not otherwise available. There is little doubt that the educational system created by the churches thus contributed to the consolidation of Protestantism in Brazil and Chile.

Secularization of Protestant Schools

The availability of Protestant education to non-Protestants and the effects it had, either on the social position of the churches or on the mobilization of a once rigid class structure, gradually reduced the role of the Protestant school as an instrument of evangelization. The continuous presence of large numbers of non-Protestant students, seldom motivated by religious curiosity or interest in anything but a secular education, imposed certain restrictions not only on proselytic activities but on the teaching of religion in general. Unless the trend were reversed, the Protestant schools would soon become secular institutions where a minority of Protestant pupils would be exposed to a few Bible classes while the rest of the student body would remain almost untouched by religious instruction.

Actually, the trend could not be reversed, and in most institutions the contact which the majority of the students had with religion was eventually reduced to a brief weekly "chapel service" whose meaning to the student body was so questionable that, for example, Mackenzie College in São Paulo recently decided to abolish it altogether.

Significant in the present context seems to be an article which *El Mercurio,* the most influential newspaper of Chile, devoted to the services of an outstanding American educator who after twenty-six years retired from the directorship of Protestant Santiago College.

Arriving here without knowing the language, the customs and the scale of values of the people of this country, she conquered the esteem of everybody and the love of all who witness her unfaltering efforts. . . .

Santiago College is heir to an honorable tradition. The couple La Fetra advanced it, under their leadership, to the top of the secondary colleges of Chile when the *liceos* for girls had barely started. Her leadership of twenty years imparted to the courses of study the characteristics of well pronounced progress and liberalism. . . .

One of the great virtues of Elizabeth Mason as an educator lay in the fact that she understood that educational structures cannot be imported from any country, not even from the United States, without adjustments to the needs, both past and present, of the nation where they are to render services. She furthermore understood that educational and formative work cannot be carried out without a psychological environment in which administration, teachers and pupils feel united by ties of comprehension, mutual respect, and happiness in the performance of a common and noble task. [Labarca, 1959.]

The article recognized indeed the successful transfer of American principles in *secular* education and the pioneer role they performed in Chilean society, but there is not even a suggestion that Santiago College is a Methodist institution whose inception most certainly involved the expectation of religious proselytism. It became a landmark in the history of Chilean secular education instead; it won countless friends in the middle and upper classes, but it hardly contributed to the evangelization of Chile.

The most powerful reason the existing trend cannot be reversed is that in recent decades the educational systems of Chile and Brazil have become the targets of steadily tightening government regulations that leave little if any leeway to denominational initiative. The curricula are rigid in form and encyclopedic in content; they are enforced by a close system of inspection and supervised examinations. Institutions that deviate from the strait jacket of government regulations fail to be "recognized" by the ministry of education and consequently their diplomas have no official status. Thus, the possibilities of "using" schools, particularly secondary schools, as instruments of religious proselytism are remote.

Furthermore, general education in Brazil and Chile is no longer what it was forty or fifty years ago. Public and private schools in both countries have changed their structure and modernized their methods; the system has lost many of its authoritarian characteristics, and the sciences are now emphasized, often to the detriment of the humanities. Os Pioneiros da Educação Nova (the Pioneers of the New Education), a secular movement of the early thirties, exercised a strong influence on the development of education in Brazil, and successive legislative reforms endeavored to adjust education to the needs of an emerging industrial society. In other words, *the Protestant schools have definitely lost their lead as pioneer institutions.* Maddox (1956:104) accurately summarized the situation when he wrote:

The nature of the problem is in part exemplified by the remarks of an executive secretary of a foreign mission board of one of the large denominations. "Thirty or forty years ago," he said, "we were leading the way in the establishment of school standards and curriculums. Today, we are kept busy complying with government regulations." In other words, Latin American governments have stepped into the educational field and have crystallized into laws and regulations many ideas that the early missionaries were sponsoring. Most of the missionary schools are therefore no longer in the forefront of educational developments. They are conforming to existing practices and procedures. Within the prevailing framework they usually maintain high standards, and the examples which they set and the competition which they give are worthwhile. To recapture positions of leadership, however, they must branch off from the traditional and develop new types of schools and new courses in their existing schools.

New types of schools and courses are difficult to develop under a system of restrictive and rigidly centralized government control. Whatever they may turn out to be, they will not be adaptable to denominational proselytism.

PART VI

Conclusions

Conclusions

✠ The introduction of proselytic Protestantism in Brazil and Chile was dealt with as a deliberate attempt at cultural transfer and diffusion. The new faith was seen in terms of its compatibility or incompatibility with traditional Latin American values. Of the three major components of American Protestantism—religion as an emotional experience mediated by revivalism, the social organization of the churches, and the Protestant ethic—the first appears to be mostly in accord with existing patterns, as the phenomenal growth of the Pentecostal sects suggests.

The particular pattern of social organization found in Protestant churches seems at first blush irreconcilable with the traditional social structure of the two countries. As a matter of historical record, however, neither country has ever been fully able to absorb, or to control sizable segments of the population that remained in a state of covert or overt rebellion. Furthermore, at least in Brazil, those segments proved to be capable of expressing their hostility in spontaneous organization as well as in religious dissent.

It has also been overlooked frequently that in both countries there is a rural middle class that could, if it chose to do so, defy traditional values and engage in organized religious dissent. In fact, religious dissent in the form of unorthodox and deviant interpretations of religious doctrine at the folk level has been extremely common and may be attributed to the weakness of the Roman Catholic church as an agency of social control and source of moral authority. Even the Protestant ethic with its emphasis on hard work, thrift, sobriety, and chastity, does not seem to be entirely at variance with existing patterns or historical precedent.

The fact that an increasing number of Brazilians and Chileans adhered to the new faith can only be understood if Latin American culture is seen as a process of continuing change. Protestantism made its first appearance in the wake of widespread secularization that dealt mortal blows to the religious and political hermetism of the colonial period. Protestant progress was slow during the first fifty or sixty

247

years of missionary endeavor, mainly because the rate of culture change was too low and its effects too restricted to make conversion a meaningful mass experience. It could be proved however that Protestantism attracted more followers as the process of culture change gained momentum and the traditional agrarian structure of Brazil and Chile entered a phase of increasing deterioration. In other words, our hypothesis of an historical concomitance between the expansion of Protestantism and the emergence of an industrialized and urbanized society was borne out by the facts.

Further corroboration of a functional relationship between these two phenomena was seen in the ecological distribution of the Protestant population of both countries. It was found that the largest Protestant populations were concentrated in the most urbanized and industrialized areas of Brazil and Chile. On the other hand, relatively small numbers of Protestants are located in areas where the traditional agrarian structure has been preserved to some extent.

Ecological data on São Paulo also indicated, however, that dissemination of Protestantism is not exclusively associated with industrialization and urbanization. There are at least two further conditions favoring receptivity to the new faith. Rural areas that for some reason were bypassed by the hacienda system, and where an independent peasantry was allowed to develop, turned out to be moderately receptive to Protestant proselytism. Secondly, agricultural frontier areas with uprooted, highly heterogeneous populations were found to be highly responsive to Protestant missionary endeavor.

Additional evidence of a functional relationship between the dissemination of Protestantism and sociocultural change is to be seen in the fact that the new faith won most of its followers among the social classes whose formation and chances of social ascent were directly affected by structural changes imposed by the emerging industrial order.

Our data further indicate that the areas of highest Protestant concentration have also received the largest numbers of rural-urban migrants who have been more exposed to the impact of culture change than any other single group.

Only under exceptional conditions can major institutions be transferred from one culture to another without undergoing at least minor changes in the process. A number of organizational and doctrinal schisms took place in Chile and Brazil which satisfied the nationalistic aspiration of the members to rid themselves of the tutelage of foreign mission boards and to pursue the cognitive and emotional objectives of their doctrine more in accord with the cultural heritage of their own society.

To judge by membership size and proselytic zeal, Pentecostalism has proved more adaptable to the aspirations and needs of the masses than any other form of Protestantism. But the adaptability of Pentecostalism can be understood only if the functions it performs with regard to its practitioners are clarified. The organizational pattern of the Pentecostal sects seems to express a protest against the Catholic church and its ally, the ruling class. It does so by pointedly stressing egalitarianism within the sect and by opposing the Catholic principle of an ecclesiastical hierarchy and a highly specialized priesthood with the principles of the primacy of the laity, the priesthood of all believers and a self-made charismatic leadership sanctioned by the Holy Spirit. Pentecostalism thus turns out to be a symbolic subversion of the traditional social order.

Adherence to Pentecostal sects also seems to be a solution to various personality problems manifest in the practice of "vices." By substituting disreputable "vices" for conventional forms of behavior, the convert cleanses himself of social stigma and becomes respectable in the eyes of the in-group and the society at large.

In the changing society of Brazil and Chile, folk Catholicism no longer serves the functions it did in the traditional rural society, mainly because folk Catholicism is a peasant religion adapted to the problems of a peasant culture. The Catholic pantheon is predominantly local; the cult of saintly helpers is centered around local shrines and concerned with rural problems. Migration to cities and rural frontiers tends to alienate people from their local pantheons, and the problems they have to face in their new environment call for different solutions. But there is apparently no solution of continuity between folk Catholicism and Pentecostalism with its heavy emphasis upon the Holy Spirit, miracles, and other mystical experiences. Pentecostalism also continues the ancient tradition of messianism in a new and more exciting way by promising the coming of the deity here and now to the individual believer.

The appeal of Pentecostalism is strengthened by the gifts or powers of the Spirit that make essentially powerless people feel strong beyond natural limits. Seizure by the Spirit also provides a temporary escape from the hopeless squalor of life to the thrills of intense emotional experiences.

The social function of the Pentecostal sect derives from its tightly woven structure in which the *crente* finds opportunity to rebuild his personal community and to find a measure of psychological and economic security.

Some of these functions are also performed by the historical churches, but to a widely varying degree. A comparative study of the three major churches suggests that their attractiveness in terms of membership is, to a considerable extent, a function of their structure. Apparently preference is given to the egalitarian denominations in which the layman is in control of church affairs and the individual congregation enjoys complete autonomy. On the whole, Protestantization may be regarded as a selective process in which functional adaptability to the needs and aspirations of the people is rewarded with the highest membership figures and the most intensive proselytic drive.

The analysis of Protestantism as a factor of sociocultural change requires a distinction between inherent changes and contingent changes. Inherent are all those modifications which are fundamentally inseparable from the emergence of proselytic Protestantism as a social institution. They are found in the organization of churches, sects, and their individual congregations. As emphasized throughout our inquiry, they consist mainly of the primacy of the laity, local autonomy, freedom of disquisition, egalitarianism, and the absence of ecclesiastical hierarchies.

Since congregation and family appear to be tightly interwoven, changes in the traditional family structure are equally inherent in or concomitant with the institutionalization of proselytic Protestantism. An autonomous congregational structure is obviously incompatible with the primacy of family and kinship prevalent in the traditional social order. Thus the Protestant family had to accept a subordinate position within the congregation. Furthermore, the web of social relationships within the immediate family had to conform to the basic norms of the Protestant ethic, a requirement which resulted in the deletion of male sex prerogatives and thus led to more egalitarian relationships between male and female members. If the cultural process comprises major changes, as it does in the emergent industrial order of Chile and Brazil, the Protestant ethic finds opportunity to provide meaning and additional impulse to changes originated by secular forces.

The practice of the Protestant virtues is conveniently rewarded by an emerging industrial civilization that promises a higher level of living to the thrifty, sober, industrious, and well educated. It makes sense to renounce expensive "vices" in order to afford better housing, better clothes, at least some contrivances of modern technology, and a better education for the children, especially if such effort is sanctioned by religious convictions and encouraged by group expectations. The economic significance of Protestant asceticism lies in the fact that it frees part of one's income for the acquisition of things that symbolize a higher level of living.

In a broader sense, being a Protestant often means having opportunities not easily available to non-Protestants. As a rule, non-Protestants assume Protestants to be dependable, honest, and efficient beyond the limit normally expected in Brazilian and Chilean society. Protestants thus become preferred business partners, employees, and servants.

There is actually an acute awareness of and belief in economic advancement among Protestants, particularly among members of the historical churches. But this belief is somewhat commensurate with actual economic achievements as observed in four different communities.

The historical Protestant churches, especially the Presbyterians and Methodists, doubtlessly played a pioneer role in the field of economic and technical development. This role however can no longer be sustained, mainly because a variety of specialized domestic and international institutions have in recent years initiated development activities on a scale that cannot be matched by church agencies, except perhaps on the level of the local community.

Economic advancement has proved equivalent to upward social mobility, and in this sense Protestantism has contributed to loosening up the once tight class structure of Brazil and Chile. If industrialism and the opening of agricultural frontiers created chances for status achievements, Protestantism provided additional sanctions and indeed showed the way by which such objectives could be attained.

Social ascent of individual Protestants also meant ascent of the church as a whole. But the historical churches have not become class-bound institutions. The study of a number of congregations shows that their class composition varies with the social composition of the parishioners rather than with the relative position which each church occupies in the social pyramid.

The historical Protestant churches have also become way-stations to further social ascent. The high aspirational level of these churches often turns out to be self-defeating because a considerable percentage of their more successful members detach themselves from the institution if such a step promises further ascent in an increasingly secularized society.

Although the historical churches have by no means become middle-class institutions, the Pentecostal sects enjoy a number of obvious advantages in their competitive effort to attract the lower classes. The churches assume a rather accomodating attitude toward class cleavages, while the sects have proved attractive to the masses, especially in Chile, by maintaining a value system apparently consistent with the way of life of the lower class.

The former attitude of abstention from political participation characteristic of all Protestant denominations has changed as the political process has undergone a gradual democratization. Except in the Pentecostal sects, participation is now deemed not only possible but even desirable, if only to protect the constitutional guarantees of religious freedom. In Brazil, this change bears a more aggressive character than in Chile, where Protestants still seem to feel that they are defending themselves against a powerful alliance between conservative parties and the Catholic church. In Brazil, thirty-four different legislative bodies have one or more Protestant members, while in Chile only now the Protestants are preparing themselves for a more active participation in politics. In both countries, Protestantism has contributed to a strengthening of democratic principles.

Strong emphasis on literacy and social progress determined the pioneer role of the historical church in the field of popular education. Especially in Brazil, the literacy rate of the Protestant population turned out to be significantly higher than that of non-Protestants. Around the turn of the century the Protestant school was beginning to be accepted by the society at large as a model of modern education deemed more desirable by the middle and upper classes than the obsolete educational system of Latin America. On the whole, the Protestant schools failed to live up to the role of proselytizing agencies assigned to them by their missionary founders. But as secular institutions of learning they succeeded in instilling respect and admiration for Protestant values, particularly among their middle- and upper-class alumni. By opening their doors to Protestants and non-Protestants alike they became significant channels of social mobility, although a general modernization and expansion of the state-operated educational systems and the gradual tightening of legal controls over private school systems have made pioneering rather a thing of the past.

Are there significant differences in the way the two countries responded to Protestantism? Although our inquiry was not focused on this question, and no specific hypotheses were put forth, a brief discussion of our findings may not be amiss. Condensed, these findings may be formulated as follows.

In spite of the fact that there are proportionally more than twice as many Protestants in Chile as in Brazil, the structure of Brazilian society has shown a degree of permeability to Protestant as well as other forms of religious dissent unheard of in Chile. The upper strata of Chilean society have been consistently unresponsive to proselytic Protestantism, while in Brazil the historical churches succeeded in recruiting followers among the traditional elite. Also, the Brazilian middle classes, particularly in the south, have been much more receptive to evangelization than their Chilean counterparts. To the extent that the historical churches cut across class lines, their success or lack thereof certainly lends support to the preceding statement Presbyterianism with its strong appeal to the middle and to a limited extent, also to the upper strata is a flourishing concern in Brazil, while in Chile it is nearly extinct. Brazilian Methodism has a relatively large and slowly expanding constituency, while in Chile Methodism is small and static. Although more successful than any other historical church, the Chilean Baptists lag far behind the Brazilian Baptist Convention insofar as relative membership is concerned.

While in both countries the historical churches reached a high level of achievement in the fields of educational and technical pioneering, the Chilean churches failed to produce the intellectual elite that so enhanced the position of Protestantism within Brazilian society, mainly because in Brazil it appeared to demonstrate the compatibility of traditional Latin American humanism with the value system of historical Protestantism.

The foregoing remarks are of course tantamount to the statement that Protestantism is more heavily concentrated in the lower classes of Chile than in those of Brazil. Lower-class Protestantism is predominantly of the Pentecostal version in both countries, but with some significant differences. The Chilean sects display a folk-like quality in their ways of worshipping and propagating the gospel by personal contact and word of mouth. Yet blended with a seemingly inherent lack of sophistication there is a pointed anti-intellectualism in the rejection of educational achievements above the bare literacy level. Of course, one also finds all this among the Brazilian Pentecostals, but in rural rather than in urban congregations. In the metropolitan areas of Brazil, the sects manifest a degree of sophistication in using the mass media which stand in singular contrast to the rusticity of the Pentecostal congregations in the Chilean cities.

Do the differences between Chilean and Brazilian Protestantism reflect basic cultural diversities between Spanish and Portuguese America? A comparative scrutiny of the available figures concerning Spanish America suggests, not only widely varying reactions to Protestant proselytism, but also an overall predominance of the historical churches over the Pentecostal sects. Chile is often considered, together with Argentina, Uruguay, and southern Brazil, one of the more westernized and progressive countries of South America, yet Chile has proportionally at least twice as many Protestants as Argentina (Damboriena, 1962: 29), and the denominational composition of the Argentine Protestants bears little resemblance to that of Chile. The Pentecostal groups of Argentina constitute only a small minority, and many of its numerous historical denominations are European in origin and designed to serve ethnic minorities of predominantly middle-class standing.

A comparison of Chile with its Andean neighbors seems even less fruitful because none of the Andean countries has been particularly responsive to Protestant proselytism, and nowhere are the Pentecostal sects more than small minorities.

Finally, Mexico has the second largest Protestant population in Latin America. Yet the denominational composition of the 897,227

Mexican Protestants (in 1961) bears no resemblance whatever to the Chilean situation. More than half of all Mexican Protestants are Presbyterians, Baptists, or Methodists, and the Pentecostal sects do not represent more than 25 percent of the total (Damboriena, 1962: 116).

Although the available data on Spanish American Protestantism are far too meager to support categorical statements, it seems reasonable to hypothesize that the way Chilean society reacted to Protestant proselytism is rather unique in Spanish America, and that it resembles the response of Brazilian society more than it does those of the other Spanish American countries.

Some Theoretical Implications

There has been a tendency among social scientists to conceive of culture change primarily in terms of disruption, disintegration, disorganization, or anomie. Customary modes of behavior are said to crumble under the "destructive" impact of innovation, leaving a frustrated and demoralized society. This, however, is presented as a temporary and transitory situation which will be resolved into a new cultural configuration when the people learn reconcile the new with the old.

The emphasis placed on disruptive aspects of change reminds one, in the present context, of the dire prophecies some critics and adversaries of Protestantism proffered about its alleged effects on Latin American culture. From Juan de Egaña's statement that "two religions in a state lead to a struggle which eventually will result in the destruction of the state or of one of its religious parties," to the widespread notion that Protestantism is alien and inadaptable to the Latin American way of life, there has been a long string of such dicta that bear little resemblance to the actual course of events but perhaps reflect the perplexity or sociological myopia of their authors.

To be sure, Protestantism brought some disarray to family and community structures. Some of its disintegrative effects were clearly pointed out on preceding pages, but on the whole there has been less disruption than current theories of culture change suggest or some prophets of doom presaged. If dissemination of Protestantism were singled out of the cultural process and treated as an isolated instance of change, in time and in space, a tendency to magnify its disruptive effects on the traditional social order might perhaps be expected. It has been clearly revealed in the present inquiry that the innovations implied by the acceptance of Protestantism were not isolated at all and should not be treated as such. In fact, they were analyzed as part and parcel of a much more ample and vastly more complex panorama of culture change. The point was made that the diffusion of Protestantism in Latin America would remain totally unintelligible if it were dealt with as a discrete and separate process. Now, the way in which it appears to be related to such complicated and disruptive phenomena as internal migration, urbanization, and industrialization, or, more specifically, to the state of anomie generated by these processes, seems to offer a plausible explanation for the fact that its adoption proceeded with relatively little conflict. The new creed, particularly its sectarian varieties, has found the most widespread acceptance among the less privileged strata of the society, those most affected by the disruptive aspects of culture change. It served, as we have seen, to attenuate frustrations, to solve certain personal and social problems resulting from the breakdown of the personal community, from disease and poverty, from the disorienting amorphousness of the modern city and the rural frontier. *Protestantism thus seems to perform an adaptive function with regard to a series of highly disruptive changes which cannot otherwise be controled or averted. And it seems capable of performing that function because it is change itself—a new, although certainly not the only available, resource for the solution of new problems.* One might anticipate little opposition to cultural devices, however new, which promise relief from pressures, frustrations, and anxieties caused by the massive disruption of traditional ways of life.

This function of Protestantism is by no means unique. In complex situations of change there usually emerge new institutions designed to solve social problems attributable to change, but Protestantism perhaps possesses a unique versatility and scope in the way its adaptive functions are performed, that run from active reform to almost complete withdrawal and otherworldiness.

The preceding interpretation shows Latin American religious pluralism in a slightly new light, at least so far as Protestant denominationalism is concerned. There is probably the assumption that a multiplicity of conditions and circumstances may contribute to the emergence of religious pluralism. Some of the contributing conditions spelled out by Lenski—growth of international trade, increase in economic specialization, and the heightening of class distinctions—were extant in the more advanced areas of Latin America long before religious pluralism began to assume its present shape. (Lenski, 1965: 30–31) It would seem that "state-church alliances" and "political suppression of rival faiths or factions" considerably delayed the deployment of religious pluralism (Lenski, 1965: 31). When freedom of religion was finally established, the differentiation of religious faiths has been following the dividing lines of economic specialization and class distinctions in the broad sense that the less privileged classes became more receptive to Protestant dissent, and that the sectarian versions of the new faith attracted mostly members of the lowest social strata. But structural differentiation obviously fails to explain the almost explosive multiplication of new sects that recruit their numerous followers *among the same social strata*. The objection may be raised at this point that these sects stand essentially for the same beliefs and therefore represent a single movement. Actually, very few students of the Pentecostal sects have paid attention to the internal differentiation of Pentecostalism, and no one—so far as we know—has recognized the structural differences that constitute one of the major analytical themes of our inquiry.

The point we are trying to make is further illustrated by the peculiar sort of religious pluralism found in Brazil. Earlier it was said that, in addition to numerous Pentecostal sects, two other religious organizations, Spiritualism and Umbanda, have recruited their numerous followers, too, among the lower social classes. The Pentecostal sects share with Umbanda and Spiritualism the belief in spirit possession, but otherwise they differ in doctrine and practice from Pentecostalism and from one another. (Willems, 1966:205 ff.). There is no intention here to depict the several million followers of all these sectarian bodies as an entirely homogeneous mass, but whatever structural differentiation there is, it fails to account for the proliferation of discrete religious formulations.

Whatever the answer to this problem may be, it seems unlikely that religious pluralism of the "intra-class" variety could possibly be attributed to any single factor or condition. Inadequate as our data are, they at least suggest a few hypotheses:

1. Quoting Gibbon's remark that the "common people" of ancient Rome reacted to the prevalent religious pluralism by assuming that all existing creeds were equally true, Lenski presents some evidence that the "common people have often reacted in this way." (Lenski, 1965:36.) It is not only that "in much of Latin America . . . Indian and Negro 'converts' to Catholicism have often retained an allegiance to their ancestral faith." (Lenski, 1965:36), but folk Catholicism itself, even without African and Indian ingredients, seems to have an un-limited capacity for the absorption of religious innovations at variance with the teachings of the Church.

Faced with the promising alternatives provided by the Pentecostal sects—promising in terms of previous experiences—and untrammeled by ecclesiastical and political controls, the "common people" of Brazil and Chile have proved highly receptive to the new religion. In contrast to Umbanda and Spiritualism, however, the Pentecostal sects or any other Protestant denomination make no allowance for religious syncretism. Whatever its version, Protestantism insists on doctrinal purity and, more often than not, aggressively opposes com-peting faiths. The very large turnover in sect membership seems to indicate, however, that such exclusiveness is not to the liking of many people. In Brazil, the number of exclusions from Protestant congregations (mostly sects) rose from 66,335 in 1956 to 116,975 in 1960 (*Estatística do Culto Protestante,* 1956, 1960). A similar tendency seems to prevail in Chile, although no comparable figures are available. The way in which many people drift back and forth between various forms of religion, perhaps without ever developing a lasting allegiance to any faith in particular, especially the naiveté with which many Brazilians profess to be Catholics while participating in Umbanda or Spiritualist cults, suggests, not that all existing faiths are perceived as equally true, but that all are regarded as *poten-tially* true. Thus the pattern of religious experimentation, traceable to folk Catholicism, set the stage, so to speak, for the proliferation of new sects.

2. This experimental attitude toward religion developed under conditions known as anomie. This term refers to the weakening or breakdown of traditional social controls as doubts and conflicting attitudes arise about the validity of their underlying moral tenets. In an environment of skepticism and perplexity, the individual finds it

increasingly difficult to choose between modes of thought or courses of action that seem inconsistent, not only with traditional orientations, but with each other as well. This situation is exacerbated if, as in the case of the modern Latin American city, the lower classes represent a mosaic of subcultures which, as a rule, are ill-equipped to cope with the bewildering contradictions and internal clashes of an anomie society. The various alternatives open to the individual run, roughly speaking, from conformity to past traditions—in our case mostly folk Catholicism—to rebellion which would mean adherence to the most radical form of religious deviance available. Religious radicalism, as seen in the perspective of Latin American lower-class culture, is probably to be understood in terms of intransigency with structural and doctrinal tenets of the Catholic church and what it is perceived to stand for within the general society. Thus the Baptist church seems to be more radical than Methodism, and most Pentecostal sects are more radical than any of the historical churches. Yet among the Pentecostal sects *there is a gradient of radicalism,* and to underrate its significance means to misunderstand the kind of religious pluralism under scrutiny. Each schism may be interpreted as a welcome opportunity to express the need for a more radical departure from principles suggesting compromise with the status quo. *In this sense, the organizational schism seems to be a more adequate means of expressing rebellion against the traditional social order than the doctrinal schism.* The sect that breaks away from the authoritarian leadership structure of the mother institution performs an act of rebellion that is probably more meaningful to its followers than the rejection of purely theological principles. To cut down the power of the ministers, or to do away with a professional clergy, to give full recognition to potentially subversive prophets, to dilute financial control among elected boards of elders, and to prevent such activities as the care of the poor, invalid, and old members of the sect from assuming rigid institutional features (and thus from becoming separate power structures); these and similar innovations are perceived as radical departures from the more traditional forms of religious organization. In this sense, there is a relevant connection between the extraordinary adaptability of Protestantism and the form of religious pluralism under scrutiny.

To sum up: Two major characteristics of anomie can be identified in this process: (1) The proliferation of sects exhibiting structural and sometimes doctrinal discrepancies, all competing with one another, the Roman Catholic church, and, in Brazil, with Spiritualism and Umbanda. (2) A floundering mass of followers drifting between religious experiences of various kinds without ever developing a lasting allegiance to any particular sect or faith. (This is not meant to imply that most sects do not have a hard core of loyal followers.)

It has often been recognized, of course, that anomic conditions—once termed social or cultural disorganization—are favorable to the emergence and dissemination of innovations, religious and otherwise. On the other hand, it could be argued that, if schismatic movements experience little difficulty in attracting large followings, it may prove considerably more difficult to hold the fickle crowds and to convert them into hard-core, loyal adherents.

Thus religious pluralism has come a long way, From being geographically and culturally identified with ethnic minorities—mostly German immigrants in Brazil and Chile—it has become a highly pervasive characteristic of both countries, at least in the sense that it is now, or has been for some time, a permanent fixture of all major regions and most communities.

Appendix

TABLE I
SIZE OF AGRICULTURAL HOLDINGS IN BRAZIL

Size	1920 No. of Holdings	1920 Area	1940 No. of Holdings	1940 Area	1950 No. of Holdings	1950 Area	1960 No. of Holdings	1960 Area
Fewer than 10 hs			654,557	2,893,439	710,934	3,025,372	1,499,545	5,923,077
10 hs to fewer than 100 hs	463,879	15,708,314	975,438	32,112,160	1,052,557	35,562,747	1,494,548	47,679,859
100 hs to fewer than 1,000 hs	157,959	48,415,737	243,818	66,184,999	268,159	75,520,717	315,119	86,291,939
1,000 hs to fewer than 10,000 hs	24,647	65,487,328	25,539	62,024,817	31,017	73,093,482	31,175	72,794,549
10,000 hs or more	1,668	45,492,606	1,273	33,504,832	1,611	45,008,788	1,710	52,743,376
No Information	.....	.....	2,964	.....	364	.....	7,387	.....

Information concerning holdings of fewer than 10 hs. were included in category of ten to fewer than 100 hs. (*Anuário Estatístico*, Rio de Janeiro I.B.G.E. Conselho Nacional de Estatística, 1963, p. 55)

TABLE II
AGRICULTURAL HOLDINGS FROM 10 HS. TO FEWER THAN 100 HS. IN FOUR BRAZILIAN STATES

State	1950	1960
Pernambuco	41,296	50,850
Bahia	119,233	161,673
São Paulo	124,778	139,620
Minas Gerais	149,080	199,405

TABLE III

NUMBER OF FARMS AND AGRICULTURAL AREA BY PROVINCES IN CHILE (1916)

Provinces	Under 5 hs	From 5 to 20 hs	From 21 to 50 hs	From 51 to 200 hs	From 201 to 1,000 hs	From 1,001 to 5,000 hs	More than 5,000 hs	Total
Tacna	1,060	159	66	58	3	2	....	1,348
Tarapacá	1,241	27	11	7	3	....	....	1,289
Antofagasta	7	1	1	2	4	....	....	15
Atacama	924	143	51	53	24	8	3	1,206
Coquimbo	3,214	435	122	145	89	37	18	4,060
Aconcagua	2,792	769	126	96	36	8	13	3,840
Valparaiso	1,505	380	196	138	65	51	10	2,345
Santiago	2,457	343	194	260	153	73	15	3,495
O'Higgins	1,616	358	147	115	72	45	6	2,359
Colchagua	5,599	1,019	378	287	149	49	17	7,498
Curicó	3,014	1,138	715	542	253	63	13	5,738
Talca	1,688	1,058	611	448	255	74	17	4,144
Maule	1,926	2,448	1,309	939	307	44	2	6,975
Liñares	1,628	1,274	624	534	263	40	14	4,377
Ñuble	2,037	2,456	1,131	996	362	77	14	7,023
Concepción	2,129	2,387	1,044	748	286	30	....	6,675
Arauco	290	291	320	350	169	40	3	1,473
Bio-Bio	768	1,107	764	680	329	84	24	3,756
Malleco	258	306	727	730	346	97	13	2,477
Cautín	161	373	909	1,185	370	56	5	3,059
Valdivia	967	1,091	1,855	1,667	381	82	14	6,067
Llanquihue	683	1,581	807	1,018	542	105	4	4,740
Chiloe	2,768	3,957	343	76	32	8	....	7,184
Magallanes	27	56	44	28	8	10	43	216
Total	38,759	23,101	12,495	11,122	4,501	1,083	248	91,309

Source: Central Statistics Bureau. Statistical Abstract of the Republic of Chile, Santiago: Sociedad Imprenta y Lito-

TABLE V

PROTESTANTISM IN BRAZIL (1958)
(ACCORDING TO THE EVANGELICAL CONFEDERATION OF BRAZIL)

Churches, Missions & Religious Organizations	I—Organizations				II—Members			III—Workers					IV Sunday Schools			
	Regional Councils	Organiz. Churches	Organiz. Congreg.	Preach. Points	Communicants	Minors	Comm. & Minors	Ordained Ministers and Pastors	Ordain. Mission	Lay Evangelists	Lay Miss. (Teachers, doc, etc)	Students in Seminaries	Number of Schools	Employees or Teachers	Students	Total Enrollment
Brazilian Episcopal Church	3	42	50	43	10,437	39,210	49,647	74	3	25	2	12	102	451	7,211	7,662
Evangelical (Synodical Federation) Lutheran Church	4	1,063		276	212,852	345,233	558,085	202				39	500	500	6,820	6,820
Methodist Church of Brazil	5	311	306	1,017	44,453	21,232	65,685	116	30	69	30	47	647	4,170	44,854	48,994
Free Methodist Church		13		48	1,018	1,000	2,018	8					40	200	1,877	2,077
Presbyterian Church of Brazil	6	504	798	1,887	88,154	70,025	158,179	385		33		74	1,450	10,581	115,182	125,763
Independent Presbyterian Church of Brazil	3	207	190	240	23,733	23,005	46,738	114				34	280	1,600	25,000	26,000
Reformed Christian Church		3	4	6	3,000	2,000	5,000	3				1	1	7	69	76
Presbyterian Mission (Center)		19	344		2,767	1,645	4,412	6	28	10	46	8	83	274	3,365	3,639
Presby. Missions-North, East and West		141	545		7,985		7,985		130	347			210			12,239
Crusade of World Evangelization	3	24		50	960	1,500	2,460	9	25	20	40		45	125	2,100	2,225
Brazilian Baptist Convention		1,411	1,399	2,516	155,865		155,865	899		157			2,381		146,915	146,915
Evangelical Lutheran Church of Brazil			493	231			106,332		108		120	19	57	160	2,572	2,732
Conservative Presby. Church		19	41	76	2,316	2,111	4,427	14	4		3	10	29	118	1,716	1,834
Union of Evangelical Congregational & Christian Churches of Brazil	6	151	98	193	12,619		12,619	112					214	1,250	16,309	17,559
Assembly of God		1,200	2,800		500,000	500,000	1,000,000	600	40	720			4,000	10,000	500,000	510,000
Christian Congregation of Brazil		928			250,000	250,000	500,000						61	87	1,681	1,768
Salvation Army				61			1,321	85					120	230	10,500	10,730
Others					8,000	8,500	16,500									
Totals		6,036	7,068	6,644	1,324,159	1,265,461	2,697,273	2,627	368	1,381	241	244	10,220	29,753	886,171	927,633

TABLE IV

NUMBER OF FARMS AND ARABLE AREA IN CHILE, 1955

Size of Farms	Number of Farms	Percent	Arable Area in hs.	Percent
Fewer than 5 hs.	28,600	23	93,738	1.7
5 to 49.9 hs.	61,700	49.6	672,708	12.2
50 to 199.9 hs.	21,100	17.0	942,894	17.1
200 to 999.9 hs.	10,300	8.3	1,571,490	28.5
1,000 hs. or more	2,700	2.1	2,233,170	40.50
Total	124,400	100	5,514,000	100

Source: Censo Agrícola de Chile, 1955:26

(see fold-out for table V)

TABLE VI

GROWTH OF PROTESTANTISM IN CHILE

Year	Population	Number of Protestants	Per Cent of Total Population
1920	3,753,799	54,165	1.4
1930	4,287,445	62,267	1.4
1940	5,023,539	115,502	2.3
1952	5,932,995	240,856	4.1
1960	7,374,115	411,530	5.6

Source: Censos de Población, 1920, 1930, 1940, 1952, 1960. Dirección de Estadistica y Censos. Chile.

TABLE VII

DISTRIBUTION OF PROTESTANTS IN BRAZIL
BY REGIONS (1960)

Region	Population [a]	Percentage of Total Population	Number of Protestants [b]	Percentage of number of Protestants
North	2,601,519	3.7	50,913	2.7
Northeast	15,677,995	22.1	174,727	9.2
East	24,832,611	35	459,373	24.2
South	24,848,194	35	1,167,484	61.5
Center-West	3,006,866	4.2	45,164	2.4
Brazil	70,967,185	100	1,897,661	100

a. I.B.G.E. Anuário Estatístico, 1962
b. I.B.G.E. Estatística do Culto Protestante, 1960

TABLE VIII
PROTESTANT POPULATION OF ELEVEN CITIES OF MORE
THAN 100,000 IN THE STATE OF SÃO PAULO (1960)

City	Population	Protestant Population	Percent Protestant
Campinas	219,303	6,221	2.84
Guarulhos	101,273	4,081	4.03
Juandiaí	105,335	1,731	1.64
Mogí das Cruzes	100,194	1,603	1.60
Piracicaba	104,309	2,625	2.52
Ribeirão Preto	147,361	2,681	1.82
Santo André	245,147	6,209	2.53
São Caetano	114,421	9,735	8.51
Santos	265,753	8,865	3.34
São Paulo	3,825,351	152,841	4.00
Sorocaba	115,536	12,921	11.18
Total	5,343,983	199,513	3.73

Sources: I.B.G.E. VII Recenseamento Geral do Brasil—1960. Estado de São Paulo Sinopse Preliminar do Censo Demográfico.
I.B.G.E. Estatística do Culto Protestante, 1960.

TABLE IX
GROWTH OF PROTESTANTISM IN BRAZIL BY CULTURAL AREAS,
1956–1960 [a]

Area	Protestant Population 1956	Protestant Population 1960	Increase Absolute	Increase P.C.
North	37,625	50,913	13,248	35.2
Northeast	181,093	221,480	40,387	22.3
South	723,439	936,202	212,763	29.4
Center-West	28,839	45,164	16,325	56.6

a. Excluded are Rio Grande do Sul and Santa Catarina. The Protestant population in these two states increased from 570,082 in 1956 to 643,207 in 1960. The growth rate was therefore 12.8 percent, the smallest on record for a Brazilian region of that size and population density.

TABLE X
GROWTH OF INDUSTRIAL LABOR FORCE IN BRAZIL

Year	Number of Workers	Growth Percentages
1920	275,512	
1940	781,185	183.54
1950	1,177,644	50.75
1960	1,509,713	28.20

Sources: I.B.G.E. Anuário Estatístico, 1956, 1962.

TABLE XI
GROWTH OF INDUSTRIAL LABOR FORCE IN SOUTHERN BRAZIL [a]

State	1920	1940	1950	1960 [b]	Percent growth 1920–40	Percent growth 1940–50	Percent growth 1950–60
Espírito Santo	1,005	4,066	7,232	—	304.58	77.87	—
Minas Gerais	18,522	74,267	110,477	—	300.97	48.72	—
Rio de Janeiro	16,794	45,483	77,035	—	171.10	69.37	—
Guanabara	56,229	123,459	165,957	—	119.56	34.42	—
São Paulo	83,998	272,865	484,844	687,982	224.85	77.69	41.90
Paraná	7,295	20,451	38,243	—	180.34	87.00	—
Total	183,843	540,591	883,788	—	194.05	63.49	—

a. Not included are Santa Catarina and Rio Grande do Sul.
b. Figures for 1960 are not available, except for the state of São Paulo.
Source: I.B.G.E. Anuário Estatístico 1956, 1962.

TABLE XII

DISTRIBUTION OF POPULATION AND PROTESTANTS BY ECOLOGICAL AREAS IN THE STATE OF SÃO PAULO 1960

Area	Population	Percentage of Total Population	Protestants	Percentage of Protestant Population
Vale do Paraíba	465,424	3.6	9,405	2.3
Serra do Mar	115,864	1.0	1,862	.5
Litoral	560,720	4.3	15,796	3.9
Paranapiacaba	178,993	1.4	4,652	1.2
Zona Industrial	5,975,260	46.0	233,175	58.1
Mantiqueira	443,231	3.4	6,953	1.7
Campos Gerais	258,366	2.0	9,678	2.4
Campos Cerrados	217,398	1.7	3,432	.9
Terras Roxas de Ourinhos	187,906	1.4	6,668	1.7
Invernadas de Botucatú	158,462	1.2	4,464	1.1
Pastagens de São Carlos	127,434	.9	2,413	.6
Terras Roxas de Ribeirão Preto	495,758	3.8	6,679	1.7
Alta Mogiana	185,044	1.4	3,554	.8
Baixa Araraquarense	194,470	1.5	4,329	1.6
Douradense	215,688	1.7	1,967	.5
Noroeste e Alta Paulista	379,415	3.0	12,023	3.0
Alta Araraquarense	445,799	3.4	11,971	3.0
Invernadas de Barretos	270,775	2.1	4,159	1.0
Alta Sorocabana (Assis)	236,236	1.8	7,586	1.9
Alta Sorocabana (Pres. Prudente)	240,780	1.9	6,669	1.7
Alta Noroeste e Alta Paulista	781,060	6.0	17,559	4.4
Sertão da Alta Sorocabana	238,376	1.8	4,250	1.1
Sertão da Alta Noroeste e Alta Araraquarense	602,240	4.7	21,692	5.4
Total	12,974,699	100.0	400,936	100.0

Sources: I.B.G.E. VII Recenseamento Geral do Brasil—1960 Estado de São Paulo. Sinopse Preliminar do Censo Demográfico I.B.G.E. Estatística do Culto Protestante 1960

TABLE XIII

DISTRIBUTION OF PROTESTANTS IN THE STATE OF SÃO PAULO
IN 1956 AND 1960, BY ECOLOGICAL AREAS.

Area	Protestant Population 1956	1960	Percentage Increase
Vale do Paraíba	6,034	9,405	55.7
Serra do Mar	1,095	1,862	70.0
Litoral	12,972	15,796	21.7
Paranapiacaba	3,265	4,652	42.5
Zona Industrial	130,914	233,175	78.1
Mantiqueira	4,560	6,953	52.5
Campos Gerais	5,333	9,678	81.1
Campos Cerrados	2,452	3,432	39.9
Terras Roxas de Ourinhos	5,075	6,668	31.2
Invernadas de Botucatú	3,254	4,464	37.2
Pastagens de São Carlos	2,247	2,413	7.4
Terras Roxas de Ribeirão Preto	4,513	6,679	47.9
Alta Mogiana	2,703	3,554	31.2
Baixa Araraquarense	2,113	4,329	104.8
Douradense	1,733	1,967	13.5
Noroeste e Alta Paulista	7,412	12,023	62.2
Alta Araraquarense	6,337	11,971	88.9
Invernadas de Barretos	2,783	4,159	49.4
Alta Sorocabana (Assis)	6,375	7,586	19.0
Alta Sorocabana (Presidente Prudente)	4,770	6,669	39.8
Alta Noroeste e Alta Paulista	15,857	17,559	10.8
Sertão da Alta Sorocabana	3,476	4,250	22.3
Sertão da Alta Noroeste e Alta Araraquarense	8,020	21,692	170.4
State of São Paulo	243,283	400,936	64.8

Source: I.B.G.E. *Estatística do Culto Protestante*, 1956 and 1960.

TABLE XV

GROWTH OF THE INDUSTRIAL LABOR FORCE IN THE THREE MOST INDUSTRIALIZED PROVINCES OF CHILE

Provinces	1916		1952		1960	
	Number of Workers	Percentage of Total Industrial Labor Force	Number of workers	Percentage of Total Industrial Labor Force	Number of Workers	Percentage of Total Industrial Labor Force
Valparaiso	10,887	18.5	42,679	10.4	42,258	9.9
Concepción	3,613	6.2	34,583	8.4	39,344	9.2
Santiago	24,405	41.6	201,035	49.2	224,157	52.0
Total	38,905	66.3	278,297	68.0	305,759	71.1
Chile	(N = 58,593)		(N = 408,713)		(N = 428,862)	

Sources. Statistical Abstracts of the Republic of Chile. Oficina Central de Estadística República de Chile. XII Censo General de Población y de Vivienda. Tomo 1, 1952. Dirección de Estadística y Censos. Población del Pais. Santiago, 1964.

TABLE XIV

GROWTH OF URBAN POPULATION IN BRAZIL

Year	Total Population	Urban Population	Percent Urban
1940	41,236,315	12,880,182	31.2
1950	51,944,397	18,782,891	36.2
1960	70,967,185	31,990,938	45.1

Source: I.B.G.E. Anuário Estatístico 1962:10–11

CHILE: POPULATION AND PROTESTANTISM
(Población Y Evangelicos Segun Los Censos De 1940, 1952 Y 1960)

Provinces	1940 Inhabitants by Provinces	1940 Percent of total Population	1940 Protestants by Provinces	1940 Percent of total Protestant Population	1952 Inhabitants by Provinces	1952 Percent of total Population	1952 Protestants by Provinces	1952 Percent of total Protestant Population	1960 Inhabitants by Provinces	1960 Percent of total Population	1960 Protestants by Provinces	1960 Percent of total Prctestant Population
Tarapacá	104,097	2.07	1,815	1.57	102,789	1.73	1,522	0.63	123,070	1.67	3,468	0.84
Antofagasta	145,147	2.89	3,078	2.66	184,824	3.12	4,417	1.83	215,219	2.92	8,801	2.14
Atacama	84,312	1.68	1,048	0.91	80,113	1.35	1,378	0.57	116,235	1.58	3,682	0.89
Coquimbo	245,609	4.89	1,495	1.29	262,169	4.42	4,072	1.69	308,991	4.19	7,079	1.72
Aconcagua	118,049	2.35	1,407	1.22	128,378	2.16	2,613	1.08	140,543	1.91	3,653	0.89
Valparaiso	425,065	8.46	10,627	9.20	498,254	8.40	17,615	7.31	617,510	8.37	26,207	6.37
Santiago	1,268,505	25.25	26,767	23.17	1,754,954	29.58	60,974	25.32	2,437,425	33.06	107,005	26.00
O'Higgins	200,297	3.99	2,768	2.40	224,593	3.79	5,260	2.18	259,470	3.52	8,710	2.12
Colchagua	131,248	2.61	693	0.60	139,531	2.35	1,952	0.81	158,509	2.15	3,705	0.90
Curico	81,185	1.62	713	0.62	89,432	1.51	2,753	1.14	105,802	1.43	5,420	1.32
Talca	157,141	3.13	2,081	1.80	173,693	2.93	5,178	2.15	206,154	2.80	9,768	2.37
Maule	70,497	1.40	589	0.51	72,181	1.22	2,053	0.85	79,736	1.08	3,537	0.86
Linares	134,968	2.69	1,151	1.00	146,257	2.47	2,766	1.15	171,350	2.32	6,625	0.61
Ñuble	243,185	4.84	5,371	4.65	251,342	4.24	10,630	4.41	285,639	3.87	18,148	4.41
Concepción	308,241	6.14	10,197	8.83	411,566	6.94	30,598	12.70	539,521	7.32	64,491	15.67
Arauco	66,107	1.32	1,718	1.49	72,289	1.22	5,076	2.11	89,460	1.21	13,305	3.23
Bio-Bio	127,312	2.53	1,964	1.70	138,292	2.33	5,360	2.22	168,718	2.29	11,817	2.87
Malleco	154,174	3.07	4,176	3.62	159,419	2.69	9,232	3.83	174,300	2.36	13,894	3.38
Cautin	374,659	7.46	21,524	18.64	365,072	6.15	33,672	13.98	394,654	5.35	38,784	9.42
Valdivia	191,642	3.81	8,026	6.95	232,647	3.92	18,256	7.58	259,794	3.52	27,672	6.72
Osorno	107,341	2.14	4,193	3.63	123,059	2.07	6,573	2.73	144,005	1.95	10,263	2.49
Llanquihue	117,225	2.33	3,768	3.26	139,986	2.36	6,147	2.55	167,671	2.27	3,653	0.89
Chiloe	101,706	2.02	742	0.64	100,687	1.70	1,208	0.50	99,211	1.35	2,156	0.52
Aysén	17,014	0.34	211	0.18	26,262	0.44	541	0.22	37,770	0.51	1,477	0.36
Magallanes	48,813	0.97	1,350	1.19	55,206	0.93	1,010	0.42	73,156	0.99	2,145	0.52
Antárdida	—	—	—	—	—	—	—	—	202	0.00	5	0.00
Chile	5,023,539	100.00	115,502	100.73	5,932,995	100.02	240,856	99.96	7,374,115	99.98	411,530	98.51

TABLE XVIa

DISTRIBUTION OF PROTESTANTS IN CHILE, BY PROVINCES

Provinces	Protestant Population in Percent of Population				
	1920	1930	1940	1952	1960
Tarapaca	2.0	1.1	1.7	1.5	2.8
Antofagasta	2.4	1.7	2.1	2.3	4.1
Atacama	1.5	1.1	1.2	1.7	3.2
Coquimbo	1.6	0.6	0.6	1.5	2.3
Aconcagua	0.5	0.8	1.2	2.0	2.6
Valparaiso	2.4	2.3	2.5	3.5	4.2
Santiago	1.1	1.3	2.1	3.4	4.4
O'Higgins	0.6	0.6	1.4	2.3	3.4
Colchagua	0.2	0.6	0.5	1.4	2.3
Curico	0.1	0.4	0.9	3.1	5.1
Talca	0.2	0.4	1.3	2.9	4.7
Maule	0.2	0.3	0.8	2.8	4.4
Linares	0.2	0.3	0.9	1.8	3.9
Ñuble	0.4	0.5	2.2	4.2	6.4
Concepción	1.0	1.5	3.3	7.4	12.0
Arauco	0.6	0.6	2.6	7.0	14.9
Bio-Bio	0.9	0.6	1.5	3.9	7.0
Malleco	2.2	3.5	2.7	5.8	8.0
Cautin	3.4	3.5	5.7	9.2	9.8
Valdivia	3.6	2.7	4.2	7.8	10.7
Osorno	3.1	2.7	3.9	5.3	7.1
Llanquihue	3.2	1.7	3.2	4.4	5.8
Chiloe	0.3	1.7	0.7	1.2	2.2
Aysén	0.3	1.7	1.2	2.0	3.9
Magallanes	7.2	4.2	2.8	2.0	2.9
Chile	1.4	1.4	2.3	4.1	5.6

Source: After d'Epinay, 1965–66:35–36. Based on National Censuses.

TABLE XVIb

PROTESTANTISM IN THREE INDUSTRIAL PROVINCES OF CHILE

Provinces	Protestants in Percent of Total Population			
	1920	1940	1952	1960
Valparaiso	14.2	9.2	7.3	6.4
Santiago	13.4	23.2	25.3	26.0
Concepción	4.8	8.8	12.7	15.7
All Three	32.1	41.2	45.3	48.1

TABLE XVI c

URBANIZATION OF CHILE

Urban Population in Percent of Total Population			
1907	43.2	1940	52.5
1920	46.4	1952	60.2
1930	49.4	1960	68.2

Sources: Republica de Chile, Dirección General de Estadística, *X Censo de la Población 1930*, Santiago, 1933; Republica de Chile, Dirección Estadística y Censos, *Población del Pais*, Santiago, 1964.

TABLE XVI d

POPULATION OF THREE INDUSTRIAL CITIES OF CHILE

	1940	1952	1960
Valparaiso	209,945	218,829	250,020
Santiago	952,075	1,350,409	1,907,378
Concepción	85,813	120,099	165,525
Satellite cities of Concepción (Tomé, Talcahuano, Penco, Coronel, Lota)	90,185	145,473	248,714
Totals	1,338,018	1,834,810	2,571,637

Source: Republica de Chile, Dirección de Estadística y Censos, *Población del Pais*, Santiago, 1964.

TABLE XVII

PROTESTANTISM AND SIZE OF LANDHOLDINGS IN
66 MUNICIPIOS OF MINAS GERAIS

	Fewer than 10 hectares	10 to 100 hectares	100 and more hectares	Total
High Protestant	4,613 12.8%	23,658 65.9%	7,616 21.2%	35,887 100%
Low Protestant	4,276 19.5%	11,256 51.4%	6,353 29.0%	21,885 100%
Total	8,889	34,914	13,969	

TABLE XVIII

CLASS DISTRIBUTION IN 34 PRESBYTERIAN CONGREGATIONS
(Sao Paulo and Neighboring States)

Percentage of Membership	Lower	Transitional	Middle
0	1	2	12
1–10	3	4	17
11–20	2	10	3
21–30	3	4	2
31–40	1	4	0
41–50	2	0	0
51–60	4	3	0
61–70	4	3	0
71–80	10	1	0
81–90	0	2	0
91–100	4	1	0
Total	34	34	34

TABLE XIX

CLASS DISTRIBUTION IN THREE PROTESTANT PARISHES
IN RIO DE JANEIRO

Class	Methodist I	Methodist II	Presbyterian Cathedral
Lower	86.7 percent	54 percent	25.2 percent
Transitional	9.8 percent	25 percent	33.9 percent
Middle	3.5 percent	21 percent	40.9 percent

TABLE XX

CLASS ORIGIN OF THREE CLERICAL GROUPS
(Brazil)

Class	Presbyterian Pastors	Presbyterian Seminarians	Methodist Seminarians
Lower	30.6 percent	39.2 percent	37.2 percent
Transitional	47.2 percent	32.4 percent	16.3 percent
Middle	22.2 percent	28.4 percent	46.5 percent

Reference matter

Bibliography

Anuário Estatístico do Brazil. Rio de Janeiro: Conselho Nacional de Estatística, 1958.

Arms, Goodsil F. *El Origen del Metodismo y su Implantación en la Costa de Sud America.* Santiago de Chile: Imprenta Universitaria, 1923.

Azevedo, Thales de. *Ensaios de Antropologia Social.* Bahia, Brazil: Publicações da Universidade da Bahia, 1959.

Barbosa da Silva, José Fábio. "A Sociological Analysis of Internal Migration in Brazil." Unpublished doctoral dissertation, University of Florida.

Barclay, Wade Crawford. *History of Methodist Missions. Part One: Early American Methodism 1769–1844. Vol. II: To Reford the Nation.* New York: The Board of Missions and Church Extension of the Methodist Church, 1950.

Bartolomeu, Floro. *Joazeiro e o Padre Cicero.* Rio de Janeiro: Imprensa Nacional, 1923.

Braga, Erasmo, and Kenneth G. Grubb. *The Republic of Brazil: A Survey of the Religious Situation.* London, New York, and Toronto: World Dominion Press, 1932.

Brazil. Conselho Nacional de Geografia e Estatística. *Recenseamento Geral de 1960. Resultados preliminares.* Rio de Janeiro: Imprensa Nacional, 1962.

Buyers, Paul E. *Historia do Metodismo.* São Paulo: Imprensa Metodista, 1945.

Candido, Antonio. *Os parceiros do Rio Bonito.* Rio de Janeiro: Livraria José Olympio, 1964.

Cânones da Igreja Metodista do Brasil. São Paulo: Imprensa Metodista, 1950.

Carvalho, Alceu Vicente Wightman de. *La population du Brésil dans le passé, le présent et l'avenir.* Institut Brésilien de Géographie et Statistique. Conseil National de Statistique. Laboratoire de Statistique. Rio de Janeiro, 1958.

Clark, Elmer T. *The Small Sects in America.* New York and Nashville: The Abingdon Press, 1937.

Coleman, William J. M. M. *Latin American Catholicism.* Maryknoll, New York: World Horizon Reports Maryknoll Publications, 1958.

Conselho Nacional de Estatística, Censo Demográfico. *Seleção dos principais dados.* Rio de Janeiro: Serviço Gráfico do Instituto Brasileiro de Geografia e Estatística, 1953.

Considine, John J. *New Horizons in Latin America.* New York: Dodd, Mead & Company, 1958.

Crabtree, A. R. *Historia dos Baptistas do Brasil.* I Volume. Rio de Janeiro: Casa Publicadora Batista, 1927.

Cunha, Euclides da. *Rebellion in the Backlands.* Chicago: The University of Chicago Press, 1945.

Damboriena, Prudencio. *El Protestantismo en América Latina.* Tomo II, Friburgo (Suiza) and Bogotá (Colombia): Oficina Internacional de Investigaciones Sociales de FERES, 1963.

Davis, J. Merle. *How the Church Grows in Brazil.* New York and London: Department of Social and Economic Research and Counsel. International Missionary Council, 1943.

Demographic Yearbook of the United Nations. New York, 1959.

Donoso, Ricardo. *Las Ideas Políticas en Chile.* México: Fundo de Cultura Económica, 1946.

Duarte, Raymundo. "Um movimento messiânico no interior da Bahia," *Revista de Antropologia,* Volume II, No. 1-2, 1963.

Dusen, Henry P. van. "The Challenge of the Sects." *Christianity and Crisis.* Volume XVIII, No. 13, 1958.

Eduardo, Octavio da Costa. "O Protestantismo em Sertão Novo, Comunidade Rústica do Interior Pernambucano." Unpublished manuscript.

El Heraldo Evangélico, Ano XXXVIII, No. 1526. Santiago, 1909.

Encina, Francisco. Historia de Chile. Volume XVIII. Santiago: Editorial Nascimento, 1951.

Encina, Francisco A. *Nuestra Inferioridad Economica.* Santiago: Editorial Universitaria S.A., 1955.

Erasmus, Charles J. "Culture Structure and Process: The Occurrence and Disappearance of Reciprocal Farm Labor." *Southwestern Journal of Anthropology,* Volume 12, No. 4., 1956.

Ferm, Vergilius, ed. *Encyclopedia of Religion.* Paterson, New Jersey: Littlefield, Adams & Company, 1959.

Ferreira, Julio Andrade. *História da Igreja Presbiteriana do Brasil* Volume I. São Paulo: Casa Editora Presbiteriana, 1959.

Firth, Raymond. "Some Principles of Social Organization." *Journal of the Royal Anthropological Institute of Great Britain and Ireland.* Volume 85, January-December, 1955.

Francescon, Louis. *Resumo de uma ramificação da obra de Deus, pelo Espírito Santo, no século atual.* Chicago, 1958.

George, Kathleen. *Among the Araucanians of Southern Chile.* London: South American Missionary Society, 1931.

Gillin, John L. "A Contribution to the Sociology of Sects." *American Journal of Sociology,* Volume 16, 1910.

Gillin, John P. "Some Signposts for Policy" in Richard N. Adams, John P. Gillin, Allan R. Holmberg, Oscar Lewis, Richard W. Patch, Charles Wagley, *Social Change in Latin America Today*. New York: Harper, 1960.

Goldschmidt, Walter R. "Class Denominationalism in Rural California Churches." *American Journal of Sociology*, January, 1944.

Hall, Thomas Cuming. *The Religious Background of American Culture*. Boston: Little, Brown and Co., 1930.

Henry, Jules. "The Personal Community and Its Invariant Properties." *American Anthropologist*, Volume 60, No. 5. October, 1958.

Higgins, Benjamin. "An Economist's View," in UNESCO, *Social Aspects of Economic Development*, Volume II. Paris: Desclée & Company, 1963.

Hoover, W. C. *Historia del Avivamiento Pentecostal en Chile*. Valparaiso: Imprenta Excelsior, 1948.

Hudson, Winthrop S. *American Protestantism*. Chicago: University of Chicago Press, 1961.

Hutchinson, Bertram. *Mobilidade e trabalho*. Rio de Janeiro: Centro de Pesquisas Educacionais. Ministério de Educação e Cultura, 1960.

I.B.G.E. (Instituto Brasileiro de Geografia e Estatística). *VI Recenseamento Geral do Brasil, 1950. Estado de São Paulo. Censo Agrícola*. Rio de Janeiro: Imprensa Nacional, 1955.

Instituto de Economia: Universidad de Chile. *La Migración interna en Chile en el periodo 1940–1952*. Publicaciones del Instituto de Economia, No. 20. 1959. *La población del Gran Santiago*. Publicaciones del Instituto de Economia, No. 19. 1959.

Kidder, D. P., and J. C. Fletcher. *Brazil and the Brazilians*. Philadelphia: Childs and Peterson, 1858.

Krause, Francisco. "Posibilidades industriales de la provincia de Cautin," in *Seminario de Investigaciones sobre el Desarrollo de la Provincia de Cautin*. Ediciones del Departamento de Extensión Cultural de la Universidad de Chile. Santiago, 1956.

Labarca H., Armanda. "Miss Elisabeth Mason en el Santiago College" *El Mercurio*. November 18, 1959.

Lalive d'Epinay, Cristián. "La expansión protestante en Chile." *Cristianismo y Sociedad*. Ano III–IV No. 9–10. Montevideo: Junta Latino-Americana de Iglesia y Sociedad, 1965–66.

La Voz Bautista. Organo de la Convención Bautista de Chile. Volume LI, No. 6. 1959.

Leite, Antonio Attico de Souza. *Fanatismo religioso. Memoria sobre o reino encantado na comarca de Villa Bella*. Second edition. Juiz de Fora, Brazil, 1898.

Lenski, Gerhard. "Religious Pluralism in Theoretical Perspective." *International Yearbook for the Sociology of Religion*, Volume I. Religious Pluralism and Social Structure. Köln and Opladen: Westdeutscher Verlag, 1965.

Léonard, Émile. "O Protestantismo Brasileiro" in *Revista de História*, Ano II, No. 7. 1951.

———"O Protestantismo Brasileiro" *Revista de História* Ano II, No. 8. São Paulo, Brazil, 1951.

———"O Protestantismo Brasileiro." *Revista de História* Ano III, No. 11, São Paulo, 1952.

———*L'illuminisme dans un Protestantisme de constitution récente* (Brésil) Paris: Presses Universitaires de France, 1953.

Linton, Ralph. "Acculturation and the Processes of Culture Change," in Ralph Linton, ed. *Acculturation in Seven American Indian Tribes.* New York: D. Appleton-Century Co., 1940.

Lopes, Juarez Rubens Brandão. "Zonas ecológicas do Estado de São Paulo" *Educação e Ciencias Sociais*, Ano II, Volume 2, No. 5 Rio de Janeiro, Brazil, 1957.

Lourenço, Filho, M. B. *Juazeiro do Padre Cícero.* Third Edition. São Paulo: Edições Melhoramentos, 1959.

Maddox, James G. *Technical Assistance by Religious Agencies in Latin America.* Chicago: The University of Chicago Press, 1956.

Manual Presbiteriano. São Paulo: Casa Editora Presbiteriana, 1960.

McLean, J. H. *Historia de la Iglesia Presbiteriana en Chile.* Santiago: Escuela Nacional de Artes Graficas, 1954.

Mecham, J. Lloyd. *Church and State in Latin America.* Chapel Hill: The University of North Carolina Press, 1934.

Medina Echavarria, José de. "A Sociologist's View," in UNESCO, *Social Aspects of Economic Development*, Volume II. Paris: Desclee & Co., 1963.

Mesquita, Antonio N. de. *Historia dos Batistas do Brasil.* Rio de Janeiro: Casa Publicadora Batista, 1940.

Milliet, Sergio. *Roteiro do Café.* São Paulo: Coleção Departamento de Cultura, Volume XXV. 1939.

Monbeig, Pierre. *Pionniers et Planteurs de São Paulo.* Paris: A. Colin, 1952.

Moore, Robert Cecil. "These other Americans to the South." Unpublished manuscript.

Moura, Epaminondas. *Estudo Bíblico sobre o Dízimo.* Juiz de Fora: Campos Bretas e Cia, Editora, 1938.

Muller, Nice L. *Sítios e sitiantes do Estado de São Paulo.* São Paulo: Faculdade de Filosofia, Ciências e Letras da Universidade de São Paulo. Boletim 132, 1951.

Nash, June. "Protestantism in an Indian Village in the Western Highlands of Guatemala." *Alpha Kappa Delta.* Winter 1960.

Nida, Eugene A. "The Relationships of Social Structure to the Problems of Evangelism in Latin America." *Practical Anthropology*, Volume 5, No. 3. 1958.

Niebuhr, H. Richard. *The Social Sources of Denominationalism.* New York: Henry Holt and Company, 1929.

Olavarria Bravo, Arturo. *Chile entre Dos Alessandris.* Volume V. Santiago: Editorial Nascimento, 1962.

Oliveira, Vianna. *Populacões meridionais do Brasil.* Volume I. Rio de Janeiro: Livraria José Olympio, 1952.

Padre Agnelo Rossi. *Diretorio Protestante no Brasil.* Campinas: Tipografia Paulista, 1938.

Pearse, Andrew. "Some Characteristics of Urbanization in the City of Rio de Janeiro," in Philip M. Hauser, ed., *Urbanization in Latin America.* New York: Columbia University Press, 1961.

Pereira de Queiroz, Maria Isaura. "Tambaú, Cidade dos Milagres." Anhembí Vols. XIX and XX, Nos. 57–58. 1955.

———La Guerre Sainte au Brésil: *Le Mouvement Messianique du Contestado.* Universidade de São Paulo, 1957.

———"L'influence du milieu social interne sur les mouvements messianiques brésiliens." *Archives de Sociologie des Religions.* No. 5. 1958.

Pierson, Donald. *Cruz das Almas. A Brazilian Village.* Smithsonian Institution, Institute of Social Anthropology, Publication No. 12. Washington, D.C.: U.S. Government Printing Office, 1951.

Pin, Émile. *Elementos para una Sociologia del Catolicismo Latinoamericano.* Friburgo y Bogtá: Oficina Internacional de Investigaciones Sociales de FERES, 1963.

Pinto, L. A. Costa. *Lutas de famílias no Brazil* Editora Nacional, São Paulo, 1949.

Primeira Iglesia Metodista Pentecostal de Chile. 50 Anos. Santiago, 1959.

Ramirez, Humberto Muñoz. *Sociologia Religiosa de Chile.* Santiago: Ediciones Paulinas, 1957.

Read, William R. *New Patterns of Church Growth in Brazil.* Grand Rapids, Michigan: William B. Eerdmans Publishing Company, 1965.

Republica de Chile. *XII Censo General de Población y de Vivienda.* Tomo I, Santiago: Servicio Nacional de Estadistica y Censos, 1952.

Republica de Chile. Dirección General de Estadística. *X Censo de la Población,* Vol. II. Santiago, 1933.

Ribeiro, Favila. "O latifúndio na conjuntura urbana." Fortaleza: Manuscript.

Rossi, Agnelo. *Diretório Protestante no Brasil.* Campinas: Tipografia Paulista, 1938.

Saunders, John van Dyke. "The Social Organization of a Protestant Congregation in the Federal District, Brazil." Unpublished master's thesis, Vanderbilt University, Nashville, Tennessee.

Serviço de Estatística Demográfica, Moral e Política. *Estatística do Culto Protestante do Brasil,* 1956, 1957. Rio de Janeiro: Servico Gráfico do Instituto Brasileiro de Geografia e História, 1959, 1960.

Stagno, Luis Picasso. "La propriedad agricola y su extensión." in *Seminario de Investigaciones sobre el Desarrollo de la Provincia de Cautin.* Ediciones del Departamento de Extensión Cultural de la Universidade de Chile. Santiago, 1956.

Statistical Abstracts of Latin America for 1956. Committee on Latin American Studies, University of California, Los Angeles, 1957.

Sweet, William Warren. *The American Churches.* New York and Nashville: Abingdon-Cokesbury Press, 1947.

Taylor, Clyde W., and Wade T. Coggins. *Protestant Missions in Latin America.* Washington, D.C.: Evangelical Foreign Missions Association, 1961.

Tognini, Eneas. *Batismo no Espírito Santo.* São Paulo: Renovação Espiritual, 1960.

Tucker, Hugh C. *The Bible in Brazil.* New York: Fleming H. Revell Co., 1902.

United Nations Department of Economic and Social Affairs. *Report on the World Social Situation.* New York: United Nations, 1961.

Vasquez de Acuña, Isidoro. *Costumbres religiosas de Chiole y su raigambre hispana.* Santiago: Universidad de Chile. Centro de Estudios Antropologicos, 1956.

Vergara, Ignacio. "Es Chile un pais catolico." *Mensaje,* No. 41 August, 1955.

————*El Protestantismo en Chile.* Santiago: Editorial del Pacifico, 1962.

Wagley, Charles. "Regionalism and Cultural Unity in Brazil." *Social Forces,* Vol. 26, No. 4. 1948.

————*An Introduction to Latin American Culture.* Washington, D.C.: Foreign Service Institute, Department of State, 1953.

————*An Introduction to Brazil.* New York: Columbia University Press, 1963.

————*Amazon Town: A Study of Man in the Tropics.* New York: Alfred A. Knopf, 1964.

Walker, Helen M., and Joseph Lev. *Statistical Inference.* New York: Henry Holt and Company, 1953.

Weber, Max. *Wirtschaftsgeschichte.* München and Leipzig: Verlag von Dunker & Humbolt, 1924.

Willems, Emilio. "A formação da Santidade." *Sociologia* Vol. II, no. 3. 1940.

————*A aculturação dos alemães no Brasil.* São Paulo: Companhia Editora Nacional, 1946.

————"Acculturative Aspects of the Feast of the Holy Ghost in Brazil." *American Anthropologist,* 1951, 400–408.

————*Uma vila brasileira.* São Paulo: Difusão Européia do Livro, 1961.

————"Religious Mass Movements and Social Change in Brazil," in Eric N. Baklanoff, ed. *New Perspectives of Brazil.* Nashville: Vanderbilt University

Glossary

CABOCLO—In southern Brazil, a person of mixed racial origin, usually engaged in some sort of primitive subsistence agriculture. In northern Brazil, a synonym for native Indian.

CAUDILLISMO—Authoritarian form of leadership, frequently but not necessarily military, with paternalistic overtones and strong emphasis on charismatic qualities.

COLÉGIO—The three last years of Brazilian secondary school.

COLÔNO—Resident laborer of an agricultural estate (southern Brazil).

COMPADRE—Godfather in relation to the godchild's parents, or child's father in relation to the godparents.

CRENTE—Literally: Believer. Generic term applied to Protestants by non-Protestants in Brazil.

DIVINO ESPÍRITO SANTO—The Divine Holy Spirit.

EL HERMANO PROFETA—Literally, brother prophet. Expression used by members of certain Chilean sects in relation to co-members believed to have the gift of prophecy.

ENCOMIENDA—In colonial Spanish America, a landed estate, including its Indian inhabitants, granted to a Spanish settler for evangelization and economic exploitation.

ESMOLA—Alms

ESCUELA ESPIRITUAL—Group of lay evangelists in charge of an expansion project.

FAZENDA—A large agricultural estate in Brazil.

FAZENDEIRO—Owner of a fazenda.

FUNDO—Agricultural estate in Chile.

GINÁSIO—First four years of Brazilian secondary schools.

GLÓRIA A DIOS—May God be praised.

GUIA DE CLASE—Lay missionary directing a specific project of evangelization. Used in certain Pentecostal sects of Chile.

INQUILINO—Resident laborer of an agricultural estate in Chile.

LATIFÚNDIO—Very large agricultural estate.

LICEU—Secondary school in Chile.

MINIFÚNDIO—Agricultural holding too small to provide for the needs of its owner and his family.

MUNDANISMO—Worldliness, or worldly pleasures.

283

OBRERO—See PASTOR PROBANDO.

PASTOR PROBANDO—Pentecostal missionary not yet ordained, in charge of a new congregation.

PATRÃO—Actual or potential employer of laborers, especially in rural areas of Brazil.

ROTO CHILENO—Collective name applied to the lower class in Chile, particularly in a rural context.

SANIDAD DIVINA—Literally, divine health, health bestowed by God.

SITIANTE—Owner of a sítio or small agricultural holding in Brazil.

TOMADA DEL ESPIRITU—Trance-like state attributed to seizure or possession by the Holy Spirit.

Index

Adaptation: of Protestantism to Latin American culture, 103

Anglican missions: in southern Chile, 90

Anticlericalism: characteristics of, 40–43; in Chile, 41

Arms, Goodsil F.: on reaction to Protestantism in Chile, 62; on economic status of early Protestants in Chile, 202

Assemblies of God: in Sertão Novo, 82; emergence of in Chile, 112–113; founding of, in Brazil, 118 ff.

Authoritarianism: in Pentecostal organization, 113–115, 141–144

Baptist: opposing Catholic and Anglican traditions, 8; origins of, in Brazil, 63; and German immigration in Chile, 64; growth of, 65; in southern Chile, 90; schism among Brazilian, 106–108; comparative growth of, 154; consistent with aspirations of common people, 155; appealing to lower classes, 206; loss of members in Chile, 216; against emphasis on schools, 235

Barbosa da Silva, José Fábio: on internal migration in Brazil, 84–85

Barclay, Wade Crawford: on religion as emotional experience, 108, 109

Bartolomeu, Floro: on Father Cicero, 33

Braga, Erasmo, and Kenneth G. Grubb: on Protestant growth in Brazil, 65

Buyers, Paul E.: on religious intolerance in Brazil, 59; on Methodist growth in Brazil, 66

Caciquism: and Pentecostalism, 113–115

Candido, Antonio: on rural middle class, 28

Catholic church: associated with state, 25; participation in, 34–38; associated with upper class, 42, 98–99; membership in, 43; and union with state, 220

Caudillism: and Pentecostalism, 113–115; and schisms in Brazil, 120

Charity: practice of, in Pentecostal sects, 147–149

Christian and Missionary Alliance: in Southern Chile, 90

Christian Congregation: growth of, 65; founding of in Brazil, 118 ff.; and Italian heritage, 119; and validation of authority, 142–143; and practice of charity, 148–149; worship in 151–153; discouraging political participation, 226

Church of God: in Chile, 113

Clark, Elmer T.: on Pentecostalism as class religion, 134

Coleman, William J. M. M.: on patronage system, 38–39; on nature of Latin American Catholicism, 43

Community: structural changes in, 165–168; expectations of, as means of control, 200

Considine, John J.: on anticlericalism, 41; on Protestant labor, 176

Conversion: motives determining, 126–130; and spirit possession, 135–136

Co-operative labor: organization of, 29–30; and diffusion of Protestantism, 29–30; withdrawal of Protestants from, 167

Crabtree, A. R.: on Brazilian Baptists, 63; on prestige of Brazilian Protestants, 202; on importance of Protestant schools, 235; on cultural conflict between Protestantism and Catholicism, 236

Culture change: generated by Protestants, 12; self-induced by sects, 52–54; in nineteenth century Brazil and Chile, 57–58; and distribution of Protestants in Brazil, 69–71; and distri-

Culture change (*cont.*)
bution of Protestants in São Paulo, 71–80; as consequence of conversion, 164 ff.; disruptive effects of, mitigated by Protestantism, 256

Culture conflict: between Protestant and Latin American values, 103; and differing values, 105; in the field of education, 235 ff.

Cunha, Euclydes da: on rebellion in Canudos, 31–32

Damboriena, Prudencio: statistics on Protestantism, 66–67

Davis, J. Merle: on Pentecostal worship, 150; on loss of members among Protestant congregations, 215; on level of living of Pentecostal missionaries, 219

Democracy: in Pentecostal organization, 113, 141–144; and political process, 220–221; advocated by Protestants, 228

Donoso, Ricardo: quoting Juan de Egaña on religious liberty, 61–62; on reactions to Protestantism in Chile, 62

Duarte, Raymundo: on Brazilian folk asceticism, 53; on sects and economic development

Durkheim, Émile: on religion, vi

Economic behavior: and gambling, 46–47; and tithing, 174–175; reflected by Protestant working habits, 176–179; and level of living, 179 ff.; and "Protestant virtues," 198–200

Economic development: and Protestantism, 81–82; in Protestant communities, 179–189

Eduardo, Octavio de Costa: on Protestantism in Sertão Novo, 81–82

Education: characteristics of Latin American, 233–234; Anglo-Saxon model of, 235; public schools gaining dominance, 242

Elections: Protestant participation in, 222 ff.

Encina, Francisco: on insecurity in Chile, 31; on transfer of European education, 234

Erasmus, Charles J.: on co-operative labor organization, 29

Evangelical Congregational Church: social mobility in, 207

Evangelical Pentecostal Church: emergence of, in Chile, 111; and validation of authority, 141–142

Familism: in traditional Latin America, 169

Family: change in the relative position of, 170; as a cult group, 172

Ferm, Vergilius: defining sect, 108

Ferreira, Júlio Andrade: on religious intolerance in Brazil, 59; on beginnings of Presbyterian church in Brazil, 63; on upper-class Protestants in Brazil, 203

Firth, Raymond: on function of spirit possession, 144

Folk Catholicism: characteristics of, 35–36; continuity with non-Catholic sects, 37, 133; in Chile, 91; and religious deviance, 96; limitations of, 132

Francescon, Louis: on growth of Christian Congregation, 65

Frontier: and distribution of Protestants in Brazil, 78–80; and Pentecostalism, 79; and development of Chilean Protestantism, 90–92

George, Kathleen: on technological change among Mapuche Indians, 190–191

German Protestantism: nonproselytic nature of, 69

Glossolalia: and conversion, 136; alleged nature of, 136–137

Goldschmidt. Walter R.: on "emotional religion," 140

Hall, Thomas C.: on American Protestanism, 6, 8, 9, 10

Henry, Jules: on personal community, 83

Higgins, Benjamin: on internal migration in Brazil, 84–85

Hoover, W. C.: on spirit possession in Chile, 109, 135; on sectarian spirit, 115–116

Hudson, Winthrop S.: on American Protestantism, 6–8; defining parish system, 165

Hutchinson, Bertram: on social mobility in Brazil, 124

Immigration: of German Protestants in

Immigration (*Cont.*)
Brazil and Chile, 3–4; of German Lutherans in Brazil, 59
Industrialization: and distribution of Protestants in Brazil, 71–72; in Chile, 86–89
International Church of the Foursquare Gospel: in Chile, 113
Intolerance: in Brazil, 60–61; in Chile, 61–62

Kidder, D. P.: on religious tolerance in Brazil, 59
Krause, Francisco: on industry in Temuco, 90

Labarca H. Armanda: on Methodist education in Chile, 241
Lalive d'Epinay, Christián: commenting on Protestant growth in Chile, 68; on religious pluralism, 89
Legislatures: Protestants elected to, 223
Lenski, Gerhard: on religious pluralism, 257–258
Léonard, Émile: on Protestantism and internal migration, in Brazil, 80; on differing values, 105; on attitudes toward freemasonry among Brazilian Presbyterians, 106; on schism among Brazilian Baptists, 106–108; on Christian Congregation, 143, 153; quoting a Pentecostal leader, 149; on Methodist organization, 155–156; on reputation of Protestants, 199; on upper-class Brazilian Protestants, 203–204; on professional versatility of Protestant clergy, 208–209; on *embourgeoisement* of Christian Congregation, 219; on Baptists opposing emphasis on education, 235
Life histories: of Protestant converts, 126–130
Linton, Ralph: on culture transfer, 163
Literacy: importance attributed to, 117; required for Bible-reading, 231; of Protestants, 231–233
Lopes, Juarez Rubens Brandáo: on eceological regions of São Paulo, 71, 78
Lourenço Filho, M. B.: on Father Cicero, 33
Lower classes: and emergence of Protestantism in Chile, 111; preferring Pentecostalism, 117; attracted by

Pentecostalism, 125–130, 140–141; role of upper brackets of, 202; defined, 204; among Protestants, 205; and religious radicalism, 259
Lutherans: nonproselytic attitude of, 389

Maddox, James G.: on technological changes in Chilean agriculture, 191; on status of agricultural college, 194; on changing role of Protestant agricultural schools, 194; on teaching of agricultural techniques in Brazil, 195; on Protestant schools, 242
Mapuche Indians: and Protestant missions, 90, 92; technological changes among, 190–191; graduates of agricultural college, 192
McLean, J. H.: on problems in Protestant congregations, 52; on Presbyterians in Chile, 64
Mecham, J. Loyd: on state-church relationships, 39–40; on religious tolerance in Chile, 62
Medina Echavarria, José: on exercise of authority, 22
Mesquita, Antonio de: on religious intolerance in Brazil, 59; on growth of Brazilian Baptist Convention, 65; on schism among Brazilian Baptists, 158
Messianism: and Pentacostalism, 134
Methodist Pentecostal Church: as a sect, 108; founding of, 110; and validation of authority, 141; and Radical Party in Chile, 227
Methodists: and revivalism, 9; beginnings of, in Brazil, 63–64; growth of, 65–66; in southern Chile, 90; comparative growth of, 154; structural aspects of, 155; and technical development in Chile, 191–193; and agricultural development in Brazil, 195; and social class, 206; and political participation of clergy, 214; and attitudes toward political participation, 224–225; political leadership of in Chile, 230
Middle classes: existence of, in Latin America, 26; in Paraíba Valley, 77; in São Paulo, 79; composition of, 201; instability of, 201; key role of, 202–203; as residual category, 204; among Protestants in Chile and Brazil, 205; accepting Protestant education, 235

Migration: and concentration of Protestants, 84–86; history of, in Brazil and Chile, 84; and problems of adjustment, 86
Minifundia: in southern Chile, 91
Missionizing: as a specialisation, 145; in Pentecostal sects, 145 ff.
Monbeig, Pierre: and social mobility in São Paulo, 79
Moore, Robert Cecil: on Baptist development in Chile, 64
Moura, Epaminondas: quoting testimony on generosity, 175–176

Nash, June: on nonparticipation of Protestants in community life, 167
Nationalism: and schism, 104 ff.; and schism among Brazilian Baptists, 106–108; of Protestants as adjustment to cultural matrix, 163
Nida, Eugene H.: on social composition of Protestants, 208
Niebuhr, H. Richard: in denominationalism, 197
North American Protestantism: missions in Latin America, 4–5; evangelisation and revivalism, 6; and the Great Awakening, 9; and English Dissent, 9; question of compatibility with Latin American culture, 235 ff.

Olavarria Bravo, Arturo: on lawlessness in Chile, 31

Parish: as a monolithic structure, 25; as a system, 165–166
Pastor: authority of, 171–172
Paternalism: as part of traditional society, 21–25
Patronage system: characteristics of, 38–40
Peasantry, and development of Protestanism, 94
Pentecostalism: as mass movement, 20; origins and growth of, in Brazil and Chile, 64; development of, in Chile, 67; distribution of, in São Paulo, 76; and frontier, 79; and thaumaturgy, 85; in southern Chile, 90; emergence of, in Chile, 109–111; division of, in Chile, 112; as religion of the lower classes, 117, 123 ff.; 157; division of in Brazil, 120–121; differences of, in Brazil and Chile, 121–122; and historical churches, 121–122; turnover in membership, 123; and messianism, 134; and rejection of conventional values, 139–140; and concerted action, 145 ff.; functional compatibility with lower-class culture, 218; competing with historical churches, 216 ff.; and political participation, 233; and abstention from politics, 228
Pierson, Donald: on reputation of Protestants, 199
Pin, Émile: in religious deviance, 34; on cult of saints, 35–36, 38; on position of Catholic priests, 41; on Chilean sex patterns, 51
Pluralism: ethnic and religious in southern Chile, 89; accompanying introduction of Protestantism, 166; characterists of, in Brazil, 256 ff.
Political participation: as means to maintain religious freedom, 117; of Protestant clergy, 213–214; meaning of, to early Protestants, 220; and democracy, 220; conditions of, in Brazil and Chile, 221–222; encouraged by historical churches, 222–223; attitudes toward, 224 ff.; of Chilean Protestants, 226 ff.
Political parties: in Chile, vii, 221; in Brazil, 221; Protestant attitudes toward, 222–223; ideological commitments of, in Chile, 226
Presbyterians: in Valparaiso, 3; in frontier areas, 8; and revivalism, 9; beginnings of, in Brazil, 63; development of, in Chile, 64; growth of, 65; and schism in Brazil, 104–105; and freemasonry in Brazil, 106; comparative growth of, 154; structural aspects of, 156; and modernization of Brazilian agriculture, 193, 196–197; and middle classes, 206; and political participation of clergy, 214; encouraging political participation, 222; and attitudes toward political participation, 224–225; schools maintained by, in Brazil, 238–240
Prophetizing: as "power of the Spirit," 137; social functions of, 139
Protestant clergy: social extraction of, 206; status achievements of, 208–214; professional versatility of, 208–212; social mobility of, 210; status aspirations of, 212–214

Protestant congregations: autonomy of, 11; cohesion of, 145; varying organization of, 154–157; nonparticipation of, 166–168; as miniature communities, 168; sociability in, 168; versus family, 170 ff.; social composition of, 204 ff.

Protestant ethic: rewarding in industrial society, 13; and personal behavior, 45–46; and sex morals, 49–51; and folk asceticism, 52–53; rejection of, 52; as culture change, 164; and family life, 172–173; and economic success, 198–200, 215

Protestantism: receptivity and opposition to, 58 ff.; growth of, in Brazil and Chile, 65–68; statistics of, 63–67; distribution of, in Brazil, 69–71; distribution of, in São Paulo, 71–80; rural, 77–80, 89; functions of, 86; in traditional areas, 92, 96–99; as factor of social mobility, 201; and political representation, 222 ff.; and democracy, 228; disruptive effects of, 225–256

Protestant missions: as extension of American frontier missions, 10; and nationalism, 104 ff.; and education, 235 ff.

Queiroz, Maria Isaura Pereira de: on "Holy War," 32

Racial composition: of Brazilian congregations, 207–208

Racial discrimination: absence of, in Brazilian Protestant churches, 207–208

Ramirez, Humberto Muñoz: on Catholicism and upper class, 42

Read, William R.: on Methodist membership, 64; on growth of Assemblies of God, Presbyterians and Methodists, 65–66; on background of Pentecostal leaders, 122; on Pentecostal representatives in legislatures, 223; on political participation of Pentecostal sect. 225

Religious consensus: meaning of, in Brazil and Chile, vi; in emerging sects, 53–54

Religious deviance: and Protestantism, 33–34; and folk Catholicism, 45–46

Research techniques: used in present volume, vi–vii

Residential segregation: by social class and distribution of churches, 216–217

Revivalism: in American Protestantism, 6; and Latin American culture, 20; and Chilean Pentecostalism, 108; originating schism, 109–110

Revolution: as part of traditional culture, 24

Ribeiro, Favila: on occupational structure of Fortaleza favela, 23

Rossi, Agnelo: quoting José Felicio dos Santos on anti-Protestantism, 60; on patriotism and anti-Protestantism, 60–61

Rural middle class: Extension of, 26–28; and Protestantism, 28; in southern Chile, 91; in southern Brazil, 94; in Minas Gerais, 96–99

Saunders, John van Dyke: on social control in Protestant congregations, 170, 200; on premarital sex among Protestants, 171–172; on race attitudes in Protestant congregations, 208; on education and social mobility, 237

Schism: directions of, 14; expressing cultural incompatibilities, 104; and nationalism, 104; among Brazilian Presbyterians, 106; organizational and doctrinal, 106; and Methodist Pentecostal Church, 108; defined, 108; expressing cultural preference, 157–158; as rebellion, 259

School: Protestant system accelerating mobility, 237; Protestant system weakened by government controls, 242

Sect: and schism, 108; spirit of, 115 ff.

Secularization: of Protestant schools, 240 ff.

Self-government: lack of, in traditional society, 24–25

Seventh Day Adventists: in southern Chile, 90

Sexual behavior: patterns of, in Latin America, 49–51; changes of, in Protestant family, 169

Social ascent: of Pentecostal leaders, 115; of historical churches, 204, 206; of Protestant ministers, 210; aspirations of, among Protestant clergy, 212–214

Social class: and economic behavior, 47–48; and thrift, 49; fluidity of, 201; in composition of Protestant congregations, 204–206; and extraction of Protestant clergy, 206

Social mobility: as reward for conversion, 203; of historical churches, 206; ministry as channel of, 210; aspirations of among Protestant clergy, 212–214; leading to religious indifference, 215; and Protestant schools, 237

Social structure: of Pentecostal sects, 141 ff.; and validation of authority, 141–144; of Baptist congregations, 155; of Brazilian Methodist church, 155–156; of Presbyterian church, 156; interstitial penetration of, 202; of Protestant congregations, 204–206

Spirit possession: functions of, vi, 137–138; and revivalism in Chile, 109–110; continuity with cult of Holy Spirit, 139; as messianism, 134; and trance, 137–138; and authority, 144; as common trait of various sects, 257

Spiritualism: competing with Protestantism, 123; compared with Pentecostalism and Umbanda, 257

Stagno, Luis Picaso: in land tenure in southern Chile, 91

Sweet, William W.: on frontier churches, 8–10

Syncretism: examples of, 132

Taylor, Clyde W., and Wade T. Coggins: on statistics of Brazilian Protestantism, 67–68; on German Evangelical Church in Chile, 89

Thaumaturgy: and folk Catholicism, 20, 96; role of in Brazilian Pentecostalism, 120; and spirit possession, 134–135

Tithing: rejected by Christian Congregation, 153; among Protestants, 174–175

Tognini, Eneas: on baptism by the Spirit, 158–159

Tolerance: in Brazil, 59–60; in Chile, 61

Transitional class: defined, 201; instability of, 201; key role of, 202; in Chilean and Brazilian congregations, 205–206

Tucker, Hugh C.: on difficulties of conversion in Brazil, 60

Umbanda: competing with Protestant sects, 123; compared to Spiritualism and Pentecostalism, 257

Upper class: in traditional society, 21 ff.; associated with Catholic church, 42; anti-Protestant attitudes of, 99; attracted by Protestantism, 203–204; local, defined, 204; ambiguity of concept of, 204; accepting Protestant education, 235

Urbanization: and distribution of Protestants in Brazil, 71–72; and internal migration, 85; and distribution of Protestants in Chile, 86–89

Vasquez de Acuña, Isidoro: on folk Catholicism in Chiloe, 92

Vergara, Ignacio: on Protestants in Chile, 3; on lower-class co-operation in Chile, 29–30; on introduction of Protestant schools in Chile, 62; on Presbyterians in Chile, 64; on growth of Pentecostalism in Chile, 67–68; on German-Chilean Protestants, 89; on Pentecostals in Chile, 110–113

Vianna, Oliveira: on rural proletariat in Brazil, 31

Wagley, Charles: on economic behavior, 46–47; on Brazilian folk asceticism, 53

Walker, Helen M. and Joseph Lev: on statistical correlations, 97

Weber, Max: on modern capitalism, 15

Weigel, Gustave: on Latin American Catholicism, 43–44; on leisure in Latin America, 47

Willems, Emilio: on German Protestants in Brazil, 4; on thrift, 49; on sex roles, 50–51; on Protestantism in rural society, 77, 94; on anti-Protestantism in upper class, 95; on folk Catholicism, 96; on cult of Holy Spirit, 133; on nonparticipation of Protestants in community affairs, 167; on Pentecostalism compared with Umbanda and Spiritualism, 257